BARBARA R. KIRWIN, Ph.D.

D0126763

ND THE INNOCENT

THE CRIMINAL MIND ON TRIAL

LITTLE, BROWN AND COMPANY

Boston New York Toronto London

First Edition

Library of Congress Cataloging-in-Publication Data

Kirwin, Barbara R.
    The mad, the bad, and the innocent : the criminal mind on trial / by Barbara R. Kirwin, Ph.D. — 1st ed.
        p. cm.
    ISBN 0-316-49499-2
    1. Psychology, Forensic. 2. Criminal psychology. 3. Insanity — Jurisprudence 4. Criminal liability. I. Title.
RA1148.K56 1997
614' . 1'092 — dc21
[B]   97-7833

10 9 8 7 6 5 4 3 2 1
MV-N Y
Book design by Julia Sedykh

Published simultaneously in Canada by Little, Brown & Company (Canada) Limited
Printed in the United States of America

For

ZIA EMMA

in loving memory

True! — nervous — very, very dreadfully
nervous I had been and am; but why *will* you
say that I am mad? The disease had
sharpened my senses — not destroyed —
not dulled them. Above all was the sense
of hearing acute. I heard all things in the
heaven and in the earth. I heard many
things in hell. How, then, am I mad?
Hearken! and observe how healthily —
how calmly I can tell you the whole story. . . .

— Edgar Allan Poe,
"The Tell-Tale Heart"

CONTENTS

A Note on Methods

All of the stories in this book are true. Most involve defendants whom I personally examined. When an individual enters an insanity plea, he waives any and all rights to confidentiality. Every official record, personal letter, drawing, writing, memento, or scrap of information pertaining to that person throughout his entire lifetime becomes open to public scrutiny. At the start of every forensic exam, I am ethically bound to inform the defendant that anything he says to me can and will be used against him in a court of law. All test results or notes that I make during the exam must be turned over to the court. Any conversations that I have with a defendant's family, friends, treating doctors, or associates in the course of an insanity defense evaluation are likewise subject to public view. This holds whether I am retained by the prosecution or the defense.

The dialogue I quote is verbatim. I have taken it directly from police crime reports, defendants' confessions, psychiatric hospital records, forensic reports of other examiners, and my personal notes taken while interviewing the defendants.

When it is a matter of public record in an insanity defense trial, I use the defendant's actual name. In the cases of juveniles, the families of the victims, or others where the insanity defense was not raised, I have chosen pseudonyms to protect privacy. The real names of the prosecutors, defense attorneys, judges, and testifying experts are mentioned when they are also part of the public record of the trial.

In some notorious cases where I have not participated directly as a forensic expert, I have consulted newspaper accounts, published books, or professional journals for information.

Acknowledgments

This book started to take shape in my mind many years ago when I was retained by the late Alfred Annenberg, forensic bureau chief of the Queens district attorney's office in New York City, to evaluate my first insanity defendant. In the course of my career as a forensic psychologist, I have benefited from the wisdom, experience, and support of countless dedicated professionals in the fields of mental health, law, and criminal justice. Like Tennyson's Ulysses, "I am a part of all that I have met," and I am grateful to all the forensic psychologists, psychiatrists, lawyers, assistant district attorneys, judges, detectives, parole officers, and corrections personnel who have generously guided and assisted me along the way.

I thank David Groff, not only for the expert editorial assistance he provided throughout this entire project, but for his devotion to the vision of the book and his unflagging loyalty and inspiration. His dedication exceeded all boundaries — he was virtually on twenty-four-hour call and as consumed with this tale of good and evil as I was. I believe he deserves much credit for helping me tell this story in the best way I could.

My special appreciation goes to my agent, Elyse Cheney, who saw the potential in my story from our first conversation and whose enthusiasm and support has never waned. I am grateful to my original editor, Catherine Crawford, for her belief in the message of the book. The book is much richer for her provocative questions and insistence on careful details. I want to express my appreciation to senior editor Jennifer Josephy, who shepherded me through the final nerve-racking days of the edit with consideration and forbearance. I appreciate copy editor Peggy Leith Anderson's thorough but gentle review of my manuscript. I thank publisher Sarah Crichton and all the staff members at Little, Brown whose interest and attention have made this a very rewarding experience for me.

I am deeply grateful to my family for their ceaseless devotion to me and the many sacrifices they made throughout the long hours I was chained to the computer writing. Without their love and encouragement, I could not have persevered through the rough times.

The staff at Harborview Psychological Services deserves special recognition for carefully organizing and tracking down the voluminous forensic records that would allow me to reconstruct these cases in such accurate detail. My heartfelt thanks also go to my private patients for their understanding and unselfish acceptance of my need to write this book even when it seemed to overshadow my identity as a therapist.

Last, most respectfully, I owe a debt of gratitude to those suffering from mental illness, their families, and the innocent victims of these tragic crimes for trusting me with their stories. I hope that my retelling here may reach out to others and bring them some measure not only of justice but of compassion and healing.

THE MAD, **THE BAD, AND THE INNOCENT**

THE MAD AND THE BAD:
INSIDE THE CRIMINAL PSYCHE

She wore a red sari with intricate gold filigree. He wore a jewel-encrusted turban and a black silk suit. An orange sash, symbolic of the bond between man and wife in Hindu marriage rites, yoked the coffins in which the two twenty-year-olds lay. After the cremation, their ashes would be taken to India and scattered on the Ganges.

Shaleen Wadwhani was starting medical school on a full scholarship; Hema Sakhrani was aiming for a degree in chemistry. The parents of the engaged couple, immigrants from India and Pakistan, listened over the clouds of incense and glowing candles as a Brahman priest intoned the funeral verses. They sprinkled the bodies with sandalwood oil, colored powders, and clarified butter.

Noticeably absent from the funeral was the Nathan family. Mohes Nathan had been Hema's godmother. Her oldest son,

Chandran, had always been something of an uncle to Hema. He used to baby-sit for her and more recently had helped her with her homework and studies.

Now Chandran Nathan sat in a jail cell in Mineola, New York, fifteen miles away, charged with second-degree murder in the killing of Hema's betrothed, Shaleen Wadwhani. When Hema was told of her fiancé's death, she leaped from the window of her family's sixteenth-floor apartment. Her last words were, "Why did this happen?"

Why *did* it happen? When I first heard about the killing on the eleven o'clock news, I had a premonition I would be called upon as a forensic psychologist to answer that question. According to the news report, Nathan, a thirty-five-year-old Sri Lankan immigrant and actuary for the City of New York, obsessed with a young woman, had gone berserk, confronted her fiancé at his home on suburban Long Island, and emptied forty-one rounds from an assault rifle through the heavy oak door, riddling the body of the young medical student who stood behind it. I watched the television footage of Nathan being taken away in handcuffs by police; I saw how the media were already in the process of turning this swarthy man with his heavy-lidded, glowering eyes into a parody of the evil foreign terrorist.

Nearly a year would pass before my premonition proved true and it became my task to try to get inside the mind of this enigmatic, fearsome man and to reconstruct what might have been going on for him at the moment he opened fire with an MAK-90, on Monday, May 24, 1993.

For more than two decades, I have attempted to straddle two disparate, often conflicting wings of the ever-evolving science of psychology. I've maintained a private psychotherapy practice named Harborview, for its scenic location on Long Island's north shore. My patients are usually high achievers, often pillars of the community, but inside they wrestle with the pain of depression, anxiety, or memories of childhood incest and abuse. Quietly, even heroically, these ordinary folk come week after week to face their problems. When I leave the safety of my therapy office for the courts and the jails, I am grappling with the minds and motives of people who may have the same sources of emotional pain but who have acted it out tragically, often violently.

The profession of forensic psychology, a recent fusion of psychology and the law, is practiced by a minority of licensed psychologists in the United States and taught in a handful of graduate programs. I am usually called upon by prosecutors in all five boroughs of New York City and in its suburbs to venture into the tortured folds of the minds behind crime — minds like Chandran Nathan's. I use the traditional tools of my trade — trained observation, clinical interviews, detailed history-taking, and psychological tests — combined with the street smarts I've gained as a narcotics parole officer and by interviewing hundreds of murderers. But sometimes I must rely on psychological guerrilla tactics, like agreeing with a psychotic's delusions, entering his hallucinations, or stoking a defendant's enthusiasm about drugs, sex, or guns. In these ways, I cull the killers who have no inkling of the wrongfulness of their crime from those who know exactly what they have done. In other words, I try to separate the mad from the bad.

As a woman, a wife, and a mother, I feel like I go through a sort of decompression chamber when I shift from holding a young rape victim's hand during a therapy session in my office to spending hours in a urine-reeking lockup, exploring with a killer the reasons why he gunned down his romantic rival on his doorstep. Sometimes I feel as if I almost have to change in a phone booth.

Certainly I felt that way in the case of Chandran Nathan. Nathan's attorneys were planning to plead not guilty by reason of insanity, but the psychiatrist retained by the defense, an exceptionally scrupulous professional named Stu Kleinman, couldn't quite put his finger on a diagnosis for Nathan. He asked me to consult as a "fake-buster" to ascertain whether Nathan was truly mentally ill or a psychopath who might just be malingering — trying to pretend he was psychotic to get acquitted under the insanity defense and not face criminal responsibility for his act. I am usually called in as a last resort, when the stakes are high and the mind of the killer on trial eludes other experts.

I pride myself on being painstakingly thorough. I always arrange to spend a minimum of ten hours face to face with the accused, giving him or her tests while I closely scrutinize behavior, body language, emotional reactions, style of relating, and thought patterns. This is called the clinical observation stage of an examination. Next, I take a careful and detailed history. Not only am I searching for any symptoms of mental illness in the past, I am also gleaning other sources of information perhaps overlooked by the police, any of which might shed light on the defendant's mental state at the time of the crime. I always administer at least four hours of standardized psychological tests aimed at pinpointing a defendant's psychiatric diagnosis, analyzing personality structure, and revealing covert attitudes, thoughts, and beliefs, all of which might have a bearing on his or her attempt to fake mental illness and elude criminal responsibility. My specialty is subjecting the data I obtain to successive mathematical corrective formulas to filter the truly psychotic from those who are malingering.

Whenever I can, I interview family and friends extensively both to corroborate the history given me by the defendant and to gain insight into his behavior and personality. Sadly, I often undertake interviews with families of the victims, especially when they are well known by the defendant. The "shopping list" of information I seek from the district attorney always includes Motor Vehicle Division records, rap sheets, medical and psychological records, employment history, and school records as far back as kindergarten. I leave nothing to speculation.

After I have reviewed all of this information about the defendant, I go about tailoring the crux of my examination — the session during which I lead the defendant step by step through the days leading up to the crime, the killing itself (virtually all the defendants I evaluate have been charged with murder), and the events immediately following that culminated in his arrest. This is the point in my forensic examination where my opinion crystallizes about the defendant's ultimate criminal responsibility and his ability to tell right from wrong.

My forensic workup is a good deal more intensive than that of most other forensic psychologists, but anything less would not satisfy my standard for formulating an opinion "with a reasonable degree of psychological certainty," which is what New York's insanity defense statute calls for. What goes on in the mind of a murderer at the moment of his crime will always remain unknowable. But I believe it is my professional mandate to make the most thorough, informed, and educated judgment I can.

Although they are all experts in a court of law, mental health forensic experts perform a role different from that of nonpsychiatric medical doctors, fingerprint or DNA specialists, and ballistics experts. Experts in other fields merely testify with a "reasonable degree of scientific certainty" that a defendant could or could not have *committed* the crime. The psychological expert in insanity defense trials, however, already knows that the defendant has committed the crime. When I am examining a defendant, I know very well that the hands that are marking "true" and "false" on my test grids have taken the life of one or many human beings.

The psychological expert has the unenviable job of assessing not the probability that the defendant committed the crime but his state of mind at the split second the criminal act was performed. Rather than employing scientifically precise and quantifiable methods like those enjoyed by DNA scientists, ballistics experts, or medical examiners, the behavioral scientist possesses rudimentary, inferential tools that can only even up the odds over hunches.

Despite popular conceptions, the psychological expert is not asked to describe for the court *why* someone committed a certain crime. Our job, and one we are well equipped to confront, is simply to ascertain the presence or absence of incapacitating mental illness at the time of the crime. State-of-the-art standardized tests can provide us with answers and approach reliabilities and validities of close to 90 percent accuracy. If in our psychological opinion a defendant has a psychosis, we can declare that belief, providing some description of the way in which the defendant's illness affects his ability to function and to form the requisite intent for his crimes. Those tasks should be the total limit of a forensic psychologist's expertise in an insanity defense trial.

Unfortunately, lawyers like to corner the expert into answering the ultimate question of insanity. Judges also don't mind hanging their decisions on the already burdened shoulders of the expert. The media tend to personalize and simplify the battle of the experts in insanity defense trials. Yet even in my most expansive moments, I never assume that a verdict in an insanity defense trial rests entirely on my testimony.

I knew from the first that Chandran Nathan was a "messy" defendant for an insanity defense — not psychotic looking enough, not raving, talking to himself, or gesturing wildly, and not sympathetic, pathetic, or likable. Moreover, he was a cultural alien, not someone with whom a jury could easily identify. The Nassau County district attorney would have a field day pointing out what seemed to be Nathan's premeditated violence, his motives for revenge, and his attempts to elude capture and possibly even flee to the Philippines. It seemed like an open-and-shut case of homicide. But in my twenty-two years of grappling with the human psyche behind jailhouse bars and behind the closed doors of the therapy room, I have learned that in the extremes of murderous behavior things are seldom what they seem.

I first met with Nathan on April 11, 1994, in the Nassau County jail. He was a well-groomed and pleasantly round-faced man with smooth skin and blue-black hair. His small stature and compact build gave him a disarmingly boyish appearance for his age. "I've been looking forward to meeting you," he said courteously, with a hint of a British accent. "Joel Rifkin has told me all about you."

Some reference! I thought to myself. Joel Rifkin, whose exam I had just finished, was a serial killer who had murdered seventeen prostitutes. His trial would become such a media circus that any question of his sanity would be lost in the frenzy to convict him.

At first, Nathan was shy, cautious, and guarded around me. I took out a roll of Lifesavers and offered him one. He refused politely and said, "At this point I need more than a candy lifesaver."

I smiled back at him, unsure if Nathan knew the full implications of his pun.

As we talked, I discovered he had a large fund of information about computers, electronics, and all sorts of machines. He was curious about the type of car I drove and was impressed with my choice of a five-speed Mazda RX-7 with its rotary engine. He would later mail me an incredibly detailed letter instructing me how to tune up a turbocharged Wankel engine. I felt like he was sending me a love letter.

He worked intently on the paper-and-pencil tests I gave him but frequently asked peculiar, almost inappropriate questions or made strange statements. At one point I looked up from checking his answers in the test booklet to catch him staring admiringly at me. "It was my destiny to have a female doctor who has had a great deal of success," he told me. "I knew this because the last three letters of your name are *win*. This means I have a winner — you're good!" Nathan was utterly serious.

Such was his magical, childish world. Random events in the news, rock 'n' roll songs heard over the radio, coincidence, dreams, and private fantasies — everything, no matter how trivial or unrelated, bore a special message pertaining directly to him, or so he thought. This symptom is called "ideas of reference." Chandran Nathan, who bragged to me that his family called him Raja, was indeed the center of his own universe, where every occurrence had portentous meaning for him.

Nathan liked to compare himself to Mr. Spock from *Star Trek*.

"I am very controlled, unemotional, logical, and intelligent," he informed me. "Nonhuman." Obsessed with the image of himself as a superhero, he declared, "I assume a dual identity as a crime fighter, like Batman, standing on a rooftop and surveying my domain, thinking to myself how I helped make this world a better and safer place to live in." Whenever I got him off the subject of electronics and machines, which was his expertise, his thinking was always strange, disjointed, and fantastic. Emotionally incapable of realizing the horror of his crime, Nathan struck me as a grotesque but pitiable Peter Pan, lost in his personal never-never land of postpubescent sexual fantasies and sci-fi superheroes. Chandran Nathan was like a child playing murderous games in a man's world.

When I went over Nathan's test results, what emerged was the most classic form of paranoia I had ever seen. Chandran Nathan manifested a distinct absence of emotion, an inability to connect with people, suspiciousness, and illogical, loose, and delusional thinking. He was a nitpicker, a collector of trivial details, but was incapable of seeing a larger perspective. The *Diagnostic and Statistical Manual of Mental Disorders (DSM-IV)*, the bible of the American Psychiatric Association, calls this symptom of paranoia "loss of appreciation of context."

Nearly a month after our first meeting, I visited Nathan again. I'd been unhappy with the lapse of time since our last visit — an occupational frustration for me, since I am always juggling several forensic cases at once. Moreover, interviewing a defendant requires something of an incubation process, in which the accrual of information and detail is central to my forensic determination. Nathan was delighted to see me, having followed Joel Rifkin's trial in the news and chatted about it with Rifkin, his cell neighbor, on several occasions. After all, we have made serial killers into cultural antiheroes of sorts, and as the sole witness for Rifkin's defense, I had a starring role in that drama. As a result, I was being incorporated into Nathan's fantasy life; I was his cartoon avenger, his Wonder Woman.

Beaming, he produced a white linen handkerchief. "I made this for you," he said. Gingerly unfolding it, he revealed an elaborate drawing, which he presented to me like a posy of flowers.

I recoiled. The nude female figure he had drawn was the type you would see in a *Penthouse* cartoon. It was penciled in garish red, with huge projecting breasts, black stiletto boots, long gloves, and spiked leather choker. The satanic pointed ears, horns, and tail bespoke the glaring label printed beside it: EVIL. The face, I realized, resembled mine.

Was Nathan so socially obtuse and detached that he could not anticipate how a female doctor who was retained to evaluate him psychologically might react to this? That single, bizarre, and unnerving gesture defined how Nathan operated, especially with women.

"What does this mean?" I asked, as evenly as I could.

"I'm good at drawing," was all Nathan said to me.

Regaining my composure, I focused on the principal purpose of this visit, which was to take Nathan's psychological history and to continue piecing together the puzzle of this man. Chandran Nathan, born in Sri Lanka, moved to America at age ten. He grew up in an Archie Bunker neighborhood of Queens with a father who was a physics professor and a mother who was a math teacher. Nathan, who claimed that almost into his teens he still believed that "babies came out of the belly button," was especially unprepared to deal with the pervasive sexuality of Western culture. He found his early sexual outlets in the form of exhibitionism. At age fourteen, he would hide in the stairwells of nearby apartment buildings and expose himself to women as they got off the elevator. I knew how those women felt. When he handed me that lewd handkerchief, I suspected, he was doing to me what he had done to them. The thrill for Nathan lay in the ambush, the element of surprise.

Nathan was embarrassed that I should even think of him as ever having been a sweaty-palmed adolescent. As a psychologist, I did not dismiss Chandran Nathan's early sexual exhibitionism as lightly as the juvenile courts and his family ultimately had; they had believed that the situation would correct itself as he became an adult. To me, his exhibitionism meant he was suffering from one of that class of sexual disorders called paraphilias — like fetishism, pedophilia, and bestiality — which signal real disturbance in a person's ability to have intimate relationships. These sexual hang-ups tend to become chronic and lifelong, the fantasies often growing more elaborate over time.

Pressured by his family, who like members of so many immigrant groups before them viewed higher education and a profession as the ticket to success and acceptance in America, Chandran Nathan excelled in the classroom and entered college at age sixteen. He lived at home, supported by his parents, until he completed his master's degree in computer science. Nathan was hired as an engineer by the Harris Corporation but was dismissed for incompetence before the six-month probation period ended. After a lengthy search, he landed a job with the City of New York Human Resources Administration. Again, he was fired for poor performance after a few months. Nathan believed he had lost his job because his Chinese supervisor had it in for him as an Indian.

Nathan began systematically harassing his former boss. He threw garbage, old tires, auto parts, and finally a string of firecrackers on his front lawn. Painstakingly, Nathan put together a video — a pastiche of clippings from porno movies, Batman, and sci-fi thrillers — which he left on his former supervisor's car hood.

He giggled as he recounted to me the elaborate preparations he had gone through, each detail seemingly a credit to his cleverness. He hot-wired his supervisor's car and drove it around the block and parked it — just so he could scare the man into believing that his car had been stolen. Finally he threw a rock with a menacing note through the plate glass storm door.

"What if one of your supervisor's children had been standing behind the glass door and had gotten hit by the rock?" I asked him. Nathan looked at me and blinked, wide-eyed. "Why would they be standing behind the door?"

Chandran Nathan had been arrested and charged with aggravated harassment and criminal trespass, both misdemeanors. He had told the police about his weapon collection; yet, in a tragic misdiagnosis, the court-appointed psychiatrist at the time concluded that there was no psychiatric basis for preventing Nathan from getting his gun collection back.

After this legal problem, he settled into a job as an actuary with the City of New York. Now over thirty years old, he had never dated or even associated with women. Following the dictates of his Indian culture, he agreed to an arranged marriage with a young woman of East Indian heritage who lived in the Philippines. (With a bitter civil war raging in Sri Lanka, his options for a bride from his own land were limited.) Nathan told me he was unable to make love to the woman he eventually married. He didn't even know her.

Over four years, as his life became more complicated — with a wife, a home, financial burdens, demands for sex he could not meet — Nathan withdrew more to the sanctuary he had created in his basement. After a while, he did not even come up for meals or to sleep with his wife. He surrounded himself with automotive and woodworking projects, superhero and porno videos, and his ever-growing collection of guns.

It took two months of a very hot summer before I could arrange another visit with Nathan. It had been reported to me that he was becoming increasingly agitated, and his mother was even more concerned about his welfare. I met in my office with Chandran Nathan's parents the week before my next interview with him, to verify the details of his life and psychological history. Nathan's father was convinced that Hema Sakhrani had been thrilled about her upcoming marriage and that her relationship with Nathan was innocent: "After all, Chandran already had a wife," he told me conclusively — as if in Western society that was enough to put an end to any sexual possibilities between his son and Hema. However, Mrs. Nathan, who rarely spoke up without a nod of permission from her husband, confided to me in private that Hema had expressed uneasiness about her approaching marriage.

His case had preoccupied me. I needed to know more about Nathan and his crime, and every day moved us further away from his state of mind the night he killed Shaleen Wadwhani. Now, at last, on my third intensive day of interviewing him, I would have more than five hours just to go over his feelings and thoughts about Hema and what happened the night of the fatal shooting. Nathan was relaxed; he seemed comfortable with me and lost no time launching into his story.

He started by claiming that he and Hema had been "affection-ate" with each other. "Might you have misinterpreted Hema's flir-tatiousness?" I asked carefully.

"*No!*" Nathan pounded his fist on the jailhouse table. "I would have known if she really wanted to marry Wadwhani."

Was his bond with Hema a figment of Nathan's imagination, or was it possible that the young girl flirted with her older "uncle," who lavished her with attention and gifts? Was Hema, like Nathan, caught in the clash of two cultures, longing to be free? Did Hema leap to her death in grief or because, as Nathan sug-gested to me, "she would have to make a full confession that there was another man in her life"? Did Hema commit suicide to spare her family and herself shame and disgrace? Nathan pointed out with perverse righteousness that in their Indian culture, such a confession would have left Hema all but an outcast and unmar-riageable.

He had to rescue Hema from an unsuitable marriage, Nathan told me. So preoccupied was he with this dilemma that he could not keep his mind on the woodworking project he was attempting in his basement workshop. He was carelessly spraying paint in the poorly ventilated room when the spray can slipped out of his hand and hit the floor, jamming the nozzle open. Nathan tossed the wildly spraying can into a bucket of water near the pilot light of the gas hot water heater. His clothes went up in a flash. He man-aged to put the fire out but suffered second-degree burns to his legs and hands. At the emergency room he was prescribed Tylenol with codeine for pain.

The following day, suffering from the painful burns and disoriented from lack of sleep and codeine, Nathan created a plan. Shaleen was hiding something. Nathan, the secret agent, would confront Shaleen, expose the truth, and save the heroine.

As I listened, Nathan's detached, usually almost singsong travelogue of events in his life gave way to an impassioned narrative and plea. On the night of the murder, preoccupied, distracted, in pain with his burns and taking codeine, Nathan fell into a daze, deliriously dreaming about Hema: making a movie with her, having sex with her — "nothing abnormal," he assured me.

Getting dressed for his confrontation with Wadwhani, Nathan took pains to look good, even donning elevator shoes for additional intimidation value. To be "more persuasive," Nathan carried an MAK-90 assault rifle. Dissatisfied with the effect because the gun seemed small and compact, he put a large magazine on it. He had trouble holding it, but he wanted Wadwhani to "see it — the impressive magazine," he recalled. "It was all for show — all plastic — like something from a James Bond movie."

As he left his home to drive to Shaleen's house in Manhasset, Nathan felt like he was on a "covert mission — like special forces in Vietnam." Fully entrenched in his commando fantasy, he parked on the grass outside the Wadwhani home, making no attempt to conceal either the car or the gun. He rang the doorbell and Shaleen answered. "Hi, we have to talk," Nathan said to him. Shaleen saw the gun and, according to Nathan, "didn't look scared. He just laughed." Then, in that curious turn of mind characteristic of paranoids, Nathan projected his own motives onto Shaleen: "It was like he was playing a game. I had not intimidated him! He said not even one word and slammed the door in my face."

Slamming the door was clearly the blow that pushed Nathan over the edge.

Nathan was flooded with competing and raging emotions. He

wished Hema had seen Shaleen "so disrespectful standing there in the porch light." His rival was not fit to marry Hema.

Now Nathan stopped in his narrative. He put both his hands on the table, palms up, as if in supplication; his eyes misted over. "I guess I just lost control. I didn't mean to shoot him."

All I could do was look him in the eye and listen. He choked out the words. "I never thought he would be behind the door waiting. I shot — possibly to scare him. I never thought I was hitting him. I was out of control of my emotions."

As Nathan related this tragic move, I recalled how he had flung a rock through his supervisor's storm door eight years earlier. Though he thought of himself as a careful thinker and schemer, Nathan acted on impulse. He was a machine not unlike his chosen MAK-90 — set to fire automatically, repeatedly, and with a vengeance.

He was talking more that day than he had in our previous two meetings, trying hard to connect with me and make me understand. I struggled to follow the frayed thread of his logic. Nathan did have some comprehension of time and the orderly sequence of events. But as he spoke, I could see how all of his thinking became derailed by his paranoid assumptions: Hema loves me; Hema does not want to marry Wadwhani and is being forced into it; Wadwhani is a fraud with dishonorable intentions; Hema needs and wants me to protect her from him and the marriage. Once Nathan veered off from reality enough to accept this interpretation, he could leap into the fantasy world of the Ramboesque avenger. The sheer childishness and stupidity of his plan to "impress" Shaleen is ludicrous. If Shaleen had been frightened or taken him seriously and acquiesced to his wishes to talk, might his life have been spared?

Nevertheless, Nathan's disturbance had more of a literary than a clinical quality about it. Chandran Nathan was a foolish incarnation of Othello — a tragic, pompous, bumbling fool who had by his own hand destroyed what he most loved in life. But Nathan's Iago was inside his head: his own paranoid, delusional belief system, which goaded him into seeing Shaleen Wadwhani as his enemy and Hema's devotion to him as passionate love.

"How did you know Shaleen was a bad man?" I asked him.

As if offering clear and conclusive proof, Nathan shook his head in emphasis. "It was obvious that Wadwhani was a fraud. He drove a manual sports car!"

The acid test of Nathan's delusional system was that he clung to his beliefs even in the face of overwhelming evidence to the contrary. Even if Hema had risen from her grave in her burial sari to express her love for Shaleen, Nathan could still explain it away. Many months after the killing, Nathan was still convinced he was in the right; in my opinion, he would always be.

The night he killed Shaleen Wadwhani, was Chandran Nathan in full possession of his faculties? Did he know the nature of his actions? Was he aware that what he was doing was wrong? When I am faced with making this sort of sad, complex determination, I constantly ask myself several basic questions, ones that will resonate throughout the pages of this book. Could this person have chosen another course of action? Were the consequences what he or she intended? Was the killer able to think far enough ahead to even know what the consequences might be? Did he or she have any kind of reasonable and informed choice at all?

It is a challenge for me to answer those questions, not only because of the twists and turns taken by the criminal mind but because of the vagaries of the criminal justice system itself. The insanity defense in practice can be as crazy and venal as those who plead innocent under it, as we struggle to distinguish the bad from the mad, the sane from the insane.

Eleven years before Chandran Nathan fired into Shaleen Wadwhani's front door, in a jurisdiction with an easier insanity defense statute, another defendant sat slumped at the table, facing the jury but somehow staring through them. Blond, blue-eyed, all-American looking yet very pale, he was strangely smaller than life in the imposing courtroom — and seemed younger than his twenty-seven years. Throughout the long days of testimony, he alternated between rolling his eyes and looking bored and out of touch.

The defendant had been born into an upwardly mobile, solidly middle-class midwestern family with traditional moral and religious values. Their home had a swimming pool, and the family room was equipped with its own Coke machine. As the trial progressed, the man in the docket would hear himself depicted as a whining, pouting mama's boy, "a wealthy, pampered suburban child who never grew up."

As adolescence approached, the young man seemed to withdraw to the sidelines — he dropped out of all sports, avoided social contacts with his peers, and was content to stay home with his mother. The family's fortunes continued to prosper. "We were the family whose American Dream had come true," he would say bitterly, after the trial had been concluded. He did not date in high school. His seclusiveness and dependence on his mother were creating conflicts in his parents' marriage. After a disastrous college experience, for the next seven years of his lonely life he bounced back and forth between pursuing various pipe dreams of success in the music business and living in his parents' home. He entered a process of withdrawal into his own world of fantasies, precipitating what psychologists call "downward drift," when mentally ill persons become less and less able to negotiate the real world and sift ever further into the cracks of society. He was being treated by a private psychiatrist who failed to realize the depths of the depression, rage, and deluded thinking that roiled his young patient.

The young man developed a rabid interest in guns and right-wing paramilitary groups. Many times he did not have money to buy food, but he continued to add impressive weapons to his personal arsenal. Even more fatal than his love of guns was his fixation upon a young movie star, whom he had met briefly on a trip to California in 1976. He became obsessed with the movie in which she played a young prostitute: *Taxi Driver.*

On March 30, 1981, John W. Hinckley, Jr., standing in the mist outside the Washington Hilton Hotel, sighted up his .22 caliber pistol loaded with exploding-head Devastator bullets and squeezed the trigger. Hinckley's first shot hit White House press secretary James Brady in the face, piercing his brain. His second shot struck police officer Thomas Delahanty in the back. The third shot whizzed over the head of President Ronald Reagan and lodged in a building across the street. Hinckley's fourth shot caught Secret Service agent Timothy McCarthy in the chest. A fifth bullet hit the bulletproof glass of the presidential limousine, ricocheted off the rear panel of the car, and tore through the president's chest, grazing a rib and lodging in his lung, just inches from his heart.

Was the shooting a political plot, an act of terrorism, the angry outburst of a spoiled rich brat, or the delusional plan of a demented person who wished to impress an inaccessible movie star? Over the following months and the weeks of the trial, both the nation and the jury would decide: Was John Hinckley mad or bad?

The answer to that question decided far more than the fate of one troubled young man. When the jury declared Hinckley not guilty by reason of insanity and the judge bundled him off to St. Elizabeth's Hospital, in Washington, D.C., America went berserk that Hinckley "got off." The resulting public outcry led to a massive stampede to "reform" the insanity defense.

Forensic examiners and the justice system go about making arbitrary, complicated, and yes, often corrupted determinations of sanity or insanity. Insanity in the sense that we discuss it in this book is not a psychological entity residing within the individual offender. In fact, the term "insanity" is not even part of the lexicon of psychiatry. No treating psychiatrist or psychologist would ever diagnose someone as "insane." The term is a legal construction. As demonstrated by the Hinckley case, the Nathan case, and many cases that are described almost daily in the pages of newspapers, insanity itself is a malleable concept, constantly remade by judges, lawyers, jurors, the media, the public, and the experts according to their own personal agendas, whether they be honest or venal.

Today, the Hinckley case is most people's point of reference for the intersection of insanity and the law. Since that 1982 verdict, all of us in the arena — the accused, the experts, the judges, juries, and attorneys — as well as the media and general public have been forced to play by different rules. And many killers fall through the cracks — from the truly mentally ill who end up in prisons, to the criminal psychopaths who fake being crazy, work the system, and elude the law.

The insanity defense has always taken on the shape of the displaced emotions of a society. Our outrage in the post-Hinckley era about the insanity defense arises from both our fear of escalating violent crime and our frustration at the failure of the criminal justice system to do anything about it.

American jurisprudence recognizes no uniform definition of insanity. Instead, there exists in America a hodgepodge of statutes and regulations across fifty states that are further affected in practice by many irrelevant variables: the sympathetic qualities of the offenders; their sex, wealth, ethnicity, and status; the emotions and prejudices of the jury; the attractiveness of the experts; the frenzy of the press; and, last, something approaching blind luck. Is it any wonder that this obscure, rarely used, and even more rarely successful defense should become a symptom for a society in disarray over the fundamental issues of individual responsibility, law over lawlessness, and personal safety and security over justice?

The insanity defense boasts a checkered past. The concept that certain mental disorders might relieve a person of responsibility for criminal conduct was first recognized as a defense in 1275 by English common law. Starting in the reign of Edward II (1307–1327), a criminal could be found insane if his defenders could demonstrate that his mental abilities were no greater than those of a "wild beast." Medieval judges and juries were assumed to have a commonsense understanding of the mentality of a wild beast.

In the mid-seventeenth century, Sir Matthew Hale, chief justice of the Court of King's Bench, redefined the notion of total insanity as having "no free will," a condition that prevailed only when "there is total defect of the understanding." A defendant could be judged insane if he possessed the understanding equivalent to a child of fourteen — not terribly restrictive in an era of short life spans, when human beings had to mature quickly. During the eighteenth century, the Age of Enlightenment, a defendant's level of knowledge of wrongfulness, his capacity to distinguish good from evil, became the touchstone of a definition of insanity.

John Hinckley's verdict was by no means the first to spur public outcry. Insanity defense standards have historically tightened as backlash against acquittals in particularly gruesome or emotional cases. In 1800, James Hadfield fired a shot at King George III as the king entered the royal box at the Drury Lane Theater in London. Hadfield believed that God wanted him to sacrifice himself for the world's salvation, yet he also believed that suicide was a mortal sin; he reasoned that attempted treason would ensure his execution while avoiding suicide.

Hadfield was defended by Lord Thomas Erskine, who convinced the court of the importance of the assailant's delusional beliefs. Erskine claimed that Hadfield's disease "consists in not merely seeing with a prejudiced eye, or with odd and absurd peculiarities . . . but his whole reasoning and corresponding contact, governed by ordinary dictates of reason, proceed upon something which has no foundation or existence." Erskine argued — as attorneys for Chandran Nathan and John Hinckley would argue nearly two centuries later — that although Hadfield knew that shooting the king was a capital offense, his act was based upon false beliefs and delusions, symptoms of his mental illness for which he could not be held responsible.

In 1843, Daniel M'Naghten, beset by longstanding delusions of a Tory conspiracy, shot the secretary to Sir Robert Peel, mistaking him for the prime minister himself, who was his intended victim. In a decision that outraged Queen Victoria (probably because it might signal open season on government officials and royalty), he was acquitted by reason of insanity. In that case the English judiciary formulated the rule that bears M'Naghten's name and remains into the 1990s an insanity standard in America in twenty-five states. "To establish a defense on the ground of insanity," the judges maintained, "it must be clearly proved that at the time of committing the act, the party accused was laboring under such a defect of reason, from disease of the mind as not to know the nature and quality of the act he was doing, or if he did know it that he did not know he was doing what was wrong."

The M'Naghten Rule evolved at a time when the dominant perception of human behavior was that people, as rational beings, made free choices informed by conscious considerations. The M'Naghten standard has been criticized for being too restrictive. Put simply, the M'Naghten Rule recognizes only one aspect of personality — cognitive reasoning — as the determinant of conduct: Did the defendant know what he was doing and that it was wrong? If so, no matter how mentally ill he is or how long his psychiatric history, he is sane.

In 1954, a different rule, Durham, was decreed by Judge David Bazelon, chief justice of the U.S. Court of Appeals in the District of Columbia. In ruling on the case of Monte Durham, the court of appeals wrote: "The rule we now hold is simply that an accused is not criminally responsible if his unlawful act was the product of mental disease or mental defect." The Durham Rule's purpose was to bring into the courtroom the legitimate knowledge that mental health professionals possess and to restore to the jury its traditional function of applying our cultural ideas of moral responsibility to those accused of crime. The marriage of psychiatry and law may have provided a temporary honeymoon of enlightened humanitarianism, and let many judges off the hook, but it eventually produced much dissatisfaction and disillusionment.

The American Law Institute standard, drafted in 1962, was designed to end what was perceived as the experts' domination over the question of moral responsibility. A major change in the test involved the ability of a defendant to conform his behavior to the law, which excluded psychopathic and antisocial behavior as mental diseases or defects. The standard envisioned that the jury would be provided with a broad range of information about the accused from a variety of sources, including but not limited to psychiatrists and psychologists. Other disciplines with special skills and knowledge in the field of human behavior would get a shot at showing the relevance of their data in the courtroom. In more than thirty years of its adoption, the ALI standard has not realized those goals.

Sixteen years ago, when I was writing my doctoral dissertation, my intention was to study the criminally insane and examine how they differed from other deviant populations. In the ensuing years, with every new case, I wonder how much closer I have really come to that intention. And I wonder whether the courts really subscribe to that same goal. Do forensic psychologists and the American judicial system even work at cross-purposes?

Because I practice in New York State, which uses the M'Naghten standard, I am mostly required to use cognitive tests in formulating my own forensic opinions of defendants — but I give as much clinical scrutiny to the issue of psychopathy as to psychotic mental illness. The essential feature of *psychopathy* is a pervasive pattern of disregard for, and violation of, the rights of others. The narrowest definition of *psychosis* refers to delusions or hallucinations that represent a major impairment in reality testing. The psychotic's break with reality interferes with his capacity to meet the ordinary demands of life. In the rare instances in which I have affirmed that a defendant was psychotic and so mentally impaired that he or she lacked responsibility for a criminal action, I have been extremely careful to rule out the presence of psychopathic tendencies.

As I will show, psychopathic criminals — who, though basically lacking a conscience, are *able* to conform their behavior to the law but *choose* not to — can get off too easily in today's courts. The insanity defense, fertilized by clever defense attorneys, has engendered numerous offspring that make a mockery out of psychology, human nature, and the law. I refer to these instances of "faux insanity" as designer defenses, whereby new and curious psychological syndromes are concocted complete with the requisite expert testimony to exonerate someone who is definitely sane, frequently psychopathic, and most frequently deserving of punishment. In my experience, the designer defense represents much of what's wrong with our entire judicial system.

Serial killer Joel Rifkin, whom I diagnosed as paranoid schizophrenic and suffering from hallucinations, did not give evidence of psychopathy in either his history, behavior, or psychological tests results. That is to say, he did not show a pattern of violating the law or of assault; in fact, he was more often the victim of cruel jokes and aggression. As a child and an adult, he was kind and tenderhearted to animals and kept many pets — in contrast to Jeffrey Dahmer, who delighted in wanton cruelty. It is unclear to me whether there were psychopathic trends in John Hinckley's personality, as the government witnesses contended. There is no doubt, however, that notorious serial killers Ted Bundy and Jeffrey Dahmer were both psychopaths. They were not crazy; they were evil.

Though all of us share a fascination with the crime of murder, the psychological literature is very sparse and inconsistent. Despite tremendous advances in the research techniques of the social sciences (much of it aided by computers), contemporary research in homicide has advanced little in the 138 years since Isaac Ray published his great *Treatise on the Medical Jurisprudence of Insanity*. Dr. Ray was called in as a consultant on the infamous M'Naghten case. He was the first to explore the psychodynamics of murder and was one of the first researchers to diagnostically differentiate between the behavior of the psychopathic murderer and the insane killer. To this day, his observations have proven remarkably accurate. Dr. Ray noted that nearly every homicide committed by an insane individual has been preceded by some signs of irrationality — people don't "just snap." He established that victims tend to be intimate associates, neighbors, family members, even the offspring of the insane murderer — who usually exhibits no remorse and freely confesses to the deed. Yet the killer's stated motive, which seems so compelling and conclusive to him, seems bizarre or inadequate to the sane person. The crimes are often superfluously brutal and gory, the result of impulse more than planning, with the killer often acting in full view of witnesses, without accomplices, using whatever weapon is handy at the time.

These sad, brutal, psychotic offenders are, regrettably, timeless. I am at once dismayed and impressed by how little psychotic crime has changed over time.

A decade and a half after the Hinckley verdict, in a courtroom in a strict M'Naghten state with the burden of proof on the defense to prove his insanity, Chandran Nathan, whose deluded crime and mental state bore a striking resemblance to John Hinckley's except in the stature and number of his victims, was convicted by a jury of second-degree murder and sentenced to thirty-three years to life in prison.

Above all, the insanity defense is a thinking person's defense. Its fair application requires a willingness and a capacity on the part of each judge and juror to be open to complicated and sometimes counterintuitive information and to apply it to a highly complex decision-making process. Sadly, especially in high-profile insanity defense cases, the jury can best be described as "sincere, serious people who — for a variety of reasons — were missing key points, focusing on irrelevant issues, succumbing to barely recognized prejudices to see through the cheapest appeals to sympathy or hate, and generally botching the job" — or so says Stephen J. Adler in his book *The Jury: Trial and Error in the American Courtroom.*

Yet I can't lay all of the problems with the application of the insanity defense on the criminal justice system or even the media. Some of the difficulties are inherent in a process of judging something as complex and unfathomable as the human mind. Unlike any other defense that can be brought into a court of law, the insanity defense not only requires reading someone's mind — it further demands that that mind be read sometime in the past. The insanity defense exacts such a gravity of thought, deliberation, and judgment that it will always carry an enormous amount of emotional freight.

In the conversations that I have had with jurors after notorious insanity defense trials, I find it shockingly obvious that they haven't even gotten a grasp of the fact that not being responsible by virtue of insanity is not the same as the defendant's claiming that he has not committed the crime or that he is innocent. Jurors can't seem to hold simultaneously in their heads the idea that the person has indeed confessed to committing the criminal actions for which he is charged and that the issue at hand is his state of mind or intent.

"Baloney!" a juror in the Nathan trial exclaimed to me as he exited the courtroom. "Everyone knew he did it." After six days on the stand justifying my careful diagnosis of Nathan's delusional thinking and trying to lead a jury through the labyrinth of his disordered mind, I was blown away. And this man was the juror who had seemed most attentive to my testimony.

When jurors can be so conceptually misguided on the fundamental premise entailed in an insanity defense, is it any wonder that Machiavellian prosecutors rely on the time-honored tactic of bamboozling them with sensational crime facts and gory photos until they lose sight of the trial's true issues? In the Nathan case, the prosecutor produced the entire bullet-riddled wooden front door of the Wadwhani house for the jury to see. For the duration of my psychological testimony, this oak door was propped up against the courtroom wall, directly behind me in the witness box, a silent but poignant reminder of the violence of Nathan's offense.

With this shameless bit of show-and-tell, it was as if this jury of mostly working-class people was being challenged to decide what was more real, the massive door perforated by forty bullets or the mumbo jumbo coming out of the lady shrink's mouth.

When it came time for me to introduce my own props, which were critical to understanding Nathan's mental state and psychology, the prosecution was able to block them. The jury never saw Chandran Nathan's psychological test profile — an EEG-type graph spiking dramatically into the abnormal, paranoid, and psychotic range. Neither were they permitted to see a comparison of his profile with that of hospitalized psychiatric patients. My thirty-two-page report systematically tracing the origin and development of his paranoid delusions about Hema and her suitor, which was at the heart of his insanity defense, never saw the light of deliberation by the jury.

On the witness stand, as I began to unfurl the linen handkerchief containing my S and M portrait, the prosecutor sprang to his feet in objection. After a lengthy sidebar discussion, which I was not permitted to hear, the judge restricted me from showing the drawing that I considered so graphic a representation of Nathan's emotional problems. The prosecutor had prevailed. The basis of his objection? I had not seen Nathan draw it with my own eyes and therefore I could not be sure that it was his. I was not permitted even to make the point that regardless of who drew the figure, Nathan's lapse in judgment and social sense in presenting it to me was what was symptomatic about it. As I leaned down from the witness stand to replace the handkerchief in my briefcase, I almost bumped my head on the oak door, which was sliding precariously toward the jury box. At that point, I knew Chandran Nathan was a goner.

Three years before I made the acquaintance of Chandran Nathan, I found myself interviewing a young man who could have been an altar boy. Twenty-five-year-old Joseph Bergamini, wide-eyed and cherubic looking, smiled politely and affably at me from across the table in the incongruously elegant examining suite of the Queens, New York, district attorney's new offices. There was something about this chubby, vulnerable-looking young man that made me want to nurture and protect him. Joseph had committed a crime of mythic proportions, and yet here I was feeling maternal toward him. I was at once puzzled and ashamed of these impulses.

On Thanksgiving morning 1990, Joseph Bergamini stabbed his mother to death with a serrated steak knife, in the kitchen of the family home where she was basting the turkey. His father, hearing screams, ran into the kitchen and attempted to stop the attack. Angela, the daughter, rushed out of the shower only to see Joseph grab another knife out of the drainboard and stab their father in the back. Cursing and mumbling, "Now I got you — you're the devil," Joseph ran out of the house. He literally bumped into his uncle on the street, then jumped on him and started beating the older man savagely around the face and head. Joseph then pursued a neighbor who had tried to pull him off his uncle, stopping long enough to assault another neighbor, throwing her to the ground and ripping off her apron, blouse, and bra while sitting on top of her.

At this point he was apprehended by two police officers. Mrs. Bergamini died of stab wounds before she got to the hospital. Mr. Bergamini, though seriously injured, survived. Joseph was charged with assaulting his father and murdering his mother — and now I was eye to eye with a young man who looked like the kind you wouldn't mind dating your daughter. Joseph was alert, intelligent, and extremely cooperative with all phases of the examination. He never complained about the difficulty he had in writing three hours of paper-and-pencil tests while his left hand was shackled to the wall.

Reverently and sometimes tearfully, Bergamini talked about his relationship with his mother. "I was my mother's first child and her favorite. She named me Joseph after her patron saint because I was born on his feast day, March nineteenth." As a child he attended mass with her daily. Her faith was not shared by his brother and sister. Religion was a bond that kept Joseph and his mother close.

By sophomore year in high school, the formerly well-behaved student had turned on to drugs. His mother was crushed when he dropped out of high school — she wanted him to be the first in their family to go to college. Still determined, she coached him and helped him pass the test for an equivalency diploma. "My mother was my best friend," he told me. "She was my protector. She'd always let me off the hook." Looking up at me doe-eyed, he sighed, "She would give her life for me."

Joseph Bergamini's mother bankrolled him through nine years of job failures and firings. She lied and covered up his drug habit to his employers — even her own brother-in-law, from whom he stole a walkie-talkie to fence for drugs. This led to a rift between her and her sister and much conflict with her exasperated husband, a gruff and no-nonsense construction worker who wanted to throw his deadbeat son out of the house. Bergamini stole from his mother, his brother, and his sister; he drank; he used crack, angel dust (PCP), and marijuana regularly. In 1987 he was arrested for robbing a gas station. His family got him into a drug rehabilitation program at Samaritan Village, in upstate New York. He was not motivated to change and continued to abuse street drugs. "Drugs and alcohol had become a way of death for me," he intoned, using the dramatic argot of recovery programs. "I wasn't the real me — a monster took over. I didn't like myself and no one else did. I lost my possessions. I lost my friends. I lost myself. I was the living dead."

Bergamini's functioning deteriorated alarmingly in 1990. He was ingesting huge amounts of angel dust regularly and mostly subsisting on handouts from his mother. A few times he experi-

enced toxic reactions to the drugs, becoming agitated and paranoid. Once he had to be detoxified at a local hospital. He described these bad trips to me as feeling like his "thoughts had been
poisoned." Joseph had used angel dust late the night before
Thanksgiving 1990.

No matter how delicately I tried to probe his memories, he
claimed to me not to recall the stabbings. The last thing he said
he remembered was asking his mother if his aunt would be there
for Thanksgiving dinner. He "came to" riding in the police car
with the two arresting officers. The police reports do not indicate
that he was disoriented, agitated, bizarre, hallucinating, or in any
way out of contact with reality during his detention overnight at
central booking. However, after Bergamini allegedly was shown a
newspaper account of what he had done by a transsexual also in
custody, he became confused, suspicious, and assaultive — the
shock of realizing what he'd done gave him a drug flashback. He
was masturbating openly on the bus to the Rikers Island prison.
Following an unprovoked attack on a corrections officer, he was
admitted to Kings County Hospital for a psychiatric evaluation.
Within seventy-two hours after his crime, when the last vestiges
of the chemical had left his system, he was again calm, lucid, and
fully oriented.

When I analyzed Bergamini's test results I could find no evidence of psychotic mental illness. He had answered honestly and
consistently, with no attempt to malinger. Curiously, I could detect hardly any trace of even appropriate depression; you'd think
a man who killed his sainted mother would be distraught, but not
Joseph. As I looked at his profile, I saw signs alerting me to his essential character. Spiking up over the normal cutoff score on his
MMPI profile sheet was the telltale elevation on scale 4, psychopathic deviate. (The MMPI — Minnesota Multiphasic Personality Inventory — is the most widely administered standardized
psychological test.) People who score high in this category are
characterized by lying, stealing, excessive drinking, and substance

abuse. For all their selfishness, impulsiveness, and superficiality, they tend to create a favorable first impression. I could understand why Kathleen Bergamini had been so seduced by her son. I had to be on guard not to let my stirrings of sympathy for him get in the way of my objective analysis of his mental state and his crime. His puppy-dog manner concealed the fact that he was essentially opportunistic and knew how to use people.

When I read one of the many harassing and manipulative letters Joseph wrote to his sister shortly after the matricide, I saw the real psychopathic killer. In the letter, he was oblivious to her grief and complained of the family's rejection of him and how much it hurt him. "After all," he wrote, "she was my mother, too!" In Joseph's mind, the real crime was not his murder of his mother but his family's treatment of him. Bergamini was what some theorists call the premoral infant. He defined goodness as what he wanted and evil as what he didn't want or like.

And what of that sainted mother "now an angel in heaven," according to her son — what role did she play in creating the agent of her death? Functioning as a classic enabler, she protected him from the logical consequences of his antisocial behavior, bailing him out again and again. Did his mother so enjoy her little companion that she attended immediately to his every whim as a child? Her devotion and attention seemed to impart to him a warped sense of entitlement, a narcissistic expectancy that he should not be required to exert himself or delay gratification. Joseph Bergamini was spoiled rotten, and in return he "loved" his mother to death.

After my encounters with this murderously good son, I was confident in asserting that Joseph Bergamini possessed all the classic characteristics of the psychopathic personality. I believe that psychopaths are not insane. Whenever I evaluate a defendant, I don't just try to ascertain whether or not he has a mental illness and has a sense of right and wrong; I try to see if he is capable of controlling himself. In psycholegal terms, I go beyond the

M'Naghten Rule to align with the ALI standard in emphasizing this distinction. Psychopaths are not mentally ill; they are "morally challenged." They know the difference between right and wrong; they just don't care.

Joseph Bergamini's case, however, was not so simple. Even though I was working for the prosecution, I declared my forensic opinion to be that at the moment of the murder Joseph Bergamini did *not* know the wrongfulness of his crime. I believe that on Thanksgiving morning 1990 Joseph Bergamini was paranoid, agitated, hallucinating — out of touch with reality. There was no motivation for the attack; he had not argued with his parents or even talked to them since the day before. The demons Bergamini wrestled with in that kitchen were products of a psychotic-like, drug-induced delirium. The poison in his brain interfered with his capacity to know the nature and consequences of his actions and their wrongfulness. He was, I believe, insane at the time of the crime.

Dr. Stu Kleinman and I, both of us working for the prosecution, independently drew the same clinical conclusions. Four psychiatrists and psychologists on the defense team reached identical diagnoses. The *DSM-III-R* (the diagnostic manual in use at that time) clearly listed PCP Intoxication 305.90 as an axis 1 mental illness. Never was a case so open-and-shut; never had I seen such agreement among experts for both sides.

Yet Joseph Bergamini was convicted and sentenced to prison for assaulting his father, uncle, and neighbors and murdering his mother. The jury did not buy his insanity defense — and rightfully so. Under the M'Naghten Rule, which governed Bergamini's trial, a state of drug intoxication, no matter how it interferes with reasoning, is *not* considered a mental illness. Although Joseph was driven temporarily mad by PCP, the jury determined that on some level he comprehended that his "guilt" lay in letting his drug habit get this far gone. Joseph Bergamini had been voluntarily intoxicated with phencyclidine, an illegal substance. No one makes a conscious decision to become psychotic, but in the eyes of the law he had exercised his free will in choosing to get high.

At its core, the insanity defense is about the distinction between evil and madness. Making this distinction is a tall order for a society that has slippery concepts and emotional misgivings about each. Now that we live in a era when religion no longer pronounces judgment and punishment of evildoers, we have turned to the new priesthood of psychiatry, experts who would determine who is "mad" and hence without "sin." Suitably chastened by the imprecision and enormity of this task, some of us "experts" are confessing that at best we even up the odds a bit in trying to figure out why people do what they do. I am still awed and not a little terrified by the moral burden thrust upon me to diagnose the mind and divine the motives of killers like Chandran Nathan, Joseph Bergamini — and Ann Green.

When Ann Green first came to meet me at my psychotherapy office fifteen years ago, she was wearing a tiny gold cherub pin on her jacket lapel. When I asked her about the pin, she said it was one of her most cherished possessions, given to her by her mother upon the birth of her first child. The cherub, she said, was a guardian angel who protects babies. Though Ann Green made this announcement matter-of-factly, I could not help but be shaken by the tragic irony symbolized in that pin: I was evaluating Ann Green because she had suffocated two of her infant children and had been caught trying to suffocate a third.

A middle-aged registered nurse from a well-to-do Philadelphia family, Green had worked in the nursery at New York Hospital and undergone the apparent misfortune of discovering two of her own babies dead in their cribs. A woman much devoted to the rituals of the Catholic Church, she made sure her children both had funeral masses, and her family rallied around her, providing a lot of attention to this grief-stricken mother. Only later would Ann Green admit she had in fact pressed a pillow into the face of her son Jamie and held it there until the baby stopped convulsing. Two years after his death, she killed her infant daughter, Patricia, the same way. She was apprehended while trying to kill her third child, Larry.

In my examination of Green for the prosecution, I could find no evidence of bona fide mental illness. Talking to her and trying to get her to answer questions or take a psychological test was like dealing with a forty-three-year-old Lolita. Ann Green's major interest in life was Ann Green. I knew in my gut that her behavior was not normal, but it was more attributable to a complicated mix of nonnurturing and nonmaternal character traits than a mental illness. There was nothing in my experience as a psychologist and a mother that could help me fathom what went on in the heart and mind of Ann Green as she snuffed the life out of her newborns, one by one, within hours of returning with them from the hospital. The high-ticket defense attorney (later indicted for fraud in a political scam) concocted a sympathy designer defense, claiming postpartum depression. I could only firmly testify "with a reasonable degree of psychological certainty" that I saw no evidence of postpartum depression in Ann Green's psychological history or profile. Astoundingly, despite the fact that she had buried two children, lost custody of the third, and was now facing the ordeal of a murder trial, I saw no evidence of depression at all. What jury would ever buy that?

Whenever the defense lawyer would huddle privately with the judge and the DA to talk strategy during the Green trial, I was excluded from the courtroom and ushered to an anteroom outside the jury's sight. Was I mistaken? Out of my revulsion for her crimes and sympathy for her infants, was I failing to see her distress? I racked my brain. I reviewed my data over and over. And last, I simply and sincerely prayed for wisdom, for mercy, and for proper humility.

Ultimately, Ann Green's jury acquitted her by reason of insanity. To kill your children willfully is an almost unimaginable crime. Only two of the last decade's 231 trials involving infanticide have resulted in verdicts of guilty. Ann Green was sent to a secure mental facility and was released within two weeks. She regained custody of her surviving son and returned to her work as a nurse.

I have seen the courts let too many people like Ann Green get away with murder and other serious crimes by saying, in essence, the devil made me do it. With killers like Ann Green, I believe that devil is a devil they *choose* to listen to. For certain people, of course, that devil really exists. There are among us those who are truly insane, like Joel Rifkin; when I examined him, it was clear he was a paranoid schizophrenic who heard voices and had no idea why he killed. Standing up to an infuriated prosecution, I testified that Rifkin was so mentally impaired that he could not know the nature and consequences of his acts and their wrongfulness. The jury went on to convict him. In my view, this was a miscarriage of justice.

The American justice system is rife with such injustices, as I have learned from two decades of face-to-face encounters with criminals of every stripe. Defense lawyers, prosecutors, expert psychological witnesses, and the media all have their own private agendas when they scrutinize the mind of a defendant. The result: more people are winning insanity verdicts for crimes they knowingly committed, and more truly insane people are being convicted of crimes they are not responsible for. When justice miscarries this way, the entire legal system suffers, and so does America's sense of the rights and responsibilities of its citizens.

Even as we seek to restore and rebalance our social sense of what is right and wrong, we need to ask how, as psychologists and as people, we can deal with the origins of the minds behind crime. How might we decipher the motivations of people like Chandran Nathan, whose chemistry and life experiences thrust them into psychosis? How do we handle an incipient criminal mentality? Are we raising a society that encourages psychopaths like Joseph Bergamini? How do we handle pathology within a family? What about the genetic factors involved in being psychotic or criminally insane? And what about the mysteries behind the people whose predispositions, choices, or environments turn them into blank-faced psychopaths, like Ted Bundy or Jeffrey Dahmer. No psychologist or philosopher can do more than begin to ask those questions, but I do believe we must keep exploring them. We might someday know enough to keep at least some kinds of crime from happening.

Issues of justice and the psyche will always be with us. Our free will — our choice to do evil — may always get us into trouble. But each of us can take more care and responsibility whenever crime and the mind converge.

2

THE TRULY INSANE

November 22, 1993, was an unseasonably warm, golden day. The AM radio station I was listening to as I drove sounded a solemn memorial for John F. Kennedy, who had been shot on this same day thirty years before. I was remembering how as a high school sophomore I felt that my generation had lost a sense of innocence that bloody afternoon.

My car sped along the causeway across Cold Spring Harbor, past entertainer Billy Joel's home. I was en route to the Nassau County jail, a thirty-five-minute journey that would bring me face to face with Joel Rifkin, the most prolific serial killer in New York State history. Rifkin had confessed to strangling seventeen prostitutes over a four-year period and dismembering a few of them. He had been arrested five months earlier after he ran into a utility pole to end a high-speed chase on the Meadowbrook Parkway.

State troopers had initially tried to pull Rifkin over because his pickup had no license plate; the stench from the back of his vehicle alerted the troopers to lift the blue plastic tarp. They found the partially decomposed body of twenty-five-year-old Tiffany Bresciani, whom Rifkin told the cops he had choked to death five days earlier.

As is my practice, I had deliberately avoided newspaper and television coverage of the Rifkin case after that late June night when I heard of his arrest on the eleven o'clock news. Since I often get called in by the prosecution in these high-profile cases, I didn't want to risk prejudicing myself further before I even got a chance to meet him — and I had long since discovered how the news media can distort beyond recognition the facts of a criminal case.

Once I did in fact get called onto the case, all I had read was a letter written by Rifkin to me and delivered via his defense attorney, John Lawrence. Despite the childlike scrawl, and the spelling and punctuation errors, the letter seemed lucid enough, which made it all the more eerie to realize that my name on the paper had been written by the same hand that had crushed the windpipes of seventeen young women.

Today's on-site exam was atypical for me. I was going to jail to evaluate Rifkin in the role of a potential witness for the defense, not the prosecution. In more than three hundred cases I have been called in by the prosecutor, and today I was working for "the enemy" for one of only two times in my career (Chandran Nathan was the other). Driving to the jail, however, I had no idea how much uproar my examination of Joel Rifkin would cause in both my private and professional lives. The dynamics of his mental state would provide a complicated yet inclusive and clear survey of what does and does not constitute "insanity" in American criminal justice.

The Nassau County district attorney's office was among my best clients. I never had to examine a defendant at the jail. Such exams would be held in the offices of the DA, where the defendant would be brought by bus and guarded by police detectives. The show would be clearly under my direction. I would be served cake and coffee, I could break for lunch whenever I wanted, and I had access to the prisoner at my convenience, into the evening if needed. It was a safe and sane environment. Now I was examining a defendant at the request of the defense. I was at the mercy of the corrections officers and the schedule of the jail.

At the same time I was working with Fred Klein, the prosecutor on the Rifkin case, as his expert in another violent homicide case that ultimately would "plead out" the night before it was slated to come to trial. Carver Johnson, age seventeen at the time of his trial, had been accused of using a baseball bat to bludgeon to death a Mexican tourist. Resorting to the insanity defense, his lawyer claimed he suffered from dyslexia, attention deficit hyperactive disorder, and other assorted learning disabilities. My examination revealed that he was a hostile, aggressive, and cunning psychopath with a long history of disruptive behavior and no organic mental illness.

Now Klein, fresh from the case of the "Long Island Lolita," Amy Fisher, had inherited Rifkin as well. After it became clear that Rifkin's attorney had interposed an insanity defense, I expected that Klein might call me in on the case. But when the call came it was from Jack Lawrence, counsel for the defense. Although I had never met Lawrence personally, I had spoken with him professionally for years because he had handled various divorce, custody, and civil cases for my private patients. Based on their reports of his ethics and professionalism, I had a high regard for his integrity.

"I want to ask you a favor," he began. Then, referring to Klein, he told me, "Freddy asked who we were going to get to do the psych part and we said 'Barbara.'"

I was floored. I respected Jack, but I also thought he was on a kamikaze mission. "I'll do it for you, Jack," I said. "But one shot in ten thousand this guy is the genuine article. He's probably a sexual psychopath — a Bundy or a Dahmer. There's little I could do for you other than suggest ways you might present the defense. Most likely what I'll find will be more supportive of the prosecution's case, and I'll probably wind up coming down on that side."

Jack was understanding, appreciative, and desperate. He said he would take care of the necessary court orders and paperwork to gain me entry into the jail. Working for the defense would be very different. I certainly could not be accused of being a hired gun — a term that I have heard mostly applied to those experts who ally only with a prosecutor, zealously pursuing a guilty verdict regardless of the defendant's actual mental state. In my experience, such experts tend to suffer from an identity crisis where they perceive themselves as police officers or district attorneys rather than as objective mental health professionals. They carefully craft their testimony to mesh with the facts of the crime and the theory the prosecution is advancing. They are usually the most highly paid, celebrated, and polished witnesses in terms of their court performance — at the expense of selling out their clinical code of ethics.

The Nassau County Correctional Center, within walking distance of the Rifkin home, had been enlarged and renovated since I had last visited in the middle 1970s, when I was a narcotics parole officer. Clearly, the jail business was booming. Jack was waiting for me in the attorneys' waiting room. I could feel the leers of the corrections officers follow me into the cubicle where the interview was to take place. I was glad Jack was with me. Brown paper had been taped over the glass enclosure in the room, presumably to provide privacy, but as it would turn out, the corrections officers were constantly standing on stools to peer over the top of the paper into the room.

There was a rap on the door, and in slouched Joel Rifkin — not at all what I expected. He appeared small, disheveled, in grungy sweat clothes. His hair was greasy and unkempt, falling over his wire-framed glasses. His most riveting feature was his slender and delicate hands. The hands of a musician, or a surgeon.

Jack Lawrence ushered Rifkin to a metal molded chair directly across from me at a rectangular table. Rifkin was distractedly polite, with a peculiar hangdog look about him. Although he listened intently, he never looked me square in the eye. He seemed to comprehend the directions for the paper-and-pencil tests, including the Minnesota Multiphasic Personality Inventory (MMPI). He said he had taken many psychological and vocational tests throughout school. Occasionally, he would steal furtive, sidelong looks at me while we spoke. Most of the time he seemed utterly absent, as if his self had long since left his body behind.

A pungent, beefy smell filled the room moments before a guard knocked on the door. Rifkin scarcely waited for the orange fiberglass tray to be placed on the table before he lowered his face to the plate and began to eat ravenously. The plate was heaped with brown chunks swimming in a gelatinous gravy of the same color. Mushy rotini tried to squirm out from under it. It smelled like Gravy Train. "The food's pretty good here," he remarked, shoveling forkfuls into his mouth. "I just have a problem with the bologna. I'm allergic to the nitrates. They make me drowsy and confused."

I spent five hours cooped up with Rifkin that day while the COs laughed, caroused, and peeked over the paper into the room like so many adolescents. Rifkin seemed to be more than a little disturbed by their behavior, which provoked several angry outbursts on his part as he would implore his attorney to talk to the sergeant and get them to stop harassing him. Rifkin complained that the COs were stealing his photo IDs and selling them as souvenirs for five dollars. Yet I could detect an undertone of self-satisfaction with the attention he was receiving. "Isn't it ironic," I observed, "that these unfortunate events have made you a hot property, more infamous and more notorious than anything good you ever did before or anything you will ever do after?"

He rolled his vacant, glazed eyes upward. "Yeah." This was an expression that I would soon come to associate with Joel Rifkin whenever I asked him any question that required insight or abstraction. I had seen that same inhuman look in the eyes of a milk shark that my friends and I had once rescued at a beach on Long Island Sound. It was the look that the press described as detached, bored, disinterested, and would later be interpreted as proof positive of his evil and predatory nature and his lack of remorse.

Rifkin never used bad language or four-letter words with me (as he did in his interviews with male doctors), nor was he ever menacing. His demeanor was highly respectful, even courtly at times. When I returned the next day to continue the testing, he reluctantly hinted that the male guards had made obscene cracks and gestures about me as they escorted him back to his cell. Reporting this to me left him confused and unable to regain his concentration on the tests. He would begin to digress and spontaneously talk about his conflicted feelings toward his father; about "working girls" as referred to in a 1959 rock 'n' roll song; or about his childhood experiences. All the while he fondled a leaf sent to him by his sister, for whom he professed great love. "She knows how important nature is to me," he told me.

Rifkin was certainly a depressed and confused misfit. He dubbed himself "herd cull" — the runt of the litter — as he recounted the many episodes of abuse at the hands of his peers throughout school. Once, on a high school track team field trip, some teammates tricked him into missing the bus, and Rifkin was left stranded in Connecticut. No one even missed him until he called his father collect to come and rescue him. His one shred of self-esteem seemed to arise from the fact that he had, as he put it, "never thrown a punch in anger or defense" — a curious contradiction for the confessed killer of seventeen prostitutes.

By the close of this second session, Rifkin had become even more of an enigma to me. Clearly he didn't fit the much-hyped FBI profile of the serial killer. He was very different from Richard Schreiner, a sexual sadist I had examined years before in Queens, who achieved orgasm during anal penetration after he slit the throats of his teenage male victims. I left this second session with more questions than when I first took the case. I raced home to score the tests.

I dropped off a copy of the tests at my office for my assistant to take to a colleague of mine, Jim Audubon, for blind scoring. Blind scoring is a way of ensuring accuracy and objectivity on a psychological test. Simply put, the answers marked by the subject are scored by another psychologist who has no information on the subject other than sex and age, the two factors that are needed to compare the scores to norms. That night, at one A.M., after two or more hours of staring at pencil marks through cardboard scoring templates, I was exhausted. I would wait to analyze the data and plot it on the profile grids tomorrow, after my third session with Rifkin.

The next day, surprised by Rifkin's intense work on the tests, the guards showed a new respect for us, giving us many time extensions before they insisted we break an hour for lunch. I retraced my way through the maze, deciding I would go to the bagel shop down the road. It was quiet there, and I could review my notes from the morning session and plan my questions for the afternoon. But first I called to check in with my office on the pay phone in the lobby — cellular phones could not be brought into the jail. My assistant told me my testing colleague, Jim Audubon, had called, saying, "It's urgent." I dropped another quarter into the phone; Jim picked up as if anticipating my call. "I scored that MMPI. Who is this guy? I never saw elevations like this — they're off the scale."

Jim didn't know he was talking about Rifkin's profile. I hung up the phone, stunned. Although the morning's session had begun to arouse my suspicions, Jim had just told me I had a near-classic psychotic on my hands. As a forensic psychologist wary of insanity defenses, I had defined myself as a debunker, a prosecution witness. What if this guy really was psychotic? Was I prepared for the risk I would be taking with my career and maybe even my life, in supporting the defense in such a high-profile case, working to demonstrate how a killer of young women was not legally responsible for his slayings?

That night, after having spent a claustrophobic afternoon in the company of Joel Rifkin's ramblings, I carefully plotted Rifkin's MMPI scores on the profile sheet. Staring me in the face were the most pathological test results that I had ever encountered in nearly twenty years of administering this test in parole offices, prisons, and the back wards of mental hospitals. What was inescapable was that they were valid: Rifkin had obtained these psychotic results by answering the way paranoid schizophrenics do — consistently and honestly. No matter how many mathematical checks I ran on his subscales for faking and malingering, his scores remained the real thing. Even his scores on the HSAS (Hidden Schizophrenia Attitude Scale), a test developed by my longtime colleague Jim Audubon to detect faking in forensic populations, proved out. The clincher for me in Rifkin's psychological profile was the absence of any antisocial tendencies. Rifkin was a misfit even among serial killers — unlike Ted Bundy and Jeffrey Dahmer, who on the same tests soared to the top of the chart as psychopathic deviates.

Jim's blind-scored profile came in by fax. With comments based solely on the test results, and still not knowing who the subject was, he confirmed my results and wrote in standard psychological language that the subject was a "poorly defended paranoid schizophrenic with defective control, massive hostility, persecutory delusions (with somatic symptoms) and given to possible periods of manic acceleration and feelings he is a special person."

With the psychological tests completed, scored, and analyzed, I spent the holidays of 1993 reviewing Rifkin's voluminous case record, which now filled four cardboard boxes at my home office: the police materials, crime photos, autopsy reports, the medical, psychological, and scholastic records, the extensive press clippings on his crimes, his reams of poetry and short stories, and the many letters he sent to me, his lawyer, and his family. Every day, in between Christmas celebrations and the challenges of therapy with my patients during what is always an emotionally tough season, I was preoccupied with tracking Joel Rifkin's mental state. "You're really into that case," my brother-in-law chided at

Christmas dinner. No one in my family wanted to hear about it; it wasn't a nice topic. I felt very isolated, even contaminated. That Christmas night, I slept fitfully, dreaming of the wild red fox my son had recently tamed to the point of being able to hand-feed her. In the dream, "Foxy" was outside the back door, digging in the flower bed on the patio. I watched from behind the screen door while she unearthed a partially decomposed female body and dragged it to my doorstep. I awoke startled. This case was coming too close to home.

After the New Year, I was in Fred Klein's office, preparing for the trial of Carver Johnson, the juvenile murderer whose status as a mentally sound psychopath was as marked as Rifkin's psychosis was confusing, when Klein entered the room and abruptly confronted me. "You don't know what you're getting into with this Rifkin case." I was on edge, cautious. It was never good practice to discuss an ongoing case with opposing counsel. Although I felt Rifkin was clearly psychotic, I hadn't yet formulated my forensic opinion on whether his mental illness substantially interfered with his ability to know and appreciate what he was doing and to know it was wrong. Establishing a diagnosis of severe mental illness was only the first step. I planned to interview Rifkin extensively on the particulars of the crimes at some later date. I was still in the hypothesis-testing stage — it was too early for me to make any commitments to either side. I explained this to Klein and tried to change the subject back to Johnson.

Klein became heated, bringing up the fact that he'd hired psychiatrist Park Dietz as the main psychological witness for the prosecution. "You'll have to listen to the forty hours or so of Dietz on tape. . . . This guy" — meaning Rifkin — "just did it because he enjoyed it, no matter what depression or mania was going on for him!" I felt Klein was already rehearsing what he would say to a jury. Dietz had notches on his belt from the recent case of serial killer Jeffrey Dahmer. Cool and collected, he would be a formidable adversary, especially if he declared Rifkin to be as sane as Dahmer was.

As I balanced my private practice, my court schedule, and the schedule of the jail, it would be nearly four months before I again saw Rifkin face to face. I arrived at the lockup on March 3, 1994, to discover that there had been a skirmish between Rifkin and Colin Ferguson, the Long Island Railroad gunman being held in protective custody. Ferguson, growing agitated as he was escorted by guards to dinner, broke loose and jumped Rifkin as he too was passing in the corridor. Rifkin's arm and neck were cut and bruised. Because he was now in protective custody — and a celebrity — circumstances had changed radically since my previous visits. Nearly forty-five minutes went by before I was cleared and sent through the first gated sally port to be searched and scanned by the metal detector. My purse contained an emery board and a perfume atomizer, which were confiscated as potential weapons. Even my blister pack of Sudafed was contraband. The sergeant passed the handheld metal detector over me from head to toe. *Bzzz! Bzzz!* I took off my bracelet — *Bzzz!* — and then my watch. *Bzzz!* I removed my belt with its metal buckle. *Bzzz!* I looked imploringly at the guard. "It must be the brass buttons on my dress!" I said.

The chief CO, who had been observing this security ritual from within his bulletproof glass booth, ambled over to see what the delay was. He was clearly from the old paramilitary school of corrections, complete with spit-shined shoes and knife-edge pleats. "Gee, Doc," he said, smiling, as he waved me through, "you look more like a stewardess than someone seeing Rifkin."

The huge steel gate creaked open and I was ushered through the cavernous prisoner's visiting hall to another guarded gate. A pleasant female officer opened the glass-encased interview room — or more accurately booth, since it could not have measured more than six feet by eight. "So you're here to see Rifkin." She shook her head as she took my pass. "Aren't you afraid?"

Rifkin slumped into the chair across from me. He was clearly annoyed that he was forced to wear the fluorescent orange prison jumpsuit required for prisoners in protective custody. There was no spark of recognition in his eyes. It was as if he were meeting me for the first time. With the psychological testing out of the way, I would have a whole day with Rifkin, just to listen to him — interrupted only by the lunch break and prisoner count, during which Rifkin would be returned to the cell tier and I would have to leave the jail. I began to converse with him, gently probing. He began to talk, easily, fluidly, almost in monologue fashion. He recounted his earliest memories, including his feelings about his father, who had killed himself when his son was twenty-seven. ("I realized after Dad died that I would hug and he wouldn't hug back.") He talked expressionlessly about finding his father slumped at the kitchen table after his suicide. He seemed disturbed at the memory of the "gurgling sound" that he heard emanating from his dying father. In our subsequent sessions, he would again refer to that sound as coming from Tiffany Bresciani, his seventeenth and final victim.

It grew hard to get a word in, so relentless was the stream of Rifkin's revelations. His memory for details of his personal history was prodigious, almost obsessive, and as the day went on, it became almost impossible for me to stem his verbal flood tide. It was as if, for the first time in his life, somebody wanted to hear what Joel Rifkin had to say. The details began to overwhelm the thread of his narrative. He started to talk about "touchstones" and the fact that he would be wearing his father's shoes in court because he needed his "presence." The logic of his discourse began to unravel. He digressed (discussing Montessori schools), went off on tangents (outlining plots from *Dark Shadows*, a 1970s gothic soap opera), and began to weave fantasy and reality so closely that it became impossible for me to distinguish whether he was talking about his dreams, his fantasies, TV shows, movies, or actual life experiences.

Suddenly, completely out of context, Rifkin leaned toward me and almost whispered in my ear. "I have premonitions. I will die at sixty-nine. My father died at sixty-eight — outlived his mother by one year." He paused as if to let his trenchant logic sink in. "I predicted my arrest . . . I was thirty-four, which is half of sixty-eight. I knew that number seventeen would be the last because two times seventeen equals thirty-four." He finished with a flourish, as if offering the definitive explanation for why he had killed exactly seventeen women. He had no grasp as to how disoriented he had become, continuing to spew out these calculations, relating each one portentously to his life and crimes. Self-congratulatory, he added, "I even calculated the extra days for leap years, like for the year the Dolphins played the Super Bowl."

One month later, I was back with Rifkin, in what was my last chance to talk to him before the trial. I now not only had to be alert to the symptoms of his psychotic, paranoid, and disordered thinking in order to make the diagnosis; I also had to lead him deftly through recounting the details of seventeen grisly murders, disposal of the corpses (and in at least one case a dismemberment), and his subsequent arrest. Only then could I know if his mental illness precluded his criminal responsibility for the murders.

But examining Joel Rifkin was like swimming upstream. He droned on for hours, in a chilling monotone, about the "events" (as he called them). He expounded on his theory of energy and how it influenced his "site selection" for the burials. After each strangling, he claimed he "had no firm idea" of where he was driving. An impulse would strike him. In choosing a location where he could dispose of a corpse, he told me, "I felt like the person liked the spot." Carting a dead woman around in his pickup truck, he believed that he had to return to the "spot of origin — a spot of comfort — a peaceful sacred place" to "release the energy." Somehow, he said, he "hadn't done the right thing with Tiffany." He kept her body for four days — first in his mother's car, then the garage — while he waited for an impulse telling him where to bury her. He was convinced that Tiffany's energy had made the license plate fall off his truck. He remembered walking to the garage to get into his truck on the night he would be arrested and being "overcome with a feeling that that was it — it was over." When I asked him why he had then fled when the troopers tried to pull him over, he looked at me incredulously. "I was dead meat!" he exclaimed. "I had no license plate, an expired registration, and no seat belt!"

Rifkin expressed no emotion at all, but his thoughts became more fragmented and disjointed. He described the last five minutes of the car chase as "the proudest" of his life because he had succeeded in transferring the engine from another truck to the one he was driving that night and making it work. Indeed, Rifkin's whole psyche was about trying to put the pieces together. But he never succeeded in welding his psychic engine into a working whole.

He claimed that he was having a "debate" with the voice that night that urged him "to complete the circle." "I never thought about it, I just accelerated." He felt that he would crash into a tree or an embankment and be killed. Now, more confused than ever, he marveled that he had crashed into a pole and was unhurt. "It was down-to-the-minute timing. . . . It was all meant to happen . . . like an act of God or fate. We all have finite time." And then, alluding to the women he killed, he said, "This was my bolt of lightning, just like I was theirs."

Based on my testing and interviews, I became convinced that Joel Rifkin was suffering from paranoid schizophrenia. Despite an IQ tested at 130, he had failed to achieve even a marginal level of social development. His employment history was spotty; he mostly lived off handouts from his mother; his bedroom and truck were strewn with debris, and he paid little attention to personal hygiene, often reeking of body odor. Not only was his thinking marked by bizarre and fragmented delusions, but he suffered from disturbances in his ability to perceive reality through his senses. He experienced repeated, transient episodes of hallucinatory experiences — suddenly everything would look very intense, with colors becoming very bright, and every detail in sharp focus, such as wood grain and scratches on wood; sounds were extremely intense. He was deteriorating fast; the whispers of his private world were growing louder, drowning out the part of his experience that still came in touch with reality. He thought he heard "voices" or "whispers" that would tell him "yes" or "no," instructing him whether or not to strangle his next victim. Sometimes, when the fickle voice said "no," Rifkin would immediately release his grasp around the girl's throat. Charlotte, a prostitute who had been with him several times, corroborated that he had his hands around her neck and was beginning to strangle her. They had not had sex. Suddenly, he just let his hands drop, thanked her, paid her, and took her home. She said he was a gentleman, "missionary position only, nothing kinky."

Talking about his victims, Rifkin told me, "They are still living. . . . No energy is ever lost, but energy can be intensified or not, like by thinking of a person on their birthday or death day. I thought of them as gifts to my dad. I started killing close to his birthday in February because the energy was intensified, so Dad would not be alone. Sometimes I can almost touch the energy, sometimes I feel their presence."

Hallucinations and delusions, the sine qua non of schizophrenia, were not well articulated for Rifkin — he was a failure even as a schizophrenic. He could never provide a coherent delusional explanation for why he strangled the women, at least nothing that a jury, schooled as juries are in talk-show psychology, could sink its teeth into. If "the devil made him do it," Rifkin was clueless as to that devil's identity.

"Why, Joel? Why did you do it?" I would probe him.

"I don't know. I don't know," he would reply, rolling his eyes upward and furrowing his brow as if searching for the answers that perpetually eluded him.

His thoughts were like so many images on a screen, a personal videotape that he could play, rewind, and play again. Rifkin's victims were like actors in his own private screenplay: even if they were dead, they could still get up for the next screening. After he strangled Mary Catherine Williamson, for example, he drove to Burger King with the corpse sitting beside him in the front seat of his mother's Toyota. The trauma of her strangulation had caused the victim to regurgitate. Rifkin related to me how he gently dabbed the edge of his Coke-moistened napkin on the corner of her mouth and on her blouse to clean her up, "so she would be presentable."

As his case snaked through murder indictments in nine jurisdictions, Rifkin went on to be examined by more than a dozen other psychiatric and psychological experts. That rarest of criminals, the serial killer, he seduced many of the doctors, who, falling victim to the hubris that characterizes some in our profession, felt they had gotten into his mind. Instead, Rifkin, whose stream of consciousness was turbid and meandering, entered the minds of the doctors. Chameleon-like, and prompted by their inevitably leading questions, he constructed the story that they wanted to hear. In psychological terms this is called confabulation; it is a symptom seen in people suffering from organic damage to the brain — chronic schizophrenics, deteriorated alcoholics, drug addicts, those suffering from senile dementia and head injuries. Confabulation is an attempt to fill in the blanks in one's experience of a sequence of events when there are large gaps in perception and memory. A confabulator is trying to make sense of events that he experiences in a random, disorganized, or confused way.

Rifkin had a flair for writing. He had composed many promising short stories. At last, he was receiving the attention and interest he craved from first-rate intellects, particularly powerful male authority figures who had replaced the father who had failed him even before committing suicide. It was a heady situation, and Rifkin reveled in it, regaling Park Dietz and other examiners with the details and explanations they most wanted to hear. Usually, he could come up with responses that were consistent with an examiner's pet theory about his psyche — adopted child syndrome (Joel was an infant when adopted), necrophilia and sexual sadism, hating prostitutes, sexual abuse and incest, or cunning psychopathy. So taken was Rifkin with center stage that he produced enormously embellished tales of perversion for Dietz, the prosecution witness, following the doctor's every lead. In his paranoid grandiosity, Rifkin was unable to realize how much he was damaging his own case. Dietz would later use some of these more lurid examples in his testimony to weave for the jury a plausible motive for Rifkin's crimes.

Throughout the course of my conversations with Rifkin I often got the impression that he was put off by my objective stance and failure to advance a trendy psychological theory for why he killed. He would almost try to bait me, saying, "Dr. Dietz said I did it because . . ." or "Dr. Ponteus believes . . ." or "Maybe Dr. Kirschner's right." Not surprisingly, Rifkin spared me the fantastical sexual details — fondling corpses, pulling out teeth and fingernails, masturbatory fantasies of bondage — or even denied them to me. In fact, as far as I have been able to determine, no corpses were ever found evidencing the mutilations described by Rifkin. The one statement of Rifkin's that I do believe was that neither he nor anyone involved in the various court cases understood why he committed the murders at all. During my fifty-six hours with him, we both were consumed by our quest for answers. We both came up empty. Or, as Rifkin would later say to the family of his victim Iris Sanchez, "You may all think that I am nothing but a monster, and you are right. Part of me must be."

The insanity plea is rarely successful, and almost never in high-profile cases, defenses set forth by serial killers, or crimes involving confessions or strong physical evidence. A verdict of not guilty by reason of insanity usually involves a diagnosis of schizophrenia and delusions or hallucinations that are actually pertinent to the crime. New York State Supreme Court Justice Charles Siragusa, who as an assistant district attorney prosecuted Arthur Shawcross, the confessed killer of eleven prostitutes, said that Rifkin's attorneys would have to work hard to show he was schizophrenic; they would have to "convince the jury that Rifkin believed God made him kill." But many instances of insanity are far more forthright than Rifkin's problematic condition.

Ameenah Abdus-Salaam, a young Black Muslim mother of five, did not have to convince a jury that Allah told her to push her children out the window of their tenth-story apartment. When I examined her I found her case to be so tragic and bizarre that I advised the Queens district attorney to assume the role of judge and jury and not pursue litigation. Ameenah's case had all the ingredients of a classic M'Naghten defense — a well-articulated delusional system, "command hallucinations," and a psychotic break with reality. She was sweet and sympathetic and appeared to be herself a victim. Most important, hers was an emotional and engaging story involving a situation and a set of delusions that would "make sense" to the general public and probably would have to a jury. The Queens DA agreed that Ameenah should be confined to a maximum-security psychiatric facility on Wards Island until she was no longer dangerously mentally ill.

Ameenah, born a Baptist, had embraced the Muslim religion in her teens. She met her husband at a mosque and bore five children over the next thirteen years. Although others described her as quiet, withdrawn, and a little odd, Ameenah had never received psychiatric treatment. Her mother felt that she was depressed and acting strangely after the birth of her last child. She made an appointment for her daughter with a psychiatrist, but Ameenah never kept it.

Ameenah, a plain woman, was almost obsessively devoted to her handsome husband. To secure her husband's love and attention, she worked ceaselessly, often exhausting herself in caring for the children, her home, and her baking business. When she discovered that her husband had a lover and was considering taking her as another "wife," Ameenah began to come unglued. Reserved to neighbors and isolated from her family in South Carolina, Ameenah made a pilgrimage to Germany to seek spiritual guidance from a Muslim holy man. He advised her to pack her husband's belongings and ask him to leave the home. The prospect of divorcing the man she idolized and being alone was a severe trauma for the fragile and dependent Ameenah. She started thinking that the world was coming to an end and that judgment day was at hand. She began having nightmares and hearing voices telling her that the world would be purged by fire and that she and her children would be saved.

Her delusion proliferated cancerously until it blocked out all semblance of normal reality for her. The voices gave very specific instructions on the preparations she was to make. The night before she was to act, she heard special messages sent to her on the radio. She found herself going "in and out" of these beliefs, first feeling that they were real and then thinking that she must have been dreaming. Soon, however, the delusions and hallucinations increased in intensity until she lost all grip on reality and began to respond obediently in accord with their commands. Buoyed by the delusional promise of salvation and controlled by the alternating voices of Allah and her "mentor," she felt euphoric. She bustled around the apartment, as she told me later, "making plans — packing things to go — like canned goods and medicine" for their life "after the fire."

In the final moments, she stripped herself and her five children naked, urinated on them, and began to push them out the window. Her seven-year-old daughter, Zainab, went first, followed by her three-year-old son. The little girl died on impact. The boy landed on top of his sister, which broke his fall and saved his life. Mercifully, firefighters racing to a nearby blaze saw the children falling from the tenth floor and radioed police. The fact that the older children resisted bought them time until the police arrived.

As the rescuers smashed down the door, a nude Ameenah rushed to attack them, shrieking, "Devils!" and babbling incoherently.

Ameenah's mental state was obvious to the officers, who restrained her and took her for psychiatric observation. Within seventy-two hours of receiving antipsychotic medication, Ameenah became lucid, coherent, and oriented to time, person, and place. When she was told the news of her children, Ameenah was so filled with guilt and remorse that she tried to kill herself.

Suffering from psychotic delusions, Ameenah intended to protect and save her children. Instead, she brought about their injury and death. After examining her, I found no question that she was suffering from a mental illness that substantially impaired what the M'Naghten statute calls her "capacity to know and appreciate the nature and consequences of her actions and their wrongfulness." The district attorney accepted this, and Ameenah was remanded to a maximum-security psychiatric hospital.

A similar clear-cut clinical picture emerged in the murder trial of Dennis Sweeney, an illustrious Peace Corps worker and civil rights activist of the 1960s, who in 1980 emptied the magazine of a Lama pistol into the head of congressional representative Allard Lowenstein of New York. Despite the promise of his college years, Sweeney had in the wake of the 1960s become a drifter, a marginal man suffering from delusions, hallucinations, and paranoid beliefs that people were talking about him and plotting against him. He believed that a transmitter had been put in his dental fillings by the CIA so that they could spy on him — a clichéd but pervasive delusion among paranoids. Although deteriorating in his functioning through the progressive worsening of untreated schizophrenia, the still boyishly handsome Sweeney could seem bright, articulate, even convincingly charming at times. He kept up a correspondence with Representative Lowenstein, whose acquaintance he had made during Robert Kennedy's 1968 presidential campaign. The receptionist could not have suspected that day when the familiar figure breezed by her directly into her boss's office that she would next see Lowenstein slumped over his desk, dead.

Sweeney was out of touch with reality, hallucinating and responding to a paranoid delusional system that made him believe Lowenstein possessed the power to destroy people. He was sure that Lowenstein had willed the murder of San Francisco mayor George Moscone in 1978, as well as the 1979 crash of a DC-10 in Chicago. When a pipe wrench fell on his head in a construction accident and his stepfather died suddenly of a heart attack,

Sweeney resolved to go to Lowenstein and beg him to stop torturing him and others. If he got sufficient assurances, he would go home. If not, he was resolved to destroy his tormentor.

Instead of humoring him, Lowenstein challenged him. He told him he needed to see a psychiatrist to make the voices stop. Sweeney drew the gun from his windbreaker and fired until there were no bullets left. A Manhattan jury acquitted him by reason of insanity, and he remains in a maximum-security mental hospital.

Rarely does a case fit the legal statute of insanity so well as those of Dennis Sweeney and Ameenah Abdus-Salaam. For better or worse, there are few textbook psychotics who manifest such clear and conclusive hallucinations and delusions relevant to their crimes. Most cases resemble Rifkin's more confusing one, where the killer operates without any clear delusions or hallucinations and has no motive or theory for his crime. In the continuing backlash of hostility against the insanity defense arising from John Hinckley's verdict, cases of more atypical schizophrenics like Rifkin have had difficulty receiving a fair and just judicial outcome. In a sense, Rifkin was too crazy to be found legally insane.

For the majority of cases, a verdict of not guilty by reason of insanity is an unlikely outcome. So some unscrupulous defense attorneys resort to "designer defenses" — carefully tailored pop-psychology excuses, such as the notorious "Twinkie defense" in the 1979 case of Dan White, the killer of San Francisco's mayor George Moscone and supervisor Harvey Milk. White's lawyers claimed he'd been eating so much junk food he'd lost his judgment. These designer defenses can sometimes hold up when a standard insanity plea does not, because they operate on logic that is specious but seductive. Yet in cases in which an acquittal by reason of insanity is justified, the public often misunderstands the meaning of the outcome and how it can serve the interests of society, the victim, and justice itself.

Even when defendants are acquitted of a crime by reason of insanity, they usually wind up spending more time incarcerated in maximum-security hospitals for the criminally insane than felons convicted of the same offense spend in prison. There are no swimming pools, law libraries, or college courses offered in psychiatric hospitals. In terms of relative cost, mental hospitals are bargains for the taxpayers. More important, there is no parole from madness. Attorneys for serial killer David Berkowitz grasped these dynamics extremely well when they advised him to eschew the insanity defense. Although the "Son of Sam" claimed that a neighbor's dog told him to do the killings, he wisely pled guilty to killing five women and one man and was sentenced to twenty-five years to life in New York. His record in jail has been impeccable and he will be eligible for parole in six years.

At a recent lecture that I presented at C. W. Post College, a poll of my upscale, educated audience revealed that almost 90 percent of them believed that sane people are using the insanity defense to get away with murder. I fear that my attempt that night to present an accurate, fact-based argument may not have penetrated the wall of fear and prejudice that surrounds madness in general and the insanity defense in particular. After my lecture, I was approached by the great-granddaughter of Stanford White, the socially prominent architect of Madison Square Garden who in 1906 was gunned down by his paramour's deranged husband. She was visibly shaken and still raging about the injustice of letting the killer, Harry K. Thaw, "get away" with her great-grandfather's murder ninety years ago. Some accounts of the day say that Thaw was acquitted because he really was insane. Others nod to the unwritten law prevailing at the time that allowed husbands to kill their wives' lovers, plead temporary insanity, and get away with it. Whichever view is correct, Thaw spent most of his life in an insane asylum — a fate that did not appease his victim's great-granddaughter.

I don't believe that a massive overhaul of the statutes or abolition of the insanity defense itself is in order. Yet it remains a popular and easy political target. Mental patients have no constituency and don't vote. Scapegoating the mentally ill has a long historical precedent. Abolishing the insanity defense amounts to revenge, not justice, in those rare cases where it genuinely applies. By unthinkingly sending people like Joel Rifkin and Chandran Nathan to prison, we are punishing the mentally ill rather than treating their illness. And we are failing as a society to grapple with the complex issues involved in distinguishing between illness and evil.

Many times when I am called upon to evaluate a defendant I do find evidence of serious mental retardation or mental illness — schizophrenia, delusional disorders, or organic psychotic states due to alcohol, crack cocaine, or other substances. Then I must carefully ascend the decision ladder to the next rung — the toughest judgment call of all: How much did this person's mental disease interfere with the ability to know what he or she was doing, what the consequences would be, and that the actions were wrong?

The case of Luc George shows how all these components must be in place for a viable insanity defense under M'Naghten statutes, even in the presence of serious, longstanding, and psychiatrically well documented schizophrenia. From his teenage years, George had manifested all the acute symptoms of paranoid schizophrenia. He had been hospitalized on many occasions for attempting to hang himself. As time went on, his outbursts became more dangerous and aggressive. I first met him while he was a twenty-three-year old patient at Creedmoor, a New York State mental hospital, where he had been committed after assaulting his two young cousins and sexually molesting his seventeen-year-old sister. Heavily medicated, he was quiet and cooperative. Robust, well-groomed, and handsome, Luc George charmed the female staff into giving him special attention and privileges.

Luc George was also his grandmother's favorite child. He lived with her and depended on her generosity. One day, four years after he had been released from Creedmoor, she turned down his request for more spending money. He decided to retaliate by setting fire to her house. Methodically, he purchased a can of gasoline, saturated furniture and draperies throughout the house, and doused the carpet covering the stairs to the second floor, where his grandmother and a three-year-old cousin slept. Beginning at the top of the stairs, he ignited the carpet behind him as he made his way out of the house, trapping his grandmother and the child. Once outside, he rolled in the dirt to smother the flames that scorched his pants. He sustained minor burns. His grandmother and cousin were burned to death, and other family members were critically burned. When I next saw Luc George, it was as a prosecution witness examining his motives and mental state surrounding the crime. Although ever the polite dandy, George did express some annoyance at having to take all these tests for me. "That's the *last* test I'm going to do," he told me, as he stamped petulantly out of the lockup after the exam.

This young man's mental illness was chronic and well documented. No one disputed that he was psychologically impaired. Nevertheless, the M'Naghten Rule revolves around knowing right from wrong. It is improbable that his express intention was to kill his grandmother and young cousin, or severely burn his relatives and the family home. In his rage and frustration at having been denied his wishes, he could focus only on wanting to punish them and teach them a lesson. But he was capable of formulating a plan that included trapping his family and permitting his own escape. He knew what gasoline could do; he knew the danger of fire. He lied to police and firemen at the scene, an indication that he was aware he had done something illegal. Under M'Naghten, his insanity defense failed and he was convicted of arson.

In an even thornier case, I had to evaluate Oliver Petrovich, age twenty-four, who shotgunned his parents in their sumptuous Great Neck home after they discovered that he had been hiding his teenage girlfriend in his bedroom closet for several weeks. The case had many of the features of the later, notorious Menendez case and might have aroused the same sort of media hype, inspired similar sympathy for the killer, and perhaps bought time for him with a hung jury, except for the fact that it was tried in the late 1980s, a few years before such designer defenses came into vogue. More pertinently, however, the defense counsel in the case,

Nicholas Marino, was a decent guy. He pled a standard insanity defense, not one based on alleged flashbacks of abuse or other "designer" elements. The Petroviches, self-made Yugoslavian immigrants, were rigid, punitive, and controlling of their only child; they were described by many as cold and eccentric. Oliver was shy, socially backward, had struggled in school, and spoke with an incapacitating stutter. My examination of him for the prosecution revealed definite schizoid disturbances in his personality and gaps in his logic and thinking. His MMPI profile showed a significant clinical elevation in schizophrenia; he reported many bizarre symptoms.

Nevertheless, a careful review of the events surrounding the crime convinced me that, mental problems notwithstanding, Oliver had hatched an elaborate plan to kill his parents, carried it out, and then attempted to dispose of the murder weapon and report the killing as a robbery-murder to the police. His girlfriend testified that he wanted to inherit the family home and money.

Petrovich had grown more exhibitionistic and bulked up from the jail's food and gym by the time I examined him. He exhibited no remorse; instead, he reveled in the attention, watched all the news coverage about himself, and chatted boisterously with the detectives. All this behavior, in a clinical sense, grew from the social inappropriateness and emotional deficits of his illness. Oliver definitely had some emotional problems, but his brashness did not inspire sympathy. The defense would have a hard time explaining subtle psychological diagnoses to a jury deliberating the fate of this swaggering, muscle-bound killer, who seemed to be amused by the whole spectacle.

The jury rejected the defense's psychiatric testimony with its depiction of Oliver Petrovich as a disturbed young man who "exploded" when his parents rejected his black girlfriend. Petrovich was convicted on two counts of second-degree murder for shooting his parents, Peter and Anna. Maintaining that he plotted the murders in a "chillingly calculated way," Judge John S. Thorp sentenced Petrovich to a maximum term of fifty years to life imprisonment.

I have seen the M'Naghten Rule applied so narrowly by prosecution experts that almost no defendant, no matter how severely mentally ill, meets the definitions in the statute. Of one severely delusional and paranoid defendant, an expert witness declared, "He said he knew it was a gun. (He didn't think it was a banana.) He said he knew it fired bullets. He said he knew bullets could kill. He said he knew it was wrong to kill." I suggested to this psychiatrist, in disbelief, that his five-year-old child could meet those criteria and be responsible for a crime. He just shrugged.

It is a well-guarded secret among professional witnesses that the tools used by psychiatrists — a defendant's self-reports and mental status exams — are not effective in determining which criminals are mentally ill and not responsible. The objective testing methods of psychologists fare somewhat better. But a criterion of insanity that is both understandable and acceptable to psychiatrists, psychologists, lawyers, and jurors has yet to be devised.

Further complicating the question is not only how we diagnose the mentally ill; it's whether we wish to treat them, punish them, or protect ourselves from them. In an impassioned plea in his book *Breaking Points*, the father of John Hinckley has questioned the logic of those who seek to resolve the issue by abolishing the insanity defense altogether: "*Nobody* benefits when a severely mentally ill felon is sent to prison rather than to a maximum-security mental hospital. . . . If sent to prison, however, he will likely receive no treatment for his sickness, yet be paroled in a few years in a worse condition than ever. Society and the ill felon are both losers."

In a letter written to his mother from jail, Joel Rifkin made this observation:

The three days with Barbara were amazing, just skimming the surface like we did. She told me things about myself I never saw. I honestly do not know how this happened. I might never know. I find that when I talk to someone like Barbara that I can concentrate or focus enough to get through. What was the point of myself ever being born? I feel like it was cursed from the start.

Are some people "cursed from the start"? Or are killers somehow created by the circumstances of their lives? These questions, of more than passing interest to society, have particular resonance for the families of the criminally insane. There are no therapy manuals written for the parents of insane murderers. How they defend themselves emotionally from the shock of their children's crimes and what responsibility they may share vary enormously with the personalities of the parents and their circumstances. And how they respond — denial, bewilderment, refusal to even recognize a problem — shows how society responds as well.

Jean and Jan Rifkin sat next to each other on the sofa in my office. At first glance, they were no different from any of the other people who might seek out my services for treatment of depression, family problems, or anxiety. The neatly dressed, white-haired older woman was gracious, well spoken; her daughter, teary-eyed, more withdrawn and fragile. In polite, conversational discourse, the older woman spoke of her son, his childhood difficulties, his gentleness, his love of animals. She referred me to a videotape she had given me to watch. The video showed Joel in the crotch of a huge tree, cutting off limbs and pruning the branches in a macabre metaphor of the dismemberments of his victims' corpses which, I realized, was simultaneously occurring in his private world. "He filmed it as a project in horticulture school," she told me, beaming. On it she had written, "Joel in a Tree — A Mother's Nightmare!"

The Rifkin family were not monsters, nor did they fail to try to get psychiatric help for their troubled adopted son. The father, Ben, had been a strong enough figure to stabilize them. When he took his own life in desperation over the pain of his prostate cancer, the family fell apart. Mrs. Rifkin turned to alcohol; sister Jan

slipped into drugs; and Joel crumbled within his "private world."
How, I wondered, were these two ordinary but broken women go-
ing to be able to go on with their lives? For families like the
Rifkins, denial seems to be the defense mechanism of choice.
There are some things in the human heart that are so unspeakable
that we can easily convince ourselves they don't exist.

Ironically, this denial is probably what prevented Joel's crimes
from coming to light sooner. His progressively deteriorating
mental state was amply reflected in the disorganization and chaos
of his room and living quarters. Little by little since his father's
suicide, Joel's ever-accumulating, senseless, and worthless belongings (books, papers, envelopes from bills, flattened pieces of chew-
ing gum tinfoil, soda cans) had metastasized through each room
of the family home, crowding Jan and his mother into smaller and
smaller living space. The garage was so full of trash that the family
car no longer fit. Literally hidden behind this wall of debris and
denial, the body of Tiffany Bresciani lay for three days until Joel
put it in the back of his truck.

Just days after meeting Rifkin's mother, I would be conferring
with the parents of Chandran Nathan, the paranoid, self-styled
superhero who had shot to death the fiancé of the woman who had
long obsessed him. Dr. Nathan, a physicist, seemed puzzled that
his son's behavior could not be solved or predicted — unlike an
equation or the movement of a molecule. In a quiet, discursive
manner, Dr. Nathan described his family as very traditional and
quite suspicious of American culture. He decried the violence,
sexual acting-out, materialism, and breakdown of the family that
he felt were epidemic in the Western lifestyle. Mrs. Nathan sat
brokenhearted, awaiting her husband's nod to speak. Sadly, she
recounted her son's obsession with weapons, science fiction, and
superheroes. She admitted that the entire family was struggling to
adjust to a vastly different culture and felt they had "no standards"
against which to compare their son's erratic, belligerent behavior.
Last, Dr. Nathan, described as "analytical and unemotional" by
his son, opined that perhaps Chandran needed a dose of Christian

religion, with its emphasis on hell and damnation, to keep him in line. The family's Hindu religion may have been too gentle and abstract to deal with the harsh realities of the Western world, or so he mused to me.

On yet another day in my office, sitting before me were a burly retired NYC sanitation worker and his withered, sullen wife. Their son, John Martin, was incarcerated in a secure facility after being acquitted by reason of insanity of vehicular homicide for running down two elderly women with his father's car. "All I know is that my wife and I did everything to help John," he boomed. "Even when he was a little kid and he did something wrong. . . . She would fill up the bathtub with hot water, and I would hold his head under for a minute to teach him a lesson. We were good parents."

Perhaps we should not be surprised that families deal with their children's crimes in the characteristic ways that they deal with all serious emotional problems. The Rifkins denied; the Nathans projected blame onto Western society; the Martins congratulated themselves. Like the Hinckleys, none of these families could bear the pain of confronting their own potential failure or culpability. But could any of us?

3

THE FACE OF EVIL:
PSYCHOPATHIC CRIME

*S*tephanie Wernick was a twenty-
year-old student at C. W. Post College, a branch of Long Island
University situated on the former estate of Marjorie Merri-
weather Post of the cereal empire. She was a petite young woman
with flowing mahogany hair and dark eyes overarched by heavy,
Brooke Shields brows. With her discreet jewelry and casual way
of dressing, in oversized tops and leggings, she fit right in with the
other coeds who attended this expensive private college in the
heart of Long Island's Gold Coast.

It was the last Monday of the fall 1990 semester at C. W. Post.
Students were cramming for their final exams and beginning to
clear out for the Christmas vacation. The December weather had
beaded the trees with ice and left the college roadways treacherous
for cars and pedestrians. Just the week before, Stephanie and one

of her girlfriends had had a minor car accident when they skidded on the ice. No one was seriously hurt. Stephanie was a little stiff and sore, but she was too preoccupied with finals to go for a medical exam.

Jeannette Lopez, a student living in Stephanie's dormitory, was doing some last-minute studying on December 17 at six A.M. in the second-floor study hall. She recognized Stephanie as a resident of the second floor when Stephanie approached and asked if she could get a tampon from her. Jeannette went to her room, got the tampon, and brought it to Stephanie in the bathroom. She handed it to her under the stall and asked if she needed anything else. Stephanie said no, and Jeannette returned to the study hall. After ten minutes she returned to find Stephanie still in the stall and asked if she was okay. Stephanie complained that she had never gotten her period so heavily before and that she was sitting in a pool of blood. Could Jeannette get her a sanitary napkin? "Do you want me to walk you back to your room?" Jeannette asked. Stephanie declined, saying that she was just going to sit in the bathroom for a while.

Twenty minutes later, leaving the study hall, Jeannette ran into her friend Laura Maher. As they were talking, Jeannette was startled by an odd sound. She turned to Laura in surprise. "I heard a cry that sounded like a baby — did you hear that?"

Laura had heard nothing. They listened intently for a few seconds until they both heard moaning coming from the women's bathroom a few feet from the staircase — and then the same cry again. This time Laura also heard it: a short little wail.

Both girls ran to the bathroom to find Stephanie still locked in the stall. They asked her if she was all right. From under the door, Laura could see that Stephanie's feet were covered with blood. So was the floor surrounding the toilet. In a calm voice from behind the door, Stephanie said, "I'm fine. I'm fine. Everything is okay."

Panicked, the two girls ran down to Stephanie's room and woke up her roommate, Jody Klein, telling her they had seen blood around Stephanie's feet in the bathroom stall. They said nothing about the sound of a baby crying; neither could be sure of what she had heard. Still uneasy, Jeannette went to shower and dress for class. Laura waited in the dorm room for a few minutes while Jody went to the bathroom to check on Stephanie. Laura had suspected that Stephanie was pregnant by her changing figure — her sorority sisters gossiped about it — but to give birth in a dormitory bathroom seemed beyond their imagining.

Jody Klein noticed blood spots on the floor inside the stall where Stephanie was. "Stef, it's Jody. Are you okay? Do you need anything?"

In a firm voice from behind the door, Stephanie insisted, "I'm all right. I've had a bad period and I'm bleeding a lot. I don't need anything. Go back to the room."

Jody did as she was told, reassuring Laura and Jeannette that their dormmate was fine. They shouldn't worry.

At about seven-fifteen A.M. Sylvia Gonzalez, a maid, entered the bathroom in the east wing of Post Hall. She saw a girl in the first booth nearest the entrance door, a puddle of blood underneath her. The blood was still dripping. Concerned, Sylvia asked if there was a problem. Through the locked door, Stephanie said, "I'm okay. I'm just having a heavy period. I'll clean the blood."

Sylvia went about her business, removing the garbage bags from the trash can inside the bathroom and replacing them with another double bag. Later, she would distinctly remember placing a brown plastic bag inside a white one.

When Stephanie did not return to her room after ten minutes, Jody became concerned. She returned to the bathroom, bringing a towel, a soap dish, and some sanitary napkins for her friend. Stephanie was still in the same stall. It was almost seven-thirty, an hour and a half since Stephanie had first gone to the bathroom. Stephanie told her to leave the items on the counter by the sink. She was going to take a shower. As Jody turned to leave the bathroom, Stephanie called out, "Bring me another towel. I want to wipe the floor up." And then, almost as an afterthought, Stephanie said, "Oh, can you throw out my clothes? They're all bloody. They're in that white plastic bag on the floor outside."

Jody was happy to help out. She picked up the plastic bag and took it down the hall to the garbage room. Jody remembered thinking that the bag was a little heavier than she expected clothing to weigh.

Sylvia Gonzalez went to clean another room and then came back to check on the young woman bleeding in the bathroom. Stephanie was walking toward the shower, wearing a sweatshirt but no pants. When she ran into Jody outside the bathroom, Sylvia was understanding and discreet. She felt that the girls were embarrassed by the indelicacy of the situation and wanted their privacy. She continued with her cleaning chores.

When Jody entered the bathroom, Stephanie was in the shower. She called out that she was better and would be back in the room in a couple of minutes.

Stephanie returned to her room with one of the two towels Jody had given her wrapped around her body and the other turbanlike around her head. She seemed woozy, out of it. Jody was worried. She offered to call a doctor, take her to the hospital, or at the very least call her mother. Stephanie refused. "I'm fine and I just want to go to sleep for a while," she told her friend. She put on blue sweatpants and a white sweatshirt. Jody glanced at the clock — it was eight A.M. Both girls then fell asleep.

Down the hall at the far east corner near the garbage room, Ireno Cruz, a custodian, called excitedly in Spanish to Sylvia. He showed her the white garbage bag with the brown plastic liner, just like the ones she had put in the bathroom trash can. There was a bloodied towel thrown on top of it. They were upset and curious and called to a second custodian, Luis Cruz. Quickly Luis opened the bag. Inside was an infant boy.

Sylvia and the custodians called campus security and the Old Brookville police, who responded within minutes. En route to the hospital, Sergeant Robert Piampiano tried repeatedly to administer CPR to the infant, but the baby's chest was not expanding. He thrust his fingers in a sweeping motion down the child's throat — and found bits of paper. He tried over and over again to clear the baby's airway.

At North Shore University Hospital, Dr. George Dunn and the emergency room staff used forceps to remove a total of seven wads of paper from the baby's throat. Pediatrician James O'Rourke raced to the ER in response to reports of the premature infant's emergency. "Has the baby been intubated?" O'Rourke asked.

"No," Dr. Dunn told him. "We can't even see the normal anatomy of the child's throat to intubate him." He motioned to the wadded-up paper on the forceps tray. O'Rourke grabbed a laryngoscope and peered deep into the baby's throat. There was still something blocking the passage. He asked for another forceps-type instrument, struggling with the blockage because it was so tightly packed. His initial tries only resulted in small shreds of tissue tearing off the matted pulp. In the course of a very long minute, after four more attempts, he was able to remove the entire mass — three or four clumps of toilet tissue that had been wadded firmly into individual balls and wedged into the child's throat. At no time did the baby show any signs of life.

On December 17, 1990, just hours after his entry into the world, the child who would become known as Baby Boy Wernick was pronounced dead. Dr. O'Rourke listed as cause of death "asphyxia by obstruction of airway with foreign matter (paper)." Under manner of death, he wrote, "HOMICIDE."

At nine A.M. Stephanie and Jody were awakened by housemother Susan Hennesey and a safety officer. A baby had been found in the east wing. The other girls said Stephanie had given birth. Stephanie was pale, somewhat agitated, and clearly nervous. She denied that she had been pregnant. "I know how to take care of myself, and besides my parents would kill me!" she told them.

When emergency medical technician Laura Plezia arrived and insisted Stephanie be transported to the hospital for her own safety, she became loud and somewhat combative, continuing to deny she had delivered a baby. Police detective Robert Ryder found Stephanie on the telephone talking to her father. "Please say good-bye," the officer said, "because I have something I want to talk to you about."

Stephanie ignored him and continued her conversation with her father. Laura Plezia turned to Detective Ryder in frustration. "This girl needs to go to the hospital but doesn't want to. Is she in custody?"

Ryder glanced at Stephanie. She was sickly looking, greenish, clearly in an exhausted state. "Consider her in custody."

He again asked Stephanie to stop her phone call — she was going to be taken to the hospital. Stephanie snapped that she didn't want to go to the hospital. She was going to leave and return to her family in New Jersey. She ordered them all out of her room. Again, Detective Ryder insisted that she get off the telephone. Stephanie tossed her still damp, wavy hair. "Am I under arrest?" she challenged.

"Yes," said Detective Ryder firmly. He began advising her of her rights.

As EMT Plezia started prepping her, Stephanie steadfastly denied to Ryder any knowledge of the baby. Finally, after a pause, she whispered, "I want to tell you something about this, but my father told me not to talk to you." Once she was in the ambulance, Stephanie told EMT Plezia that she had started severe cramping the night before. Early that morning she went to the bathroom, delivered the baby into the toilet, removed it, and wrapped it in a pink towel. "I pulled and grabbed on the cord till it came apart," Stephanie said to the female medic. "I cleaned myself up with toilet paper, then took a shower. When I finished the shower, the baby was gone." She paused, to let it sink in that the infant had disappeared. "I went back to bed to go to sleep," she added. Stephanie finished this chilling revelation simply, as if by explanation: "I bled every month. I didn't know I was pregnant."

The Wernick family rallied around her. Her grandfather claimed the deceased infant's body, while her father retained a former Nassau County prosecutor as her attorney. Stephanie was whisked off to a private rehab facility in Belle Mead, New Jersey, for psychiatric evaluation. Seventeen days after the suffocation of her baby, she was discharged and sent home to her family. Psychiatrists at the facility had diagnosed her as having "adjustment disorder with disturbance of conduct," one of the mildest admissible diagnoses, and a disorder that by its very definition goes away within ninety days, even if untreated.

The courts were not so dismissive. Stephanie Wernick was charged with six counts of manslaughter in the first degree for the asphyxiation of her infant boy.

The only possible legal recourse for Stephanie Wernick was an insanity defense. Her attorney was faced with a major challenge in building his argument. The tepid psychiatric diagnosis would not help him out very much, nor would the fact that his client had been given no medication. This young woman's record stated unequivocally that there was no evidence of psychosis, mood disturbance, or personality disorder. How could so seemingly "normal" a young woman commit such an unspeakable crime?

After the shock of the grand jury indictment, life settled into a routine at the Wernick household. Stephanie enrolled in nearby Montclair State College, worked part-time as a waitress in an Italian restaurant, and began a long-distance romance with a young man in Auburn, New York, whom she only saw occasionally. She didn't think it was relevant to mention to him anything about what she called her "legal troubles." At her lawyer's insistence, she was seen weekly by first one and then a second psychiatrist. Both doctors noted that Stephanie was limited in insight and not very motivated. Her sessions were generally pretty superficial.

One afternoon, I got a telephone call at my private therapy offices from Nassau County prosecutor George Peck. I had worked with Peck on the case of Yong Ho Hon, a Korean honor student who had savagely stabbed a sixteen-year-old friend and buried a carving knife in the brain of his thirteen-year-old sister in an altercation over a BB gun. I liked Peck's competence and his breadth of understanding on these psychological cases. Most important, I had found him to be fair — an increasingly rare commodity among prosecutors trying to make a political name for themselves in high-profile, media-saturated cases.

Peck described to me the details of the Wernick case. "Here's why it's perfect for you," he told me. There would be a tremendous outpouring of sympathy toward a young girl who had delivered a baby alone and unassisted, in fear of her parents and in the face of social stigma. I knew that, traditionally, such cases were rarely even prosecuted; in more than 285 cases in the United States and the United Kingdom, not once did a mother charged with neonaticide ever serve more than an overnight in jail. The Wernick family had means and were prepared to put up their own battery of psychological experts to explain Stephanie's crime. In Peck's view, I could present myself on the stand as a concerned clinician, not a hired gun, which might make a jury take note and listen.

Peck shared my beliefs about the utility and potential persuasiveness of psychological tests. He believed that a clean bill of health on those tests, if that's what we came up with, would go a long way to convincing the jury that Stephanie Wernick was not "crazy" and had not "just snapped." The tests also might shed some light on the character traits and personality of someone who would suffocate her own newborn.

Having cut back on my forensic work, I was reluctant to take on the case. In the post-Hinckley backlash against the insanity defense, the legal manipulations had grown more scurrilous, with the pressure on the prosecution witness to "win" more intense. But I was still haunted by the specter of Ann Green, hovering over the bodies of her asphyxiated infants and then beating the rap. And moments before Peck had called, I'd concluded a therapy session with an infertile couple desperately trying to adopt a child.

Their earnest and tearful frustration helped spur me into accepting Peck's offer. "Send me the stuff, George, and I'll take a look at it," I said. "I'll meet with her, test her, and we'll see what comes up." As always, I told Peck that even though he had hired me I could not guarantee I would ethically be able to arrive at an opinion helpful to his prosecution. Any forensic mental health professional worth her salt has to make those caveats.

The next day a huge package of material arrived from the DA's office. It contained medical records, statements of witnesses, autopsy reports, psychiatric reports by five defense experts. I left it unopened on my desk. I make it a strict practice never to read any material that could potentially bias me for or against the defendant before I have the opportunity to meet and examine him or her face to face and administer objective psychological tests.

Stephanie Wernick was scheduled to undergo her examination with me at my office on April 16, 1993. Her attorney, Steve Scaring, sent his wife, who was also his assistant and a registered nurse, to sit in on the exam. George Peck was present as well. Most of the time I prefer to examine a defendant without either counsel present, and most of the time that is how it happens. The presence of so many people during the interview tends to affect the interaction between the defendant and me, making it more tense, more stilted, and more difficult for me to get the in-depth clinical information I need to form an accurate impression of the defendant's personality and mental state. It also puts pressure on my performance. This case was starting out so acrimoniously that it was clear that every legal *i* must be dotted and *t* crossed.

Stephanie arrived late, accompanied by her older brother, Michael, a tax attorney. He complained vociferously about the traffic and was clearly annoyed at having to appear at a therapist's office. As soon as Stephanie saw Maureen Scaring, she became tearful and embraced the older woman. After Michael left the office to find a place in town to eat, a change came over Stephanie. Once quiet, she became quite petulant and demanding; clearly the examination was her show and was going to be conducted on her terms. I explained to her that today would mostly be composed of her taking paper-and-pencil psychological tests and that I would not be asking her any details of the crime or interviewing her in any way. She seemed relieved at that, although she did complain about where George Peck was sitting — directly across from her; she said he made her nervous. "I don't understand why he's trying to do this to me," she said, referring, I thought, not just to the tests but to the entire prosecution.

I could soon surmise that Stephanie was a young woman who was used to having things her way and had little tolerance for inconvenience or discomfort. Throughout the course of the exam, she variously complained about the heat in the office, the sound coming through the walls, the noise the toilet made when she used it, where George Peck was sitting, the glare from the desk lamp, the traffic getting here, and the fact that she would have to come back so I could complete the assessment. When it became clear to her that this exam was inevitable and that it was in her best interests to get it over with as quickly as possible, she did just that. Stephanie, despite her initial tears and fears, completed the first 366 questions of the MMPI psychological test in less than forty-five minutes; the average length of administration is one and a half hours. She never asked any questions, she just worked steadily, with incredible determination and alacrity. When she was finished I thanked her for her cooperation and scheduled our next appointment. Leaving quickly, she had little time for pleasantries.

I began to score Stephanie's tests as soon as I got home that evening. This woman who had murdered her newborn baby mystified me, and the results of these tests could begin to shed some light on her psychological makeup. I carefully scored the test and plotted the numbers on the test graph. The curve was markedly flat; there were no significant clinical elevations. In other words, this young woman had no mental illness, no depression, no thought disorder, no nothing. It was an absolutely unremarkable profile. Stephanie Wernick was still a mystery.

If she was not mentally ill, what made her do what she did? Never before had I seen such a seemingly normal person commit such a vicious murder on such an innocent victim. Surely, this very normality and the incomprehensibility of her crime would be the essence of her defense strategy: some combination of temporary insanity, amnesia, brief reactive psychosis, dissociation, postpartum psychosis, and Stephanie's allegedly low IQ. All of this would constitute the defendant's neonaticide designer defense.

If she could appear sympathetic, and if Steve Scaring was convincing enough, Stephanie could walk. After all, defense attorney Michael Dowd had been able to pull that off years before in the Ann Green case. In fact, at the same time as the Wernick case was beginning, Dowd was again hoping that this would work for Caroline Beale, a thirty-year-old British woman who delivered her baby girl in a hotel bathtub while on vacation in New York, drowned her, and put her into a plastic bag. She was apprehended going through customs with the bag tied around her chest at Kennedy Airport eighteen hours later.

Neonaticide cases are the single most successful use of the insanity defense. It seems incomprehensible to a jury that any mother would deliberately take the life of her own child. Steve Scaring and the Wernick family were banking on that. I recognized that the key to countering that strategy would not be found in Stephanie's lack of mental illness but in her personality and character development. In my next encounters with Stephanie — and in those with her family and friends — I would have to explore the possibility that it was Stephanie's character and background that had led her into murder.

Stephanie and her fraternal twin sister, Tracy, were born in the summer of 1970, joining twelve-year-old Nancy and eight-and-a-half-year-old Michael to complete the typical suburban middle-class family. Mr. Wernick was an accountant with a successful and prospering private practice, while Mrs. Wernick was a stay-at-home mom. The Wernicks were moderately observant Jews who celebrated the important holidays but did not keep a kosher home. Stephanie didn't remember many details about her childhood. Even Mrs. Wernick seemed a little vague about the milestones in her daughter's development. She did recall that from the very beginning Stephanie did not appear as "sensitive or scholarly" as her twin. Stephanie had little to say about her relationship with her mother. She did say that she was most inclined to go to her mother when she needed money for shopping.

Mr. Wernick described himself as "prone to threats and angry outbursts," but Stephanie vehemently denied this. She saw her father as extroverted and maybe just a "little bit harsher" disciplinarian than her mother, who was quite lenient and easygoing. This made me wonder how that squared with Stephanie's professed fear of her father's reaction if he had found out she was pregnant.

The main arena of contention in the Wernick family seemed to be Stephanie's academic underachievement. She was more concerned with her friends and social affairs than academics. She failed many classes; she squeaked by high school with special tutoring. Her father would yell at her about her grades and ground her for a few days — a punishment that was never enforced. She fondly recalled to me that her father was extremely generous with money whenever she needed it.

Stephanie and her twin sister shared a bedroom in the family home throughout their childhood years. They went to the same schools and attended the same camps. They were bat mitzvahed together. However, they never seemed to grow truly close the way some twins do. By high school they went their separate ways. Stephanie's grades were too low to gain her admission to the same college as her sister, which suited her just fine. By then, living in the shadow of Tracy's academic accomplishments irritated Stephanie in the extreme.

Stephanie seldom dated in high school, though she had a loyal circle of girlfriends. She started C. W. Post College in 1988. There she rapidly cultivated friends and adapted well to dorm life. She drank beer and wine regularly, got drunk once or twice, experimented with marijuana, and dated casually. In short, Stephanie was in all aspects a normal college student with no particularly pressing attachments, concerns, or aspirations.

Her first sexual experience occurred when she was a sophomore in college. She had just started hanging out with a young man named Dave and his group; she told me she had "just drifted into having intercourse with him," without having any special attraction or fondness for him. She hinted to me that she might have felt some peer pressure to go along with the crowd and get involved with sex. Though she thought the relationship had no future, she continued to have sex with him regularly throughout that winter and spring term. When the term ended, Stephanie returned to her family home in New Jersey for the summer. The affair very unceremoniously ended. Stephanie never saw Dave again.

"Have you ever told Dave that he was the father of your child?" I asked her.

"No," she told me, surprised at the question.

As I interpreted all of this information and integrated it into the results of the tests I administered, a profile of Stephanie's personality began to emerge. She was, I came to believe, an extremely manipulative and narcissistic young woman who was capable of being comfortable, confident, and even insouciant in social situations. Like Ann Green, she scored high on the social imperturbability scale — a "do your own thing" component of personality that in itself is not pathological and can characterize many powerful and creative people. This young woman was a law unto herself, had strong opinions, and cared little for the effects of her behavior on others. What I saw emerging, carefully concealed under her shy and naive demeanor, was a tough side to Stephanie. Although she presented herself as having extremely high moral standards and denied negative impulses, our interviews and her test results revealed that she harbored many hostile feelings and was extremely resentful of the demands placed upon her by others.

Far from being emotionally unstable, Stephanie scored impressively in ego strength and resilience. Such personalities are not prone to panic in emergencies and are known for their unusual capacity to face ordeals. I had strong evidence of this in Stephanie's ability to deliver her baby without assistance, cut and tie the cord, kill him, wipe up the blood, and take a nap. Were these the actions of a young woman who had "just snapped" in brief reactive psychosis, or who was undergoing instant postpartum depression, as her defense would claim?

Stephanie rated herself as a perfect 10 on superego strength and declared herself possessed of a scrupulous moral system and conscience. In fact, however, Stephanie scored a 2 — indicating that she had significantly failed in internalizing the prevailing moral values of our society. This was also reflected in her score on the MMPI psychopathic deviance subscales.

Stephanie Wernick was amoral. As I interacted with her and studied the descriptions of witnesses to the murder and disposal of her infant son, I was coming to conclude that she was functioning at a childish level of moral development. She saw "goodness" and "right" as what she wanted and liked. For whatever reason, Stephanie had made little progress in moving away from the normal self-centered orientation of early childhood. Morally speaking, she was a three-year-old stealing cookies and hoarding her toys in nursery school. Her emotional attachments to others were weak. She manifested a strong tendency to reject authority and to act on her own whims. Her underlying boldness was remarkable; she seemed to have a constitutional underreactivity to fear and anxiety, which provided her with a curious immunity to physical and social threats that other young women would find unbearable. This explained to me the coolness and calm with which Stephanie operated that December morning.

Somewhere in my undergraduate studies, I had read of personalities like Stephanie's being described as "walking on snow without leaving footprints." Guilt and remorse with their incumbent despair and depression were seemingly missing for Stephanie. Although she would be histrionically tearful at times (especially in the courtroom, in front of the cameras), she never once expressed regret for her actions or grief for the deceased infant. Stephanie's consistent theme was the effect of the murder rap on her. She was an extremely practical young woman with little use for abstractions or complicated conceptual inferences. Once I started to hear the convoluted psychoanalytic explanations for Stephanie's crime espoused by her highly paid defense experts — one of whom was the past president of the American Psychiatric Association — it struck me as ironic that they would have been lost on Stephanie herself. The morning she killed her baby, Stephanie was absorbed by the immediate, external environment. She had the quintessential one-track mind. She delivered an inconvenient baby, cut the cord, silenced its cries forever by systematically ramming wadded toilet paper down its throat, relegated its disposal to her friend Jody, cleaned up, showered, and went back to bed. She was intent on taking her exams and completing the semester. This is as much as we'll ever know. I doubt that Stephanie herself has reflected enough to have any insight into her own motivations — or ever will. She bore all the selfish, goal-centered traits that characterize the psychopath.

The defense team would, of course, challenge my conclusion. One of the Wernick psychological experts wrote in his assessment of Stephanie:

> She was faced with severe cramps, the rupture of her membranes and the delivery of the baby into the toilet, she could not know what was happening. What was in a sense left of her reality testing mind was completely destroyed. She clearly lacked the capacity to appreciate that she had delivered a child, that it was the child crying and that if she stuffed paper into the child's throat, it would kill the child. She did not know that was wrong, nor that asking someone

to throw the "bag" out was wrong. . . . What she did was related to menstruation and not to childbirth.

I asked Stephanie what she usually did with soiled clothes after a
heavy period. She said she washed them — she said nothing
about throwing them out.

Stephanie's case would not rest on firm psychiatric evidence.
Even a finding of postpartum depression would be more a gesture
to structure the sympathy of the jury than a clinically accurate diagnosis. The jury would have to decide whether whatever psychological distress she was suffering was exculpatory. That would
depend on the skill of her lawyer, the credibility of her experts,
and the moral elasticity of the jury. The insanity defense inevitably involves an emotional appeal to our innermost feelings and
what we want to believe about murderers or, in this case, mothers.

The medical model of psychological states has unfortunately
led us to consider bad choices such the one made by Stephanie
Wernick to be diseases, illnesses over which one has no control.
To the lay person, what is normal is equated with what is healthy,
and any abnormal behavior is equated with mental illness. Mercifully, what Stephanie Wernick did was not normal; most young
mothers, even those who are woefully unprepared to parent a
child, do not asphyxiate their infants and dispose of them in the
garbage. But she was not in the grip of mental illness either. What
was abnormal was the way she chose to behave, so egregiously did
it fall outside the realm of what we value and believe.

Over a century ago, French psychiatrists coined the term "moral
idiot" to describe the type of personality who seems to be utterly
lacking in conscience and unable to conform his conduct to prevailing cultural norms. Such people were later called psychopaths
(a term from the Greek, meaning, literally, disease of the soul).
With the rise of behaviorism, social psychology, and the emphasis on environmental influences on the shaping of an individual's

personality, the term was dropped in favor of the word "sociopath." For decades, psychologists viewed this morally nonconformist flaw as the result of deficits in a person's socialization experiences, often as a result of poverty, discrimination, or some other environmental deprivation or hardship. The person's lack of social conformity — and human caring — was now laid at the doorstep of society. Sociopaths were thought to be acting out the behaviors they had learned in adapting to harsh realities.

In the *DSM-IV*, the most recent edition of the main handbook of psychiatric diagnoses, which lists more than 3,500 mental illnesses, the term "sociopath" has been replaced by the phrase "antisocial personality disorder." The criteria have become so narrow and so behavioral that the designation really only covers people who have been arrested or have had some assaultive episodes. The standard for the diagnosis now even insists that a person must evidence this condition before age fifteen. Clearly, given these diagnostic criteria, a nice middle-class girl like Stephanie Wernick, or an upper-middle-class nurse like Ann Green, doesn't fit the bill.

The *DSM-IV* goes on to describe a cluster of personality disorders that tend to overlap and occur in a varying admixture in certain persons. The "cluster B" personality disorder contains not only antisocial persons but those who are borderline, histrionic, and narcissistic. Both Ann Green and Stephanie Wernick were described in objective psychological tests and by both defense and prosecution experts as giving evidence of those last three disorders. Yet in neither woman did it reach the full-blown level of clinical significance.

So how do we define Stephanie Wernick? She is not mentally ill — or so I would claim in my testimony in court. Nor did the jury find her insane. But she did something truly evil. What do we make of that?

To explain Stephanie Wernick, I have to set aside the rigidities of psychology and move into the realm of the moral and spiritual. In his book *Children of the Lie: Toward a Psychology of Evil*, M. Scott Peck, who is both a psychiatrist and a minister, talks about the distinction between opportunistic, brutish criminals and the subtle attitudes of so-called nice people like Stephanie Wernick and Ann Green. He urges psychology to explore the variant of human behavior that has traditionally been relegated to theologians and moralists: evil.

I entered the field of forensic psychology with the tools of a scientist. After twenty years of witnessing and analyzing so many evil actions, I see the limitations of our current systems of psychology in even being able to *name* evil, much less study it. Peck attributes this paralysis to the divorce of science and religion. Even using the word "evil" requires a judgment that science is not willing to make. Like Peck, I believe it is imperative that we as behavioral scientists, expert witnesses, and agents of social change begin taking responsibility for systematically going about formulating and asking moral questions arising around human behavior and the concept of evil.

Peck would classify evil within the cluster B personality disorders, whose common thread is denial of personal responsibility. He views evil as a subvariant of narcissistic personality disorder. Although most of us are self-interested, we relatively normal folks usually eventually get around to thinking about another person and his often different point of view, especially if we care about that person. Peck believes that people who act evilly reflect a "brand of narcissism so total that they seem to lack, in whole or in part, this capacity for empathy." In a chilling paragraph, Peck concludes:

> Their narcissism makes the evil dangerous . . . because it deprives them of the restraint that results from empathy and respect for others. . . . Narcissism permits them to ignore the humanity of their victims. As well as it gives them the motive for murder, so it also renders them insensitive to the act of killing. The blindness of the narcissist to others can extend even beyond the lack of empathy; narcissists may not "see" others at all.

Psychopathy, as I use the term in this book, is not a mental disease or defect but a global attitude of selfishness that governs a person's interactions with others. When the chips are down, the psychopath makes sure it is him over you. Exercising this attitude throughout life ultimately leads to manipulativeness, exploitation, and the inflicting of pain on others. In essence, evil. I believe the psychopath is fundamentally a self-absorbed person whose vantage point on the human community begins and ends with himself. The psychopath has no social fear, is perceived of as extroverted although lacking in true warmth and affection, grows easily bored, and is possessed of an ability to con other people, a superficial charm, and a resistance to rules and demands.

The majority of people who commit violent crimes are psychopaths — and they are dangerous. Like Stephanie Wernick, most psychopaths could pass as normal people. They hold down jobs, they have relationships, though often superficial ones, and they manage to manage, however selfishly. But in background and characterological makeup, they differ from the norm. More than most people, they are selfish, highly absorbed with securing the primitive comforts of life. They cannot delay their gratifications, or set aside their resentments. They may have been indulged by their parents or other relatives, who can join them in their crusade against persecution by an unjust world. While psychopaths come from all classes, the privileged psychopath's legal case is more often successfully acquitted. They are usually charming, eager to please, and quite often very smart. However, though they may function in the world effectively, they do not conduct their lives according to accepted moral codes and standards of behavior. They do not consider their crimes crimes. What seems a crime to us is to them an expediency, an act of entitlement. As intelligent as they may be, psychopaths lack a certain cosmic consciousness, an awareness that they are participating in the overall drama of the human species. Accused of a crime, they believe that the world that owes them a living has done them wrong. They are evil.

Serial killer Ted Bundy represents a classic example of a sexual psychopath. A superficially charming, ingratiating, and bright young man who acted out his sadomasochistic sexual impulses on from thirty to more than a hundred young girls, from rape to dismemberment, mutilation, and necrophilia, Bundy bragged that he "owned a girl like you own a Porsche." Although he unabashedly admitted to killing thirty women in six states, he never expressed any remorse. Instead he felt sorry for himself for getting caught and punished. Before he was finally executed, he married a woman who had corresponded with him while he was on death row. They have a daughter born after his death. Never underestimate the seductiveness of evil.

In Bundy's sort of criminal insouciance lies some of our ambivalence, our simultaneous attraction/repulsion and grudging admiration for psychopaths. They move through life unencumbered by the doubts, guilts, and obligations that bother most of us. When they are bright and dynamic, there is almost no end to their apparent accomplishments. They are enviably efficient in the pursuit of their goals and adept at being able to deploy people to achieve their desired ends. Many of the captains of industry, indeed the legendary robber barons, probably fall into this category; they are the prosocial psychopaths. They usually do not collide with the law — unless, made careless by too many victories, they overstep their bounds and get caught in some white-collar crime. Sometimes, like many politicians accustomed to power, they engage in sexual exploits, graft, and fraud and then brag about it in their diaries. Sometimes, they concoct huge financial scams, sell junk bonds, engage in insider trading. Yet another may be a highly respected judge who, accustomed to getting his way, cannot accept the rejection of a mistress and begins to make horrendous physical threats against her children.

Stephanie Wernick is not the only mother to have killed an inopportune child. In Union, South Carolina, Susan Smith got out of her car and propelled the vehicle into a man-made lake; inside were her two young sons. After she lied about the circumstances of her sons' deaths, she finally admitted she had killed them because her new lover didn't want children and might leave her. In Brooklyn, Abigail Cortez stood by while her husband beat her five-year-old child to death because the little girl wet her pants. Wernick, Smith, and Cortez all put themselves first. Their needs, their wants, their comfort, and their convenience superseded even the basic human breath of their offspring. In his monograph "Schizophrenia and Cosmic Insanity," forthcoming in *Psychology: The Journal of Human Behavior*, my research colleague Jim Audubon calls this behavior "cosmic inequity" — a fundamental me-first attitude that negates the rights and reality of the other. Eventually, the habitual exercise of inequity results in iniquity.

Why do psychopaths commit crimes? Very simply, because they can. Psychopaths do what has to be done — nothing personal — swiftly, efficiently, expediently. They undergo no internal dialogue, no wrestling with conscience. Rarely do I see psychopathic personalities in the therapy room, because they don't feel they have to change. But I do see them very frequently in the lockup when I undertake a forensic evaluation of a killer. When I confront these psychopathic murders, I feel what I call "thinged."

Basically, you can never connect with a psychopath. You are relegated to the status of an inanimate object to be used for a specific purpose according to the psychopath's design. You are reduced, your humanity is invalidated, you are a character in this drama. You are less than human. You become Ted Bundy's Porsche.

Sexual psychopaths, especially those who have committed lurid serial killings, illustrate this penchant in the most extreme fashion. MMPI tests administered to notorious serial killer and cannibal Jeffrey Dahmer revealed an excessively high score on the psychopathic deviate scale. Since early childhood Dahmer exhibited a monstrous lack of empathy for the consequences of his behavior on other people. This consummate self-centeredness was central to his capacity to do cold and cruel things to others, especially morbidly sadistic sexual acts. Basically, Jeffrey Dahmer thought no more about the young boys who were his victims than he would an inflatable sex doll. The testing that was performed on Dahmer in 1991 shortly after his arrest for the torture, mutilation, and murder of fifteen boys and young men revealed an astonishing lack of tension and anxiety. Far from being the twisted and tortured soul we would like to believe him to be, Dahmer was curiously at ease with himself.

This clinical picture changed when Dahmer was retested in prison a year after his conviction. Now fearful for his life — which was subsequently taken by inmates in 1995 — Dahmer manifested a great deal of anxiety and disorganization. Unable to engage in his preferred form of tension release, Dahmer was becoming more depressed and paranoid. It is untrue that psychopaths cannot feel anxiety or strong emotion — they are often exquisitely sensitive to their *own* needs. They just can't feel any emotions toward others.

Dahmer, by all accounts, was not an abused or unwanted child. An attractive, intelligent youngster of well-educated, middle-class parents (his father held a Ph.D. in engineering), he seemed to be protected and indulged, just like Stephanie Wernick, and just like matricidal killer Joseph Bergamini. Dahmer had every opportunity afforded to white Anglo-Saxon males in our society. Nevertheless, his preoccupation with death and destruction began very early. In grade school, he already had a collection of skulls from road-killed animals. Absolute control — an outgrowth of what psychologists call the grandiosity of narcissism — was central to Dahmer. The more he sought to control others, the more inconvenient became their own wills and selves.

There was no evidence that Jeffrey Dahmer was psychotic — that is, that he suffered from delusions or hallucinations, or that he had made a break with reality so extreme that he no longer knew the nature and consequences of his actions. Dahmer's crimes, as revolting and shocking as they are to normal people, were not the unintentional products of a diseased mind. They were just evil.

Andrew Delbanco, in his book *The Death of Satan: How Ameri-*

cans Have Lost the Sense of Evil, talks about the schism in our culture "between the visibility of evil and the intellectual resources available for coping with it." "The repertoire of evil has never been richer," he writes. "Yet never have our responses been so weak. We have no language for connecting our inner lives with the horrors that pass before our eyes in the outer world." What Delbanco talks about is an occupational hazard of my profession, which places me constantly in proximity with people who have committed evil acts, yet leaves me without the vocabulary to describe them for what they are. Ironically, my own science of psychology and psychiatry has probably contributed the most to the "denaming" of evil. What theologians used to refer to as "sin" or "moral evil" has now been euphemistically termed "antisocial behavior," a notion from which the concept of individual responsibility and free will has largely disappeared. Forensic psychology and psychiatry must come to terms with evil and separate it from mental illness, not shrinking from the systematic scientific study of it and how it operates on the personality. Each time I interview a serial killer, a mass murderer, or a mother who has killed her child, and my instruments and intuition fail to find any shred of what might be a legitimate mental illness, I experience what Delbanco calls "the flustered response to evil." Like fiction's Hannibal Lecter, encased in his Plexiglas cell, the killers' "normal" profiles loom at me from the test grids and their interviews as if to challenge me in his words: "Can you stand to say I'm evil?"

A nationwide debate is raging today about the decline of morals and the perceived rise of violent and inexplicable crime. Is our society creating more psychopaths? After spending hundreds of dreary hours in jails and lockups, face to face with murderers, or in conversation with their families or the families of their victims, I have come to a very basic conclusion: I believe that we are denying that we are producing psychopaths at all. Consequently, we comparatively normal people are unable to recognize them or respond with appropriate self-protection when we deal with them. Psychopathic crime is a dance of wolves and sheep. The wolves won't change, but the sheep can get smarter. Psychopathy by its very nature is resistant to peer pressure and even punishment as inducements to change. We can hope to change our thinking enough to restore our grasp of the issue of individual accountability and to regain the will to use a language that calls some behavior unequivocally evil.

If all psychopaths were as overtly menacing as Hannibal Lecter, they would not be able to victimize anyone. The hallmark of evil is deceit. Theodore Bundy used slings and casts on his arms to stir pity in his prospective victims. Jeffrey Dahmer was able to con his probation officer into being lenient with him when he violated the conditions of his probation repeatedly. The first trial of Erik and Lyle Menendez ended in hung juries (they were tried together before separate juries) because the young men were able to dazzle some California jurors into believing that the abuse they allegedly suffered at the hands of their wealthy parents mitigated their responsibility for blasting open their heads with a shotgun.

The case of Allen Hirschhorn illustrates our vulnerability in the face of the psychopath at work. Hirschhorn was a mild-mannered and unexceptional hotel employee who lived with his parents in the quiet Kew Gardens area of Queens, New York. Inexplicably, one Saturday afternoon during an August heat wave, he lured into his home an Orthodox Jewish woman, returning with her prayer book from shul. "Please help!" he pleaded from his doorway. "My wife is in labor — her first baby!" The woman had no reason to suspect the clean-cut young man. She rushed inside to help. The door slammed shut. There was no wife in labor. Suddenly, Hirschhorn's fists were pummeling her around the head and face; he knocked her to the floor, lashing a vacuum cleaner cord around her throat. As they thrashed she began to pray out loud and managed to struggle free. She dashed out into the street, where she was picked up by a motorist, dazed, bloodied, and beaten. I testified at the request of the Queens district attorney in an attempt to open the jury's eyes and demonstrate that this Clark Kent of a man could be capable of inexplicable violence. He was convicted and sentenced to eight and a half years in prison.

To equate evil with madness is tantamount to the medieval thinking that saw mental illness as demonic possession. We again do a major disservice to those truly afflicted with mental illness. We as psychological experts must do the rigorous scientific work of making our values clear, explicit, and empirically based. Then we must be prepared to be responsible for their ramifications on society and the uncomfortable moral imperatives placed on us in our roles as experts to the courts.

In the past, when psychopaths succeeded in using the mental health system to excuse them for their crimes, they were given a virtual assurance that their next criminal act would again be viewed a sickness for which they would not be held responsible. Abdul Oman, aka Joe Brown, had spent most of his thirty-nine years bouncing between the streets, psychiatric hospitals, and jail. His first arrest was for attempted homicide in the stabbing of a tourist at the United Nations. He was acquitted by reason of insanity and sent to a maximum-security facility for three years, until the doctors felt he was sufficiently recovered to be transferred to a less secure facility in New York City. Oman spent twenty-two months there, complaining every day: There was no gym, no exercise yard, the food was bad. He decided he wanted to return to the maximum-security facility upstate. The state code made no provisions for voluntary transfer, and he certainly deserved no special dispensation for good behavior. He had harassed and bothered other patients; he fondled female staff; he slipped off the ward whenever he wanted to without a pass. Yet at the same time he was able to pressure and cajole the doctors into extending all manner of unearned privileges to him. One psychiatrist had even bought him a bicycle so that he could ride around the grounds for exercise.

The one sure way he knew to get a return ticket upstate was to assault a doctor. Determined, Oman waited for Dr. Lourdes

Campos to come on duty. As Dr. Campos, a diminutive, gracious sixty-two-year-old physician from the Philippines, opened the door to her office, Oman ambushed her, struck her repeatedly in the face, knocked her to the ground, and kicked her savagely until attendants came and restrained him. Quietly and smugly, he accompanied the security officers to headquarters. He said that he'd heard voices telling him the doctor was the devil. Dr. Campos suffered a broken nose, lacerations of the forehead, and multiple contusions of the head, chest, and thigh, as well as a fractured sternum. She never returned to work. Oman had no personal animosity to her; she was simply his ticket to where he wanted to go.

I was retained by the Queens district attorney to evaluate him on this assault charge. During the exam, he was hostile and uncooperative, marking the test items randomly so that they were not valid. He made sexual innuendos. At one point, he rolled his eyes and lunged across the table at me, snarling, "Aren't you afraid of me?" I did not find him mentally ill. He was threatening and menacing for effect and not squeamish about hurting others to reach his ends. This time Oman was convicted of assault and sent to the infamous Attica prison facility — not at all the mental hospital he had been anticipating, where he would have been able to work the system to secure his release sooner. A year later, he wrote to me from jail. He was serving two to four years on the assault charge. Ever planning ahead, he realized that the Office of Mental Health still had a hold on him under provisions of the Criminal Proceeding Law for the dangerously mentally ill in connection with his attempted homicide. In a lucid, beautifully hand-scripted, four-page letter, Oman outlined his legal and psychiatric strategy and tried to cajole me into lending my expertise to help him out.

Dear Dr. Kirwin:

You will remember me and how uncooperative I was at Kew Gardens during your examination. My behavior was irreverent and, perhaps, infantile; however, after our "session" concluded, Gary (esq) told me you thought I was sane. Enheartened by that I hope to retain you as my doctor in order that you might refute the contentions of my treating psychiatrist.

Barbara, I've done some legal research, precedents and such, but you know I got to have psychs of my own at my next retention hearing if I ever hope to extract myself from this. . . . You are resourceful. What's the loophole? Something must be done about my predicament and with dispatch. For me, you are the oracle, yes, of alternatives under the mental hygiene law — Speak! Yes, I repose a lot of confidence in you (smile). . . . I've severed relationships with my live-in mate . . . she was keeping me for awhile. It was good while it lasted. Now, I'm corresponding with a young girl in Newburgh. She's a pen pal. Perhaps I could write to you socially . . . if you have the time and/or inclination. You are comely, smartly attired (I can vaguely visualize your svelte figure before me) "up and coming." You have some of the accouterments of a successful physician. . . . I've already put in for a transfer to Sing Sing. Got to wait 6 months. I'll be keeping a low profile, until then I shall patiently await your reply.

Ever Yours,
Abdul

Needless to say, his blandishments fell on deaf ears. In the case of Abdul Oman, I felt I had done my part to thwart evil and see that an evil man was properly punished.

My testimony in the murder trial of Stephanie Wernick began in suburban Mineola, New York, on a stiflingly warm day in October 1993. The prosecution had presented its numerous witnesses, including Laura Plezia and the other emergency medical technicians, Detective Ryder and the police officers, Dr. O'Rourke and Dr. Dunn, Jody Klein, the coeds who heard the baby cry, and the cleaning personnel, including the custodian who had discovered the infant. Then for several weeks the jury heard testimony from the psychiatric experts offered by the defense, along with assorted character witnesses — even Stephanie's high school guidance counselor. Now it was time to mount the psychological rebuttal, and I was center stage.

This was an emotional, highly publicized, and very tense case. The defense counsel was flamboyant and widely respected. The family was wealthy. The proceedings were televised. Stephanie looked small and vulnerable, sobbing audibly throughout the trial, her head resting on Maureen Scaring's broad shoulder.

Under questioning from George Peck, I told the jury how I had conducted my examination of Stephanie, what psychological tests I had administered, and what they showed. I discussed the clinical interviews and my in-depth discussion with Stephanie about the incident. The questioning continued over the entire day while Peck led me through the parts of my report and findings that were important to the prosecution's case.

We recessed for the weekend, and I took the stand again on Monday morning. The TV cameras were rolling. Systematically I testified as to the absence of any mental illness that could be determined from either my clinical interviews or my testing — or from any source other than the defense psychiatrists. Ultimately, rather than postpartum depression, the defense was claiming Stephanie suffered from a brief reactive psychosis. The *DSM-III-R* described this condition as a "sudden onset of psychotic symptoms of at least a few hours but no more than a month's duration: usually occurring after someone had been subjected to a major stressor or trauma." This diagnosis appears in a problematic section of the *DSM-III-R* called "Psychotic Disorders Not Elsewhere Classified" — a veritable catchall of symptoms that either don't meet the criteria for more well-articulated mental illnesses or else lack the coherence necessary to make a specific diagnosis. In my entire career as a psychologist, I have never actually seen anyone clinically given this diagnosis. (In fact, it would be officially dropped from the new edition of this manual in 1994.) Stephanie Wernick had not even been tagged as having brief reactive psychosis in any of the three hospitals where she was treated after she killed her son. The diagnosis is, however, commonly utilized by the defense in insanity cases because it seems to correspond neatly to the public's perception of normal people who, when they commit crimes, "just snap" or undergo a bout of "temporary insanity." "Temporary insanity" does not exist. Most bona fide psychoses, except for states of delirium or intoxication, do not come on out of the blue; nor, sadly, do they go away so quickly. I have always felt, cynically, that the brief reactive psychosis diagnosis should be included in a new manual called the *DSM-IV-F*, the F standing for Forensic. This manual would comprise all the diagnoses that have no clinical validity but that are perennial favorites in the courtroom as designer defenses.

In the Wernick case, the brief reactive psychosis diagnosis sounded good, and I knew that the jury, eager for an explanation of her sad crime, would find it persuasive. But as I tried to explain in court, at the time she murdered her baby Stephanie Wernick did not manifest the "rapid shifts from one intense affect to another, . . . overwhelming perplexity or confusion, . . . which can be judged from the way he or she responds to questions and requests," as the diagnostic manual states is required. In fact, none of the features necessary for a diagnosis of brief reactive psychosis were present in her case. Just the opposite behavior was documented by witnesses at the time and by the various medical and psychiatric personnel who examined Stephanie. As Peck had already made clear during cross-examination, all the experts who were bound by the diagnostic criteria of the *DSM-III-R* could not honestly say that Stephanie manifested "behavior that may be bizarre, including peculiar postures, outlandish dress, screaming or muteness," or speech that "may include inarticulate gibberish or repetition of nonsensical phrases," transient hallucinations or delusions, or silly answers to factual questions. The only thing that remained as a hook to the jury was the severe trauma of a young girl, allegedly unaware of her pregnancy, giving birth alone and unassisted. If Scaring could hammer this image home, nothing else would matter.

My direct examination by George Peck stretched over a day and a half. Periodically distracted by Stephanie's muffled sobs, and often feeling the searing glances of her family members, who appeared front row center throughout the trial, I reiterated my findings: There was no evidence of mental illness that I could detect, now or at the time of the incident. As I said on the stand, all the witnesses to Wernick's behavior that morning attested to the fact that "she was . . . lucid, coherent, oriented, able to respond to questions, not hysterical, not in a panic state, not hallucinating, not having delusions."

Peck was tying up the case. I was comfortable discussing psychosis, amnesia, dissociation, and all the other psychological symptoms. But now we were getting to the crux of the people's case: Stephanie's moral responsibility in the death of her infant. As an objective scientist, I had been taught to keep my own values out of the situation; now, having failed to find any evidence of exculpatory mental illness, I was being asked to cast the first stone of blame.

When Peck asked me about the personality traits of narcissism, I responded: "There's something that I noticed in the material, examination and test results of Stephanie . . . that's very much associated with the childish self-centered state of the narcissistic personality. As early as Stephanie's admission to Nassau County Medical Center, within hours after the delivery and death of the infant, Stephanie's comments were recorded as being 'I'm so frightened, what will happen to me? What's going to become of me?'"

I went on to say that nowhere in the voluminous records reviewed for this trial or in her hours of clinical examination with me did she ever express grief for the infant or remorse over how her actions had affected those who loved her. I was as much in disbelief as the jury must have been, looking at the fragile and gentle-seeming young woman clinging to Mrs. Scaring.

The cross-examination lasted more than a day and was vitriolic. "You're trying to trash her, aren't you, Doctor?" Steve Scaring accused me. The only person trashed here was the infant, I wanted to say. Instead, my anger dissolved into sadness. I replied quietly, "That's not a word I use to characterize anything I do in the frame of psychological assessment." Steve Scaring's fury at me would have a major impact on the outcome of the case — aggravated by the fact of those television cameras glaring at the entire cast of characters. Stephanie's trial would take many twists and turns before the jury delivered a verdict. (The media aspects of this trial, and the eventual verdict, are discussed in Chapter 6.) But from the start, the case and the crime illustrated the pervasive narcissism behind psychopathic behavior.

During a recess, I got in the elevator with George Peck, who was pushing a large metal cart with evidence. On top of the pile of police reports and witness statements was the bloodied pink towel in which the infant had been wrapped. I had trouble looking at it.

Stephanie's father and grandfather also got into the elevator. We all nodded in awkward acknowledgment. As the elevator ascended, we were arrayed around the cart with the bloody towel on it. "Shall we get corned beef or pastrami?" I overheard one Mr. Wernick ask the other.

THE DESIGNER DEFENSE

*I*t *was freakishly hot and muggy*
when thirty-one-year-old Louis Kahan woke that Saturday morning in April 1977. Pretending to sleep, he waited for his mother to
leave for work before he dialed the local police station. When the
precinct switchboard answered, he calmly gave directions. "I want
to talk to somebody about a killing. Can you send a car to pick me
up in front of the movie theater on Main Street?"

Six feet tall, heavily muscled, tattooed, and swarthy, with a Fu
Manchu mustache and a gold earring in one ear, Kahan looked
more like a biker than the ex-marine he was. He was met at the
theater by two officers who escorted him to the station house for
questioning. Methodically over the next few hours, Kahan related
the story of raping and killing a young Vietnamese girl in an
empty apartment. He had ambushed her coming out of the sub-

way on Queens Boulevard — right across from the Queens criminal court building — dragged her upstairs, removed a kerchief
from her hair and gagged her with it, and proceeded to undress
her. He punched her in the jaw, knocking her unconscious before
he penetrated her, first vaginally, then anally. During the rape, he
choked her to death. He then stayed in the room for a few hours
before he dressed her again and put her in the closet. "I don't
know why I did this," he confessed to the cops, between determined drags on his cigarette.

On the closet floor of apartment 2C in a building in the quiet
neighborhood of Kew Gardens, Queens, detectives found the
fully clothed body of fifteen-year-old Le My Hanh, the daughter
of a refugee Saigon intellectual. Her hands were bound behind
her with rope; her legs were bent behind her body until the soles
of her feet and palms touched. She was trussed as one field dresses
wild game after the kill. It was exactly as Kahan had said.

The local press coverage of the crime was sparse. Kahan had
been upstaged by the escapades of the killer who had declared that
the "son of Sam" was instructing him to blast off the heads of lovers as they necked in parked cars. Preoccupied by his public conversation with this at-large serial killer, *New York Daily News*
columnist Jimmy Breslin gave Kahan only the briefest of nods.

This was the way it always had been for Louis Kahan; he
couldn't even win attention for himself as a criminal. Despite an
IQ of 135, Kahan had done poorly in school, been truant, and had
eventually gotten around to drinking, smoking marijuana, and
snorting heroin. The fact that his father was a tyrant, had trouble
holding down a job, and moved the family from coast to coast several times in his childhood had done nothing for Louis's social adjustment as he grew into a hulking teenager who weighed as much
as three hundred pounds. A high school dropout, like many young
male working-class drifters in the 1960s, he anticipated the draft
by enlisting in the marines, where he passed all tests easily and was
promptly sent to Vietnam.

When he went on trial for the killing of Le My Hanh, Louis

Kahan told his psychiatric examiners that in Vietnam he was a commando, a veteran of countless search-and-destroy missions in which he had seen numerous atrocities committed by his fellow U.S. soldiers. He grew to believe, he told me, that in fact war is hell, and that these actions were justified because they got results. He also talked of the deceits and strategies that the Vietcong would use. He told stories of how women would be alongside the roads begging, holding infants in whose blankets would be hidden grenades ready to explode when the compassionate soldier reached out to embrace the baby. Nobody in Vietnam could be trusted — not the enemy, not our allies the South Vietnamese, not his own men. In court, Kahan claimed that in his units, rape was a combat tactic used by U.S. troops in field interrogations. He recalled that women were selected for their beauty and then threatened with sodomy and gang rape to force them to reveal any information they might have. Kahan declared that he had taken part in these "interrogations" twice as a rapist.

After just nine months overseas, Kahan was discharged and returned to his mother's apartment in Brooklyn. Nearly a decade slipped by, while Louis Kahan lived an aimless and marginal existence, crisscrossing the United States, rebounding from woman to woman, bouncing from job to job. His affair with a woman named Cindy was turbulent, ending when she left him after an episode in which he had his massive hands around her throat and was choking her into unconsciousness. Eventually, at age twenty-nine, he found himself back in his mother's apartment in Brooklyn. Kahan had begun to amass a collection of weapons since his Vietnam days. He kept them in his mother's closet, and he kept them loaded. By now, April 1977, he had become edgy, reclusive, unable to work. He would later claim he wouldn't leave the apartment except to take his dog for a brief walk each day. What prompted him to emerge from his self-described exile that April afternoon and kill a young girl less than half his size?

To the prosecution, the case against Kahan was a classic open-and-shut proceeding. He was presented as a drifter and chronic malcontent known to have trouble with people on the job and prone to violence in his relationships with women. The killing of Le My Hanh was just the culmination of an antisocial life that had finally veered entirely into vicious crime.

Defense attorney Mel Lebetkin, however, presented a startling new argument. Psychiatric experts for the defense didn't even mention the term "psychosis," nor did they claim Kahan suffered from schizophrenia, paranoia, or any other personality disorders officially diagnosable at that time. Kahan, they said, clearly suffered from post-Vietnam syndrome. In a nation racked by guilt over the Vietnam War and its callous treatment of veterans, this line of reasoning was a sure winner. The defense contended that Louis Kahan, triggered by Le My Hanh's Asian features, split off into two distinct personalities. One watched helplessly as the other, a trained killing machine, experienced a vivid flashback and went through the motions of what he was taught to do in Vietnam, raping and strangling the girl. Even though Kahan had these flashbacks ten years after he left Vietnam, that was understandable. The memories of those years still festered in the American consciousness and were accompanied by a tremendous emotional backlash of guilt. "Louis Kahan is not the only one on trial here," his defense attorney told the judge. "Society permitted the military to go over there and kill these people . . . they told him to do that!"

The prosecution's psychiatric expert, a psychoanalyst, found himself so sympathetic to the novelty of the defense strategy and to the defendant himself that even he conceded the point the defense was making:

I think when he saw the devastated buildings, the hole in the ground, the dirt; and he saw this devastated landscape and he began thinking Vietnam; and the rage at how unfairly he was dealt with by the nation, unfairly dealt with by the officers; how he was betrayed by the Marines — and enraged at the Viet Cong agents that not only caused the death of some of his friends, but made him become a killer which he didn't like to be. That rage started to build up and eventually it burst forth.

With prosecution witnesses like this, who needed a defense? The expert witness was creating a scene and scenario that made his rationalization of the crime seem plausible. The trial was not conducted before a jury but in front of Judge Bernard Dubin, who declared with considerable fury that the opposing expert witnesses were in such agreement regarding Kahan's combat-related flashbacks that he had no choice but to find Kahan not guilty by reason of insanity. Louis Kahan was sent to a maximum-security facility for the criminally insane and after twenty-seven months was sent to Creedmoor, a less secure civil hospital. Only when I met him at Creedmoor did I discover that Kahan had not been a commando in Vietnam but a cook.

The Kahan designer defense was no fluke; many defense attorneys have aroused sympathy for their clients based on unsubstantiated allegations that the defendants were themselves victims. Two brothers, Lyle and Erik Menendez, born into wealth and privilege, shotgunned their parents to death while they watched TV in the den of their Beverly Hills mansion. The older brother, Lyle, admitted shooting his father in the back of the head. When his mother didn't die in the first barrage of gunfire, he left to reload and then returned to blow off a portion of her head. Large pieces of their mother's body were blown all over the den while they kept firing. Over fifteen blasts were fired from two 12-gauge shotguns. The brothers then left the home and drove around trying to shore up alibis before Lyle histrionically called 911 to describe finding his parents dead. After their parents' funeral, the brothers embarked on a major spending escapade, purchasing a restaurant, sports cars, expensive clothing, and Rolex watches.

Months later, Erik, the younger and more suggestible brother, confessed to the killings. At that point, the brothers divulged that they had experienced years of sexual and emotional abuse at the hands of their father while their distant, alcoholic mother stood by in silent complicity. There was no evidence corroborating this abuse, nor had any allegations ever been made before the killings. Lyle Menendez said the killings had followed a week of growing tension after he had confronted his father about his continued molestation of Erik. His father, he reported, had responded with an angry death threat when Lyle announced his intention to expose him as a child abuser. The brothers grew convinced their parents were plotting to kill them to avert a family scandal. When their parents went into the den and closed the doors behind them after a heated argument, the brothers claimed, they panicked. Fearing for their lives, they got their shotguns and burst into the room firing wildly in self-defense.

The prosecution believed the brothers' motive was to inherit the family's $14 million fortune and that they had attempted to snare the police in deceptions. The defense invoked insanity. Lead defense attorney Leslie Abramson alleged that the boys suffered from a form of post-traumatic stress disorder common to abused children, whereby they become extremely sensitive to threats and imagine danger where none exists. Years of physical, sexual, and emotional abuse from constantly critical and belittling parents had caused the two young men to kill in self-defense. Abramson would try to convince the jury for each brother that the parents were monsters of perversity and that Lyle and Erik were the true victims.

The Menendez brothers' first trial, which raised the blame-the-victims defense to an art form, resulted in hung juries. It took two years, two more juries, the testimony of many more experts, and $5 million more before a prosecutor could persuade jurors that the story of these young men was a web of falsehood.

After working for an insurance company for more than twenty years, lawyer Gerald Long abruptly lost his job. When he could not find work in his field, he tried his hand at becoming a hack driver, and even bought a gypsy cab. He failed miserably and was forced to sell the car five months later to pay off debts. One morning in February 1978, after his wife had gone to work, Long struck his son William with a bat and killed him while he was still asleep. He felt sure that the first blow had killed him, but just to make sure, he struck him a second time. He then spent about two hours in his daughter's room as she watched TV in her brothers' room with her retarded brother, James. Long's daughter came in to tell her father that William seemed to be sleeping unusually late. Long then realized that it was time to kill her. He instructed her to go back to bed with her brother James. Long came into the room and told her to close her eyes so that he could play a game with her. Gleefully, she obeyed. Her father struck her in the head with the bat and killed her as she lay alongside her brother.

James, the remaining child, had been born blind, deaf, and mentally retarded. His disabilities had placed a tremendous emotional and financial strain on the family. James sensed that something was wrong. When he asked his father what was going on, Long struck him several times with the bat and killed him. With his three children dead beside him, Gerald Long sat in the bedroom for six or seven hours. He concluded that he wanted to spare his wife the pain of coming home to see her three children dead. Long had often felt threatened by his wife's attention to the children, especially her intense involvement with their disabled son. He complained that she had become preoccupied, sexually cold, and distant. Long heard her fumbling with the key in the lock and ran to let her in. He told her that he had a surprise for her, instructing her to stand in the middle of the living room with her eyes closed. Then he killed her with the same bat he'd used to kill their children.

When Long went on trial, his defense attorney depicted him as a "man with a weak underpinning" who had no feelings whatsoever during the eight hours it took to bludgeon to death his entire family. He acted like a machine, the attorney said, and machines can't tell right from wrong. The defense portrayed him as a loving family man whose devotion was "inconsistent" with his criminal acts. Clearly, therefore, the defense claimed, in a primitive version of a designer defense, Gerald Long "just snapped" under all the pressure. Psychiatrists testified that he thought he was performing an altruistic act. He was killing his children out of love so that they wouldn't have to be brought up in poverty and without respect for their father. Specifically, of killing his son William, Long said, "I was killing Billy and loving him at the same time." Once he began striking, the defense contended, the acts propelled themselves independently of Gerald Long.

Long was acquitted. The judge reflected that he had suffered enough; after all, he had lost his entire family. Long was confined at a psychiatric hospital until he was deemed no longer dangerously mentally ill, then was released. It is rumored that he went on to practice law in another state under an assumed name.

Susan Smith was another parent whose depression and self-protective instincts "just took over," according to her defense attorney, on that evening in October 1994 when she rolled her Mazda into a lake in South Carolina with her two toddlers strapped into their safety seats. The prosecution maintained that Susan Smith was a conniving, social-climbing, self-centered, vain young woman who disposed of her children to secure a failing relationship with the heir of a wealthy factory owner. Tom Findlay, the son of the owner of the plant where Susan had been employed, had sent her a letter breaking off their affair because he was not ready to assume the responsibilities of raising children. Ms. Smith was simultaneously carrying on liaisons with his father and her stepfather. Moreover, for nine days after the children were killed, Smith extorted the nation's pity and stirred up racial animosities by claiming that her children had been abducted by a young black man in a ski cap; this tale, the DA maintained, was not exactly the work of an innocent victim.

According to her defense team, Susan Smith's children were "the light of her life . . . the sunshine of her life. . . . They were everything to Susan Smith. . . . Everyone has a breaking point and she just broke. She just snapped like a dried twig!" Susan Smith had been pushed into suicidal confusion by a sense of failure in a life scarred with sexual molestation by her stepfather and the suicide of her own father. At the last second, her defense attorney declared, "her body willed itself out of the car, and she lived and her toddlers died."

Smith's stepfather took the stand in her defense, saying that he shared the guilt for the drowning death of his two grandsons, because his molestation of Susan starting at age fifteen "may have tainted her psyche for years." The prosecution countered by pointing out that Ms. Smith and her stepfather had continued their sexual relationship as consenting adults up to the time of the drownings. Dr. Seymour Halleck, a professor of psychiatry at the University of North Carolina, testified that he believed the children would still be alive if their mother had been adequately treated with the antidepressant Prozac around the time of the drownings. His testimony implied that the medical system, not Susan Smith, was to blame for her homicidal actions. The child welfare system, which did not pursue Susan's complaints of incest by her stepfather, had failed her as well.

All around, the defense portrayed the tearful Susan Smith as a victim herself — of incest, depression, a lax and negligent family court system, a careless medical establishment, and the social snobbery and stratification of a sleepy Southern town. In a final act of altruism, she killed her kids because, she said, she couldn't be a good enough mother. "But I didn't want my children to grow up without a mom," she would say later. "I felt I had to end our lives to protect us all from any grief or harm. My children, Michael and Alex, are with our Heavenly Father now and I know that they will never be hurt again. As a mom, that means more than I can say."

Susan Smith's defense — a mélange of excuses from incest to

depression to that old standby, the contention that she "just snapped" — did not exonerate her. It was not meant to. It was meant simply to stir enough sympathy among the jury and the public to rescue her from the electric chair. Toward that end, it worked just fine. She was sentenced to life.

Ann Green, the schoolmarmish and dedicated baby nurse, wished more than anything else to be a mother. She was an object of sympathy on the maternity ward of New York Hospital, where she had been employed for the last nineteen years: Poor Ann, tending to other people's newborns day after day, when her only two infants, born in this very same ward, had died within hours of being brought home. SIDS — sudden infant death syndrome — the death certificates read. Green was a trouper, and her profound Catholic faith helped sustain her. The lovely funerals — the tiny white coffins, the requiem Masses of the Angels — helped comfort her and brought her family and friends to rally around her. After the first infant's death, Green had begged the reluctant hospital chaplain to baptize her second baby before she left the hospital. Although this was only the practice in cases of imminent death, a kindly priest indulged the new mother. It was a good thing he did, for this child too was admitted dead on arrival to New York Hospital within five hours of arriving at the Green home. The autopsy revealed death by asphyxiation, SIDS.

Several years later, Ann Green gave birth to a third child, a boy. Although the child appeared to be normal and healthy in every way, hospital policy dictated that he remain in the nursery under intensive observation for two weeks in an effort to minimize the risk of another potential SIDS death. On the day of baby Larry's arrival home, a neighbor heard muffled distress cries coming from the apartment's front door, which Green had accidentally left ajar. She rushed in to find Ann leaning over the struggling infant, with a pillow covering his upper body and face.

I have already described some of my experiences in this case in

Chapter 1. When I testified for the prosecution, the defense even challenged my finding that Ann Green had what might be mildly labeled as severe deficits in her ability to nurture and bond with her infants. In meetings with me, she complained that "little Patricia didn't seem to want to nurse at all" and that baby Jamie was so "strong" that he bit her "so hard it hurt." She went on to muse, "I had taken care of so many babies in the hospital and never felt this way."

Green, the defense claimed, suffered from postpartum psychosis, which devastated her hormonal balance in the wake of each of her deliveries. Even though hospital records never mentioned any postpartum psychosis — which manifests itself in delirium and agitation so severe as to require restraint in a straitjacket — it was the only disorder that could have accounted for what the defense did agree was an unspeakable tragedy. To hear the defense tell it, Ann Green's case was a woman's issue.

Using a designer defense of postpartum psychosis — a hormonal, female variation of temporary insanity — Ann Green was acquitted of the smothering deaths of two infants and the attempted murder of a third. Her postverdict hospitalization for psychiatric evaluation quickly revealed that she no longer suffered from a mental illness and did not represent a danger to the community. She was in the hospital for less than thirty days. Upon her release, she returned to the practice of nursing and won custody of her surviving boy, Larry.

Forty-six-year-old Richard Taus, living in a suburban community through which the Long Island Railroad served commuters, would have fit Colin Ferguson's description of a white Anglo-Saxon male of the "power elite" he professed to despise. But Taus himself blamed his legal troubles on the government and the politicians, an elite group plotting to destroy him. Like Louis Kahan but in a very different era, he would mount a designer defense that would be based on his experiences in Vietnam.

Unlike Kahan, however, Taus had seen much combat. The son of a career army cavalry man who was a hardened veteran of World War II and Korea, Richard as a child was fat, uncoordinated, unhappy, and withdrawn — hardly the son for a military hero. In attempts at discipline, Taus's father would often tie the child to his chair during meals to teach him how to sit still. Mrs. Taus left her husband and returned with her son to her family home on Long Island when Richard was eight. In 1965, following in the path of a father he now barely knew, he graduated from Pennsylvania Military College with a commission as a second lieutenant in the U.S. Army. Taus was assigned to the courier service and directed to deliver classified and secret documents to command bases throughout Vietnam. He flew hundreds of missions during his first tour of duty and was shot down and crashed nine times. He won enough medals to make any father happy.

Lieutenant Taus was in Vietnam during the infamous Tet Offensive in 1968 and became very involved with a South Vietnamese colonel and his family. When the colonel and his wife were killed and their son consigned to an orphanage, Taus was tireless in obtaining food, medical care, and other help and supplies for the children at the orphanage. He had grown especially attached to the colonel's son and tangled with the bureaucracy in an attempt to adopt the boy and bring him back to the States. By 1971, at the end of his second tour of Vietnam, Taus succeeded in bringing the boy, whom he named David, to America.

Taus left active duty in 1972. For years he worked as a loan officer for Citibank in Manhattan. He found it boring and yearned for the old excitement he felt in combat situations and undercover missions. In 1978 he was inducted into the FBI, where he was assigned to investigate bank robberies. Agent Taus accumulated many citations and outstanding evaluations through the next ten years of his career, as he was alternately assigned to the criminal unit and to foreign counterintelligence. By all accounts, Richard Taus was a model agent and a beacon of his community.

When his adopted son, David, expressed an interest in soccer,

Taus became very involved in the sport. He organized a local boys soccer league in Freeport, New York, which he managed, coached, and helped sponsor long after his own son outgrew the league. Most of the boys were from dysfunctional and fatherless families and looked up to Taus and relished his attention and generosity. Their mothers were extremely grateful for this positive father figure in their sons' lives. He took the boys on trips and outings. By this point in his life, this Vietnam veteran and criminal justice professional had no adult friends. He spent his time almost exclusively in the company of children. His house became a mecca for little boys, with snacks and toys and clothing that he purchased and kept on hand for them. He also kept stacks of Polaroid pictures showing the children nude in various sexual poses.

In 1988 FBI agents, acting on the complaint of one of the boys' mothers, staked out Taus's house while Taus entered with a thirteen-year-old boy. The boy later testified that Taus fondled and sodomized him while he was in the house. Emboldened by his arrest, ten other boys on the team, from ages six to thirteen, came forward with their experiences of fondling and sexual abuse at the hands of Richard Taus. One boy, a ten-year-old being raised by his grandmother, told the agents about one episode with his coach:

> We played games and this time Rick began touching me all over, he also kissed me a lot of times. In the car, Jon [another teammate, aged nine] was in the middle of the front seat and I was sitting next to the door and he also kissed Jon and rubbed on Jon's penis, then he did the same to me — rubbed my penis and kissed me. . . . At his house, he told me that I was going to be his son one day. . . . Rick put his hands down my pants and made me sit on his lap and was feeling on my dick. . . . I remember that in all it was about five times.

Nine other boys, independently, gave similar accounts of their experiences with Taus.

Richard Taus was incensed. He hired Lombardino and Borg, a crackerjack Long Island law firm, to defend him against twenty-eight counts of sexual molestation and abuse with ten little boys on his soccer team, all allegedly occurring over a four-year period. He initially resisted any kind of psychological evaluation, even when his defense team recommended it. Taus didn't consider himself insane. He often became hostile to the doctors examining him. "Your expertise is in your billfold!" he muttered to Dr. Lawrence Siegal, a psychiatrist examining him for the prosecution. "You don't give a fuck, do you? You're talking to a war hero!" The defense hedged their bets. They maintained that Taus had never touched the kids, other than to give a fatherly hug or a pat on the back on the playing field. But in case the jury was inclined to believe he had molested them, he was clearly not responsible: Taus, they said, suffered from severe post-traumatic stress disorder as a result of his combat experiences more than seventeen years before in Vietnam.

The defense psychologist, who seemed to speak with the authority of a veteran himself and was most taken with Taus's war record, wrote the court:

> Most of his lifestyle was dominated by the war or his attempts to escape the memories of it (e.g., . . . his need to expiate his feelings of guilt through heroic community activity). His work with young boys and his desire to assist those in special need (a reminder of the orphans in Vietnam) is dictated by an unconscious desire to make up for his perceived failures to help Vietnamese children in the hour of their greatest need (the TET offensive).
>
> It is with a high degree of certainty that any fondling of children which may have taken place was an unconscious recapitulation of the traumatic episode which took place at the Go Vap Orphanage in which numerous children were killed and mutilated. That is, at such times he was operating in a state of less than full awareness and . . . his judgment and cognitive capacity were impaired to such a degree that he

was unable to appreciate the nature and consequences of his actions.

I was called in by the Nassau County district attorney to examine Taus to ascertain whether he suffered from a mental illness that would relieve him of criminal responsibility for molesting the boys. At our first meeting, Taus was jumpy, edgy, tightly wrapped. I too was nervous. Since Taus had been freed on $350,000 bail, I would be examining him in my private office, without the protection of detectives, armed guards, or prison bars — in fact, without any of the familiar trappings of my role as a forensic psychologist. I was face to face with him in the same room where I conducted hours of family therapy each week. My two worlds were threatening to converge, and I was uncomfortable.

Taus had appeared in my waiting room dressed in the standard G-man navy blue suit. His Nixon-like receding hairline revealed a deeply furrowed brow. He was miserable and defensive, clasping a portfolio of newspaper clippings about his wartime exploits and government citations and accolades as if it were a shield. He would wave his credentials at me each time we met. It took four meetings, spread out over eleven hours, before he was able to finish the psychological tests and clinical interview. He politely asked if he could tape the exam. I prefer not to record a session because it tends to change the dynamics of the interview, but this time (the only time in my career) I acquiesced. I thought it might make Taus more tractable. It was a mistake. Taus whipped out his stainless steel microcassette recorder, seizing control of the interview. With every question I asked he asked one of me, to try to get me off track. I felt as if Taus the FBI agent were interrogating me.

Richard Taus was bitter and angry at what he correctly perceived as his ruin. He would not accept any responsibility for how he had damaged his own life and the lives of his victims. He insisted to me that he was good to the boys and that he never touched them or fondled them in any inappropriate fashion. But he went beyond anger to declare that his arrest was a setup engineered by the FBI to "neutralize" him and destroy his reputation and credibility because of information he had gathered which, he told investigators, was "damaging to the establishment." Taus claimed to me to know about operations in Central America that, if revealed, would have hurt George Bush's chances in the 1988 presidential election. According to Taus, the boys' statements had been faked and the Polaroid evidence was planted. The children in the league had all been co-opted into the government's plot. "What angers me," he confided between clenched teeth, "is what the experience of this whole plot and trial has done to these little boys."

As Taus left my office after our last session, he noticed a bulletin board in the waiting room decorated with dozens of Christmas cards featuring photos of the children of my patients and staff. His tone of voice softened as he pointed out the photo of a boy with long dark eyelashes. "He is a beautiful boy," Taus remarked. "I don't know if this would be inappropriate," he asked tentatively, "but I would like to send him a soccer ball." I fell silent. The little boy Taus had selected was my son.

I coined the phrase "designer defense" while sitting in the forensic bureau of the Queens district attorney's office reading through an expert's report replete with the most nonsensical and incoherent psychobabble imaginable. I have since found far too many opportunities to employ the term, by which I mean a psychological defense used in an insanity plea which is carefully fabricated to fit all the pertinent facts of the case, and then tailored to individual characteristics of the defendant that might appeal to a jury — all regardless of whether any bona fide incapacitating mental illness exists. The nature of a particular designer defense is determined by what sympathy-evoking excuses are in vogue at the time of the trial. All designer defenses propound the idea of the defendant as victim — of battered woman syndrome, post-traumatic stress disorder, Twinkie-related sugar shock, or postpartum psychosis, to name just a few possibilities. "Victim chic" — a syndrome central to our culture of individual blamelessness — has for many years affected how we determine and dispense justice.

Designer defenses often work. Even when thy fail to secure an acquittal, as in the cases of Susan Smith and the Menendezes, they are persuasive enough to gum up the gears of the criminal justice system and warp our moral perspective on guilt, blame, and responsibility. When a crafty attorney weaves a designer defense, the sheer illusion and artifice that masquerade as psychological science — all dazzling form without substance — can easily confound and con a jury. Like fool's gold, these defenses with their trendy diseases and syndromes often seem more logical and persuasive to the layperson than responsible psychological science does. Psychology, a science still in its infancy, deals with probabilities and predictions, even as we professionals reach for what we call a "reasonable degree of psychological certainty." But claiming that postpartum psychosis caused Ann Green to suffocate her children can be a far more simple, stylish, and comprehensible explanation for that horror than saying she simply chose to do evil. The jurors can thus justify their own willing suspension of disbelief.

Many people see the famous "Twinkie defense" of Dan White in 1979 as having popularized the current trend to designer defenses. Dan White, a San Francisco city supervisor, shot and killed Mayor George Moscone and fellow supervisor and gay rights activist Harvey Milk, with a .38 special, right in their respective offices in City Hall. Pleading insanity, the defense told the jury that White's bingeing on sugar-loaded junk food like Cokes, chocolate cupcakes, and Twinkies aggravated his emotional distress to the point that his sense of right and wrong crumbled.

Defense attorneys called in a bevy of psychiatric experts, but none was as spellbinding a storyteller as Dr. Martin Blinder. Through his gift for words, Dan White's murderous behavior that day became quite humanly understandable. Another defense psychiatrist referred to the murder weapon, a .38 caliber revolver, as a "sort of security blanket" for White. A psychologist went on for hours about inkblots and scores on IQ tests.

Chronicling the Dan White trial in *Double Play: The San Francisco City Hall Killings*, Mike Weiss writes:

> Though psychiatrists claimed a scientific dispassion, their conclusions could hardly have been more subjective; and this seemed doubly true in the courtroom, where their judgments reduced them to little more than opinion-mongering.

With grudging awe, Weiss goes on to describe the testimony of another defense expert:

> Dr. Lunde had not titillated them with stories of Dan and Mary's sexual frequency, nor told them that the .38 special was really a teddy bear, nor bored them with inkblots in the shape of the defendant's father. Precise as a surgeon, the man of science laid out a body of facts and cut away the parts that offended until what was left on the operating table was a human being very nearly devoid of responsibility for his acts.

He concludes: "At fifty dollars an hour he [Lunde] was a real bargain." Eighteen years later, the going rate for designer defense experts is $300 to $600 an hour!

The lawyers and their designer experts constructed a flattering, well-constructed, comforting defense that could relieve jurors of sitting in judgment. White beat a double murder charge and was convicted of manslaughter. San Francisco erupted into riots. White served five years; within months after his release, he committed suicide.

The White defense was merely one of the most notorious

recent cases in a tradition of designer defenses that can be traced back to that icon of defense attorneys, Clarence Darrow, during the infamous Leopold and Loeb case in Chicago in 1924. Nathan Leopold and Richard Loeb were brilliant students from exceptionally illustrious and wealthy families. Arrogant and careless, they concocted a scheme to commit what would be called the "crime of the century." In a rented car, they picked up at random a boy named Bobby Franks, a small-for-his-age fourteen-year-old on his way home from school. They killed him with a blow to the head from a cloth-covered chisel and stuffed his dead body in a culvert on the Illinois-Indiana border. That evening, they called his father, Jacob Franks, a millionaire businessman, and followed up with a typed ransom note demanding $10,000 for the boy's release. They were soon caught.

The Leopold and Loeb families retained sixty-seven-year-old Clarence Darrow to defend their sons, utilizing an insanity defense based on what newspapers called the "new-fangled mental psychosis." More than six "alienists" (as psychiatrists were then called) examined the pair of young defendants and testified. William Alanson White, president of the American Psychiatric Association and superintendent of St. Elizabeth's Hospital, the government mental facility, served as a defense witness. Just coming into vogue in that era was the novel theory of psychoanalysis, with its emphasis on unconscious motives for behavior. Its concept of psychic determinism — which said that personality is shaped by crucial childhood phases — could easily be corrupted into an argument that the two young men lacked responsibility for their crimes. Sigmund Freud himself was consulted, and offered $25,000 or "anything he named" by various newspapers, eager for headlines, to "psychoanalyze" the two defendants. Responsibly, Freud turned down all offers "for reasons of health," adding, "I cannot be supposed to provide an expert opinion about persons and a deed when I have only newspaper reports to go on and have no opportunity to make a personal examination."

The report prepared by the defense psychiatrist set a precedent, the legacy of which is still seen today in insanity defense trials. The testimony consumed over three hundred pages of official transcript and dealt with every aspect in the life of the two killers — including their childhood sexual fantasies, their alleged molestation by governesses, and a vague reference to their current "perverse practices." The one limitation on testimony, which seems quaint by today's no-holds-barred standard, was any reference to the alleged homosexual nature of the relationship between Richard Loeb and Nathan Leopold. Otherwise, to present-day eyes, except in the choice of victim, the transcript bears uncanny similarity to the abuse defense proposed in the Menendez trial nearly seventy years later, and it carried a price tag every bit as steep in pre-Depression dollars. The media frenzy was termed a "vaudevillian spectacle," in which even the *Chicago Tribune* admitted "its share of the blame" in stirring up pretrial publicity that had become "an abomination."

In a nearly flawless defense, Darrow saved Leopold and Loeb from death. They were convicted and sentenced to life in prison. The verdict in the Franks case would establish the precedent for the introduction of psychological considerations as a mitigating defense. Loeb was slashed to death before his thirtieth birthday by another inmate, who claimed he made sexual advances to him. Leopold was a model prisoner who was paroled in 1958, after serving thirty-three years; after his release, he married and devoted himself to philanthropic activities and community service. Unlike his accomplice Loeb, or victim Bobby Franks, he died a quiet, natural death at age sixty-six.

Whether it's the case of Leopold and Loeb or Lyle and Erik Menendez, inherent in many a good designer defense is the legal tactic that famed defense attorney Alan Dershowitz calls the "abuse excuse," in which a criminal defendant claims a history of abuse as an excuse for a savage and usually retaliatory crime. Inventive expert witnesses have found a way of circumventing the diagnostic limitations of *DSM-IV*: the creative *syndrome*. In psychiatry, a syndrome is merely a descriptive term whereby symptoms, traits, and behaviors are observed to occur together in an individual. In cases in which I have participated, I personally have seen the defense get experts to corroborate adopted child syndrome, battered woman syndrome, Vietnam syndrome, and sexual abuse syndrome in attempts to relieve the defendant of responsibility for the crime.

An example of the misguided and far-flung application of battered woman syndrome (BWS) was brought home to me in the federal case of Jackie Everett. Everett, a young Hispanic woman, was arrested in an FBI sting operation when she acted as a cocaine courier in her jailed husband's drug operation. A local expert, a professor of social psychology, was called in for the defense. She stated that Ms. Everett suffered from BWS and therefore was not responsible for her criminal actions and was not competent to be sentenced. The absurd thing was that Ms. Everett had never even lived with her husband; they had married while he was in jail and had enjoyed exactly one conjugal visit years before. Undaunted, this expert pronounced that she suffered from emotional and psychological battering. This doctor was not licensed to practice psychology, nor was she qualified to diagnose the defendant's mental state. She provided the court with anecdotal evidence about a syndrome of questionable validity and neatly pigeonholed the defendant under its rubric. The language of the report read like a Jane Austen novel. "The course of one's life is set in an instant," wrote the doctor of Jackie's first meeting with her husband; Jackie was immediately "hypnotized" by him, according to this expert, while at the same time having "the capacity to empower him." Her report, which the sympathetic judge read with some interest, went on to cite the existence of many "counterintuitive truths in psychology" — which struck me as a poetic way of asking the court to ignore the evidence of Jackie's guilt and culpability. My assessment, including psychological tests, revealed that Jackie Everett was an angry, passive-aggressive personality with many antisocial features. It was more likely that she was the controller of her convict husband rather than the one dominated by him. In my view, the real victims of Jackie Everett's crimes were the citizens in the neighborhoods where the cocaine she couriered was sold and snorted.

Such misuse of battered woman syndrome damages the women who have in fact repeatedly been abused emotionally, physically, and sexually by their spouses or boyfriends. Many women who have been victims of domestic violence eventually find the courage and support to leave their abusive situations and reclaim normal lives. Others hang on until age, alcoholism, or other assorted physical ailments take the fight out of their mates. Most battered women are not murdered, and most do not kill. To the outrage of its vast machine of vociferous advocates, BWS has been denied inclusion in several revisions of the *DSM* since 1980. Although the 1995 murder trial of O. J. Simpson brought the social and criminal problem of domestic violence to renewed national attention, there simply is not sufficient scientific data to corroborate that such violence can actually spur a specific and diagnosable psychiatric condition in which a woman is not responsible for her actions.

I certainly believe that it is a national tragedy that so many women are victimized by the very men who claim to love them. Sadly, there are far too many battered women in America. What I don't see is a stereotyped, limiting syndrome that neatly defines and wraps up the day-to-day hostagelike existence of these women. Although their suffering at the hands of their batterer may be similar in its manifestation, each one of these women is unique and attempts to cope with whatever emotional and social resources she has. I resent that the BWS advocates have taken the suffering of these women and made it a cause célèbre, parlaying it into lucrative careers for themselves. I also might be more convinced if in over thirty-five homicides alleging battered woman syndrome, I had examined even one defendant who was not a psychopath who gave as good as she got.

It is misplaced beneficence to try to right one social ill at the expense of perpetuating another. Crusading under the guise of the objective psychological expert is the wrong way to right a wrong if it prostitutes the greater cause of justice.

Criminal defendants themselves seldom come up with these designer defenses. It is defense attorneys who summon up such creative excuses as "distant father syndrome" or "multiple-personality disorder" to excuse their clients' violent acts. However, these clever trial attorneys would not succeed without expert psychological witnesses who will obligingly tailor the "designer disease" to substantiate the defense's claim. These tailored syndromes are unknown to the *DSM-IV*, the guidebook to standards of psychological diagnosis. It is true that the *DSM-IV*, which contains more than 3,500 mental illnesses, including caffeine addiction and dysgraphia (bad handwriting), has often been criticized as being overinclusive; some critics have claimed it pathologizes ordinary behaviors so that treating psychiatrists and psychologists will have diagnosable conditions for which to receive insurance reimbursement. For example, after three weeks of sleep loss, irritability, overwork, and loss of appetite, what's to keep a working woman from killing her husband and pleading dual career stress syndrome?

None of the syndromes listed in Dershowitz's catalog of "abuse excuses" appears in the *DSM-IV* except post-traumatic stress disorder — a diagnosis that in itself points up many of the more complex issues involved in the designer defense. PTSD, as it's called, has also been criticized as being too broad, a garbage-can category into which lazy or incompetent diagnosticians and hired witnesses toss many more truly defined and more appropriate mental disorders. PTSD is real and debilitating. In my experience, however, it looks very different in the therapist's office than it does on the witness stand. One night, in a group therapy session I was running, a young Gulf War veteran who was medicated with Prozac and had been suffering from crippling depression broke down into sweating, shakes, and tears as he confessed his guilt about lobbing shells into crowds of innocent women and children. His mission was to clear the beaches for Navy Seal operations. This man was struggling to remain a productive member of society. He entered therapy on his own initiative and at his own expense; his veterans' benefits didn't cover it. He was compliant and serious about his treatment — and he recovered. Despite his arsenal of assault and hunting weapons, despite experiencing terrifying flashbacks of combat, he did not rape or murder, or throw acid in the face of his landlord, or open sniper fire on seven young fathers in a Brooklyn street as they left church with their sons, or blow away his boss with a sawed-off shotgun. In short, he did not engage in any of the criminal and violent activities that I have seen clever attorneys and experts try to explain away under the PTSD rubric. The stereotype of the returning veteran portrayed so chillingly in *Taxi Driver*, and so popular in today's courtrooms, does a disservice to the majority of young men and women who have experienced the horrors of war, battled their own adjustment problems on returning home, coped, and gone on to live valuable, upstanding lives.

Mounting a designer defense can be a travesty of justice not only because of defense-team craftiness but because of carelessness as well. Sometimes attorneys, especially public defenders, are so overworked and overwhelmed that they make tactical errors in representing their clients. Sometimes they hoist themselves onto the bandwagon of the designer defense to their clients' detriment when, sadly, a more reasonable and bona fide defense strategy exists. Such was the case in the trial of Olda Mae Calhoun, charged with murder in the stabbing death of her common-law spouse. Her lawyer was claiming battered woman syndrome. Willy Barker was a paranoid schizophrenic, an ex-con mental patient with a habit of beating and cutting Olda Mae when he got high.

I was called to examine Olda Mae by the Brooklyn district attorney, who apologized that I would have to journey to Rikers

Island, New York City's notorious prison, to interview her. I was unknown to the guards there, and despite the court order I wielded authorizing me to evaluate her, they were not going to take any unnecessary chances. "Do you have any official ID?" the captain asked gruffly.

I rummaged through my wallet, "Driver's license?"

"I'll need something more official than that," he said, scowling.

I was no longer the parole officer I had once been, possessed of the cachet of a badge. Finally I found my pistol permit authorizing me to carry a .44 magnum. I slid this under the bulletproof window to the captain. He scrutinized it, glancing several times back and forth from my face to the photo identification before relenting. "Okay," he said, as he threw the lever opening the metal grate. Almost as an afterthought, he called out, "You're not carrying, are you?"

One of several old schoolbuses shuttled me to the building that housed Olda Mae. On this beautiful August afternoon, the place had the balmy feeling of Santa Catalina Island, until the iron bars slammed shut behind me and I was locked in a low-ceilinged, dark inmates' area, more like a cave than a visitors' room.

Into this catacomb came Olda Mae, aged forty-three, toothless, disheveled, but incongruously ladylike, simple, and almost sweet. She offered me a caramel she had gotten from the commissary. I was touched by her generosity, because for indigent inmates like Olda Mae, with no family or friends, little treats from the prison commissary were precious. Olda Mae shifted her bulk in the metal chair, settling in to tell her story. "I don't get no visitors," she started. She talked in low, barely audible tones, gesturing almost triumphantly to the crisscross of keloid scars on her arms and legs, as if they were so many battle ribbons. Olda Mae had a hard life. To get through it, she told me, she relied on booze, crack cocaine, and her man, Willy. One night, she and Willy were drunk and high when they got into one of their usual arguments over a card game. Willy was really riled up. He threatened to cut her, kill her. She knew if he got her he would; he had almost severed her arteries with cuts before, as witnessed by her long record of hospitalizations. She grabbed a knife from the dish drainer. He lunged at her with his own blade, trying to corner her and block her from the only exit. Olda Mae was trapped with this maniac; this time she was fighting for her life. Crime scene evidence revealed that she stabbed him and fled through the door.

Olda Mae's killing of Willy was, I believed, clearly done in self-defense. A woman does not have to be insane to use deadly force to protect her own life when a reasonable fear exists that she is in imminent danger. This is a constitutional right, and Olda Mae had summoned up enough courage, or enough fear, to use it. I believe any desperate woman would have done the same thing when faced with this threat. Olda Mae accepted a plea bargain of manslaughter and is now serving a sentence of five to fifteen years.

Good designer defenses must not only be elegant sob stories; they must also be extremely believable dramas that speak to the day-to-day experiences of the jurors. Jurors must be so drawn into the narrative that they can easily imagine themselves committing a crime given such motivations; they must come to feel that there really is no difference between themselves and the defendant except for the extreme circumstances. True mental illness is messy, for there are few textbook cases; it is not dramatic or entertaining or easily understandable by a jury. In a designer defense plea, a defense attorney and his experts must prepare for a bravura performance. They must carefully play to their audience.

Ubiquitous in the headlines and in the language of defense attorneys and their experts are phrases like these: "He just snapped." "She cracked under the pressure." "He saw his wife with her lover and went temporarily insane." Firmly rooted in the public mythology of mental illness is the notion that seemingly normal people "just snap" in response to some terrible real or symbolic trauma in their lives. For us ordinary, law-abiding people — and certainly for those of us on juries — such a concept is pretty scary, to think that someday your wonderful neighbor, coworker, or even spouse may just crack and erupt into violence.

Purveyors of the designer defense feed on the popular notion that people do in fact "just snap" and burn, kill, rape, and pillage. But no matter what defense attorneys and newspapers declare, mental illness does not operate this way. *People don't just snap*; neither do psychopaths and antisocial character types. Any criminal is a long time in the making, and there are many clear signs along the way if anyone cares to take a look. Examine the lives of psychotics like Joel Rifkin, Chandran Nathan, and John Hinckley: their experiences, and those of the mentally ill people who do not commit infamous crimes, are evidence that psychotic illnesses are progressive diseases of gradual deterioration in functioning. They usually start in late adolescence or early adulthood. They are, if not curable, treatable and manageable. In every case of a mentally ill criminal that I have ever examined, the signs of sickness and danger were there, loud and clear, to doctors or anyone else who cared to see them, well before the violent act. And tragically, those signs arose in enough time to intervene and prevent the crime — if denial and incompetence hadn't been involved. For me as a therapist, the most difficult part about forensic work is the waste of human lives.

Neither the family of Abigail Cortez, her boyfriends, her physically battered ten-year-old son, nor Jessica, the five-year-old daughter she would eventually allow to be killed, could comprehend the intense level of rage and aggressiveness harbored by this petite, soft-spoken woman. There had been glimpses of it as early as first grade, when her public school teacher wrote that she was a "moody and difficult child." By fifth grade, the teachers described her as having "a chip on her shoulder — likes to fight — sullen and argumentative." The family ignored all recommendations for counseling. Police had evidence showing that Abigail ran drugs and sold her body and had an active life on the streets while her boyfriend was away. She often locked the children alone in the bedroom of the apartment while she went about her activities on the streets. Jessica's paternal grandmother had seen the woman's fury firsthand and had exhausted all bureaucratic channels and her meager financial resources in an attempt to get Abigail's two children away from her. Abigail won a four-year court battle when the judge ruled her a fit mother. Ten months later, Jessica was beaten to death by Abigail's live-in boyfriend, who regularly abused both her children.

The defense claimed that Abigail suffered from battered woman syndrome and "learned helplessness." Abigail was pretty, with dark, soulful eyes and a gold charm around her neck saying "#1 MOM," given to her by her mother and sisters in support. The designer defense claimed that Abigail was an innocent, in love with a monstrous, abusive man from whom she could not escape, beset by the stresses of poverty and drug abuse. Charged with murder, she eventually pled guilty to assault and manslaughter charges and was sentenced to five to fifteen years.

In his pantheon of abuse excuses, Dershowitz refers to the adopted child syndrome defense proposed by Marty Effman, Joel Rifkin's attorney for the serial killer's second trial, which was to take place in Suffolk County. This defense would have allowed Rifkin to claim that his "rejection" by his biological mother had stirred in him such intense rage that he bore no responsibility for his murderous impulses. The proposal became a moot point because after being convicted of killing Tiffany Bresciani, Rifkin, running out of money, fired Effman and went on to plead guilty in the other jurisdictions in which he had been charged, racking up combined sentences of over a thousand years.

The psychologist who espoused this syndrome, not included in *DSM-IV* or any other manual of reputable, scientific psychology, was selling it as his own product, one he claimed he had used in helping to defend ten others accused of crime. And a zealous marketer he was. During my preparations for Rifkin's first trial, he very nearly bombarded my office and the office of defense attorney Jack Lawrence with offers to participate in the defense. I avoided speaking to him, politely and honestly pointing out through Lawrence as my intermediary that the defense we were presenting, a straight schizophrenia insanity defense, was probably doomed to failure (given Rifkin's unfocused and erratic schizophrenic symptoms, I doubted we could persuade the jury he was insane) and that his novel defense would then be contaminated for the second trial. Personally, I was outraged at the bold entrepreneurialism of someone in my profession who wanted to use a high-profile case like this to advance his pet theory. More important, Rifkin may have been paranoid and schizophrenic and prone to suggestibility, but he was not hostile to his parents, angry about his adoption, or prone to blame others for his acts. When pressed on the issue of adoptive child syndrome, Rifkin expressed little curiosity about whether his birth mother had been a prostitute or a college student. He shrugged. "Who knows!" Without rage or bitterness, he said, "Look, whoever she was, she chose to give me life . . . I'm grateful for that. I could've wound up on the end of a coat hanger." Rifkin also resisted suggestions that a Menendez-like defense might be constructed out of sexual abuse that might have been perpetrated by his mother, father, or sister. Rifkin grew furious. "They were good to me . . . they gave me a good home. I loved them very much."

Shortly after Rifkin was convicted, my adversary in that case, prosecutor Fred Klein, met me for lunch in an attempt at rapprochement after the trench warfare of the trial. Klein sounded almost avuncular. "You're a good prosecution witness," he said. "You're not cut out to be a defense witness." I reluctantly had to agree. In my effort to present the truth of Rifkin's paranoid schizophrenia, I may have done my client a disservice. Though I doubt it would have made any difference in the verdict, I did not play the role of defense expert the way the jury expected. I had no easy and dramatic explanations for Rifkin's behavior. I had no anecdotes, no snap, crackle, and pop excuses. In describing for the jury the actual clinical symptoms of schizophrenia and psychosis, I couldn't even provide an account of Rifkin's madness with any juicy delusions or a riveting plot line.

I also may have missed the boat strategically in the only other trial in which I was able to support the defense with psychological testimony of bona fide incapacitating mental condition, the case of Chandran Nathan. Prominent defense experts had suggested that we employ a "Rambo syndrome" approach, maintaining that this withdrawn computer analyst had been so obsessed with film and comic-book superheroes that he lost touch with reality and believed he was in mortal combat with an oppressive enemy: twenty-year-old medical student Shaleen Wadwhani. Heavily armed, Nathan undertook a commando mission, ambushing the enemy behind his front door. "Too bad Nathan had never been in the military and was too young for Vietnam," one expert said to me, shaking his head, "or this defense could really fly!" Others suggested the "Romeo and Juliet syndrome," a scheme of reasoning in which Nathan suffered from an obsession with Hema Sakhrani, believed the families of the betrothed to be the warring Montagues and Capulets, and in a novel twist on Shakespeare, resolved to rescue his beloved Juliet from a fate worse than death. Paradoxically, Nathan, with his paranoid, deluded logic, appeared too sane to be crazy.

A 1996 feature in the *New York Times* by science writer Jane Brody advertised one more brand-new line of designer defenses. "When can killers claim sleepwalking as a defense?" she asked. The answer, of course, is, whenever a slick defense attorney feels that he can cut and weave that notion into a fabric that will excuse his client from responsibility for his actions. Brody mentions the case of a sixteen-year-old girl who, while allegedly dreaming that burglars were in her home murdering her family, grabbed a revolver and shot and killed her father and six-year-old brother and wounded her mother. A young Canadian man suffering from a sleep disorder, allegedly while still asleep, drove his car fourteen miles to his in-laws' house, where he stabbed his mother-in-law to death and severely wounded his father-in-law. Both killers were acquitted.

In both cases, sleep experts maintained that a person who com-

mitted a violent crime while sleeping should not be held responsible for it. They labeled the phenomenon of sleep-related violence as "noninsane automatism" — an act performed by a sane
person without intent, awareness, or malice. Most mainstream
sleep experts challenge the whole notion of "noninsane automatism," since even under hypnosis we cannot be made to do something we don't want to do. Yet, with millions of people suffering
from sleep disorders, like sleep apnea, in the United States, it
could well become the new designer defense of the season, a last
resort for those who have committed assaultive and murderous
acts — and a business boom for psychiatric and neurological experts.

In 1995 John E. Du Pont, of the Du Pont chemical family, the
fifty-seven-year-old heir to an estimated $250 million fortune,
fired a .44 magnum revolver at U.S. Olympic wrestler Dave
Schultz, striking him twice in the chest and killing him. Schultz,
thirty-six, lived in a home on the Du Pont estate with his wife and
two young children. After the shooting, a swarm of associates
from the U.S. wrestling team and the local police department in
the Pennsylvania county where Du Pont had his 800-acre estate
came forward with their tales of his paranoia, his delusions of persecution, his angry unpredictable outbursts, and the arsenal of
weapons he collected and armed himself with. Cocaine, pain pills,
and alcohol seemed to fuel what friends described as his "tailspin."
Gail Wenk Du Pont, who married Du Pont in 1983, alleged that
during their marriage he choked her, threatened her with a knife,
put a gun to her head, and tried to push her out of a moving car.
Fearing for her life, she left him after a year. Many who knew John
Du Pont, and are describing his emotional problems so clearly in
hindsight, admit in shame that they were just using him or hanging on for the money.

Over a year after his crime, bolstered by the expert testimony
of three psychiatrists, John E. Du Pont was wheeled into the
courthouse in Media, Pennsylvania, to begin his insanity defense
trial. Dressed in the same blue sweat suit he was arrested in, with

long and greasy gray hair and a Rip Van Winkle beard, Du Pont might have been an understudy for Howard Hughes sent from central casting. Certainly, it was someone's calculated idea to have him appear this way in contrast to the neat white shirt and tie approach used by other insanity defendants like Nathan and Rifkin. It certainly did go a long way toward making Du Pont look crazy in the eyes of the jury and to confirm defense counsel Thomas Bergstrom's notion that they had been "an eyewitness to insanity — a spectator to a kaleidoscope of madness." It was a clever coup of costuming. However, no institution in the United States would have allowed Du Pont to wear the same clothing for a year or not to bathe or wash his hair. Neither was it ever clear to me why the formerly robust wrestler and sportsman was confined to a wheelchair throughout the trial.

Just two months after his conviction, when John E. Du Pont appeared in court to be sentenced, he was a miracle of sartorial rehabilitation. Clean-shaven, well-attired, and with neatly trimmed hair, he listened attentively to the proceedings. Both prosecution and defense experts agreed that his mental health was significantly improved after eight months of treatment at Norristown State Hospital, but they clashed over whether he was fit for imprisonment. "Currently, he suffers from schizophrenia, paranoid type, which is now in partial, but tenuous, remission," Dr. Gerald Cooke testified on Du Pont's behalf. Dr. William Carpenter, another defense expert, worried that locking Du Pont in a cell might cause him to revert to violent delusional behavior.

Subliminally, fear, guilt, ignorance, and apathy toward the mentally ill allow designer defenses to proliferate and manipulate juries. When our criminal justice system plays the "blame game" — blame the victims, blame society, blame the parents, blame the war, the bureaucracy, sugar, Prozac — we all come out losers. Beyond creating a chance for a criminal to be wrongly acquitted, the designer defense perpetuates myths about mental illness that interfere with people getting timely and competent treatment. It continues to unfairly stigmatize the truly mentally ill. It cripples our capacity to predict and prevent psychotic violence. It distorts and perverts our entire social framework regarding individual responsibility and accountability. It paralyzes our ability to even believe that we have control over our decisions and our lives.

With the abuse of the insanity defense, we can come to believe that we can't help the mentally ill and can't admonish or control the psychopath. If we are led to believe that a perfectly normal person can "just snap" or be driven to murder by eating Twinkies or by being adopted, we will feel even less in control of our destinies.

I believe that psychologically a sense of loss of control is central to the collective pessimism and malaise that seems to infect us as a society. We seem to feel ourselves less than adequate to the task of daily living in a highly complicated, stress-filled technological environment. As the economic and social gulf between the haves and have-nots continues to widen, we all feel as if we have less control over our safety, our prosperity, our mortality, our inner and outer urges, and our overall life circumstances. Senseless, violent crime — serial killers, terrorist bombings, carjackings, and gang rampages — seem to scream at us from every headline, reinforcing our fears. We strike back; we say we should reinstitute the death penalty, get tough on crime, abolish the insanity defense — yet contradictorily that same sense of loss of control makes us susceptible to designer defenses. The boundaries among the mad, the bad, and the innocent seem hopelessly blurred.

The cases of the two Vietnam veterans, Louis Kahan and Richard Taus, separated by twelve years, illustrate the transient nature of designer defenses — along with larger issues of personal and social responsibility. The public had hardened to the psychological effects of Vietnam by 1990, when Richard Taus utilized the same sort of defense Kahan had succeeded with. Taus had not murdered, assaulted, or physically harmed his victims. But he had betrayed and traumatized them, stolen their childhoods. It seemed that for most of his forty-six years, Taus had been an exemplary citizen. He truly was a war hero, and his performance as an FBI agent was commendable. By all accounts, he was a devoted and loving father to his adopted son, who vehemently denied that Taus had ever molested him.

At the time of the trial, when I first met him, Taus was really falling apart — decompensating, in psychological terms. His emotional distress, paranoia, and disturbed thinking were getting the better of him. He appeared to me a somewhat tragic, ruined figure who was acutely aware of his life crumbling down around him. Taus's defense team was aggressive and thorough, and had it not been for the fortuitous appearance of a surprise witness they might have persuaded the jury that flashbacks of combat could cause a man to systematically molest little boys seventeen years later.

The prosecutor, Ken Litman, was equally well prepared and aggressive. He also had been dealt a stroke of luck. A thirty-six-year-old man living in Connecticut had read about Taus in the newspaper. He contacted the district attorney and gave a sad and chilling statement. In 1962, when he was about eight years old, he attended a summer sleep-away camp in New York State. He was assigned to the group led by an eighteen-year-old counselor named Richard Taus. When he accidentally injured his knee and was sent to the infirmary for treatment, Taus took a special interest in him and visited him. Now, a quarter of a century later, he remembered how on one of these visits, Taus kissed him on the lips. "A relationship developed between us that became very emotional and sexual in nature," he stated. Sadly he explained that he had come from a very "emotionally detached" home and that Taus had become "a role model" for him. The relationship continued for the remaining six weeks of the camp season, during which, he stated, it escalated to mutual oral sex. After camp, he remembered, Taus sought to continue their relationship and visited him several times at his family home in New Jersey. He took him for dinner and to the movies. All the attention made this little boy feel special. They would go for car rides during which, the man reported, they would "engage in touching each other's organs and performing oral sex." His parents brought him to visit Taus in Freeport twice. Once, the boy even slept over. Finally, after four and a half months, according to this witness, the cleaning woman caught them naked in bed together at his family home. When she screamed, the boy's father came home and "physically threw Taus out of our house."

For nearly twenty-five years, this man, now a husband and father, struggled with doubts about his psychosexual stability. He had tracked Taus down and gone to see him in Freeport in 1985. Taus was entertaining some young boys from the soccer team. He embraced the man lovingly and turned to the boys. "This is the Bill I told you about." Confused and sickened, Bill fled. Four years later, Bill read about Taus's arrest in the newspaper. Outraged by Taus's designer defense, Bill felt it was his responsibility to come forward and set things right. He contacted the Nassau County district attorney and gave a detailed statement about the abuse that as a child he had suffered at Taus's hands — well before Taus ever saw Vietnam. His statement convinced the jury to reject Taus's insanity defense and convict him. Bill could make sure that justice came at last to Richard Taus and that no other boys would be victimized by him — because he had finally found the courage to tell the truth.

5

THE FORENSIC DETECTIVE

*D*ay after day for two icy February weeks, four experts — three psychiatrists and myself, a psychologist — sat at the witness table in the old New York City federal courthouse while the defendant, Lilly Schmidt, glared at us sullenly from across the room. When I passed by her during a recess, she glowered at me and muttered, "I have put an old Gypsy curse on you!" For an instant, I was startled, both by the malevolence in her tone and by an irrational sense that this remarkable woman just might be capable of carrying out her threat. Lilly Schmidt was using the same sort of reckless ingenuity she'd had as a con woman as she now tried to persuade the courts that she was insane.

Lilly Schmidt, born Lili Madjarova in Bulgaria in 1951 (or 1961, as she preferred to tell it), was one of the most frustrating and confounding forensic cases I had ever examined. With her imperious, Old World ways, Garbo cheekbones, and Gabor accent, she could be as charming, engaging, and witty as an East European countess, until you reminded yourself that she had just been convicted of conspiring to kill two federal agents in a plan she had engineered to escape from Rikers Island with the help of two hit men. An inmate informant tipped the feds off to the fact that she was contracting with the killers, and her phone conversations were tapped. In thirteen hours of tapes, she is heard methodically masterminding the jail escape and the murder of the agents, to eliminate them as witnesses to her crimes.

The FBI set up a sting operation that executed her daring escape plan to the last detail. On her way to a court hearing, two men posing as marshals were hit in the head by two men posing as Lilly's rescuers, who took her out of Rikers, got her in a car, and spirited her to a local Holiday Inn. Lilly is at her best in the secret video of her taken hours after the breakout, in the Holiday Inn, sipping champagne with the two undercover agents whom she believes are hit men who have not only gotten her out of jail but also killed agent Kenneth Connaughton and another G-man.

"Brought you a little fuckin' present," one agent/hit man says to her.

Lilly Schmidt laughs. "Kenny — Kenny's chain."

The undercover man urges her to keep it as a souvenir, but ever-cunning Lilly is no amateur. "Uh, the chain maybe — but not this thing," she says, pointing to the agents' ID badges. "Someone might know." She continues to chat with the "hit men," who are now trying on the other supposedly murdered agent's glasses. "Wasn't he a clown, honey?" she asks, chuckling. "My idea was great, right? I told you those two were clowns, baby — twenty-three- and twenty-four-year-olds."

The hit man reassures her. "They died like dogs."

A relaxed and victorious Lilly continues to relate her exploits. "Well, listen, this is my life story, which is quite pictureful. I mean, out of Bulgaria in the ambassador's car with dark windows and everything, and the secret service is shooting at the diplomatic car. Don't you just love it?"

The agent/hit man chimes in, "What, we got like fuckin' James Bond here?"

"You know another woman that would have guts to do something like that?" challenges Lilly.

"You're a ballsy broad," he finally admits.

Perhaps that appraisal of Lilly is more honest and accurate than most that I encountered in the examination notes and psychiatric reports of more than twenty doctors who subsequently evaluated her as she sought to prove, by whatever zany means possible, that she was severely mentally ill, not responsible for her crimes, could not understand the charges against her, could not participate in her own defense, and therefore needed to be hospitalized psychiatrically rather than incarcerated. I had been retained by the U.S. Department of Justice to examine Lilly Schmidt and to determine whether she was genuinely suffering from a mental illness that was a factor in her crimes, or whether she was, as many suspected, malingering. If she could not demonstrate mental illness, she faced a lengthy sentence without parole in a federal penitentiary.

Back before she started trying to rub out federal agents, Lilly Schmidt had been the grand dame of "paper hangers," con artists who forge or counterfeit official documents, checks, securities, and passports. She would brag to me that she and her accomplice-husband, Lenny, even forged cashiers' checks to raise the $100,000 a day pocket money they required to maintain their luxurious lifestyle. In fact, on a previous forgery conviction, Lilly had secured her bail from Rikers Island with a forged check! By the time I met her, she had prior convictions for grand larceny and bail jumping in New York; check forging, perjury, grand theft, and making false financial statements in Los Angeles; and submitting phony passport applications, a federal offense. She had fled to London in 1988, where she was arrested for grand larceny and scheme of fraud. Returning to the States, she was convicted of bank fraud, falsifying social security numbers, and unauthorized access to a U.S. State Department device (the fraudulent pass-port). For these earlier crimes, she had been sentenced to two and a half years in a federal penitentiary.

When Lilly was released from the pen in Lexington, Kentucky, the relief was mutual. She had been an extremely difficult and de-manding inmate. She knew her rights and her way around both the correctional and mental health systems. When she wasn't in the law library composing legal briefs and complaints, she was badgering the shrinks for drugs and special treatment. Using her impressive skills, she had figured out how to forge prison docu-ments and official signatures to obtain special passes and privi-leges for herself. Despite her constant allegations of abuse and victimization from guards and fellow prisoners, it was actually she who was extremely assaultive and provocative to the other in-mates.

After her release she returned to New York and met the love of her life, Lenny, an aging con artist with a taste for elegance. The two traveled extensively, for business and pleasure, purchasing luxuries from places like Tiffany's with forged checks. On an ex-cursion to Washington, D.C., they visited the Pentagon, slipped through the cordoned-off security areas, and rifled the desk draw-ers of the security chief, stealing his credit cards, driver's license, and ID. Lilly knocked off identification showing she was the secu-rity chief's wife and began a massive spending spree at the cha-grined civil servant's expense. So much for national security. What Lilly lacked in scruples she made up for in panache.

In 1992 Lilly and Lenny decided to stick up a jewelry store in the concourse of Trump Tower in New York City. She was beau-tifully coiffed, resplendent in sable, and sported a sapphire and diamond knockoff of Princess Diana's engagement ring. On this occasion, however, their timing was off and they were arrested. In Lilly's possession was a .38 handgun, counterfeit checks, forged securities, and forged and counterfeit military and official passes and permits. Agents searching the couple's penthouse apartment found an original Renoir, two Monets, a full wardrobe of furs, jewelry from Cartier, Tiffany's, and Harry Winston, a cache of erotic Polaroids showing Lilly in provocative poses, and forged identification and securities using over forty-two different aliases.

As I sat across a conference table from Lilly Schmidt in the attorneys' room at the Metropolitan Correctional Center, I found it difficult to imagine that this disheveled-looking woman in prison denim, with long, straggly hair showing almost six inches of gray roots, had run up a $1,000-a-month tab at Elizabeth Arden. Lilly, a modern-day Moll Flanders, was temporarily down on her luck. I would soon realize that Lilly was in role — I was in the presence of a diva who made every examination a drama she directed. This time, Lilly would be giving the performance of her life. If she didn't win, she would be an old woman before she ever walked into Tiffany's again.

Evaluating Lilly Schmidt was like conducting an archaeological dig. I was confronted with layer upon layer of lies, embellishments, fabrications, and inconsistencies, all deposited along with the facts into an almost impenetrable shale. Her medical and police records went back ten years, filling two legal-size storage boxes. I would have to sort through videotapes, audiotapes, and reams of Lilly's own correspondence and writings. I would also have to sift through Lilly's accumulation of mental diseases and psychiatric diagnoses. At one time or another, based on her self-reported symptoms and behavior, she had been diagnosed with everything from schizophrenia to manic-depression. She claimed to have every psychiatric disorder in the book — even when they were contradictory or mutually exclusive. How can you be simultaneously depressed and euphoric, insomniac and hypersomniac, or agitated and vegetative? Lilly swore she was.

When Lilly took the MMPI, the computer service that scored it considered it an invalid profile. Lilly had endorsed so many inconsistent, contradictory, and improbable symptoms and attitudes that no valid interpretations could be made about her mental condition from the test — except one: that Lilly was "faking bad," i.e., attempting to present herself in the sickest way possible. The doctor who examined her for the defense, in an odd admission of confusion, asked in his report, "Could it be that she experienced all of these symptoms at one time or another in her life?"

The psychologists at the federal prison in Lexington, Kentucky, had a different explanation: malingering. During her previous stint in prison, Lilly had resisted every attempt at clinical assessment, grudgingly agreeing only to take a test used to estimate verbal intelligence. They concluded, "She performed so poorly as to leave no other conclusion than [that] she was deliberately attempting to underestimate her true abilities." Lilly claimed that she could not comprehend the words "drum," "elbow," "fence," or "cage." Her score was equivalent to that of a three-year-old. Yet Lilly frequented the prison law library, where she pored over law books, laboriously copied out cases, and drafted coherent strategy letters to her attorney. In letters she wrote Lenny from Rikers Island, she instructed him how to get the psychiatrists to send him to a hospital and get out. First, she told him, he must insist that he had a long psychiatric history. "Honey, we will play incompetent and beat the system again."

Lilly's bravado was getting the better of her; she started overplaying her hand and getting sloppy. The doctors believed she was conning them in order to appear mentally ill and incompetent to stand trial. Her contradictions were starting to catch up with her — especially now that she had moved from con games to conspiracy to commit murder. She was beginning to discover that it might not be so easy to put one over on the shrinks.

Undaunted, Lilly intensified her efforts. She told one examiner that she saw a mouse walking on the walls of her cell. The mouse laughed at her and told her she was hopeless and that everyone was against her. "How pitiful you are!" the mouse declared. She claimed that a federal agent transporting her to her court appearance had raped her and left her pregnant. Pregnancy tests conducted at that time were negative. She swore she miscarried. She began to tell the mental health staff at the jail that she was depressed and could not eat. Curiously, her weight remained stable.

The doctors discovered that she was hoarding food in her cell. Her stories of starving herself down to eighty-six pounds and being hospitalized while at Lexington turned out to be false. Slowly, the fabric of lies woven by Lilly was unraveling.

Simply put, my job on behalf of the government was to poke as many holes in her story as necessary to discover the truth. I had the whole day to spend with Lilly at the jail. She seemed to relish the contact as if I were making a social visit. We were permitted to bring in cans of soda, which to inmates was a treat. She leaned back against her chair, crossed her legs, and began to relate the long and convoluted story of her life as it progressed from a tumultuous childhood in Bulgaria, through six or seven marriages, to California and this jail in downtown New York City. Lilly emoted throughout her whole narrative as if she were a starlet at her screen test. Cringing in embarrassment, she apologized for her disheveled appearance; she was afraid to let the prison barbers cut her hair because they would "hurt" her. She said she was frightened of flushing the toilet because, like cutting her hair, it would be "losing something" of herself. Pointing to a chipped front tooth, she claimed that she was afraid to go to a prison dentist. (When I checked the medical record I found that the tooth had been capped by a prison dentist two years earlier at her request.)

Lilly talked continuously of her exploits for three and a half hours. Her face registered an incredible range of dramatic emotions. She wept as she spoke of her abusive father and the terrible childhood she had suffered in Bulgaria. She clenched her fists in rage as she recounted the injustices her wealthy and prominent family suffered at the hands of the Communists. Painstakingly, she recounted the hurts and betrayals of her many love affairs and marriages. Although she often gestured excitedly as she spoke, she was always clearly in control, calculating the effect her words were having on me. Sometimes, she would interrupt her soliloquy to ask me questions about myself: Was I married? Religious? Did I have children? I felt as one does with the carnival fortune-teller, as if she were trying to psych me out so she could tailor her approach to have maximum effect on me. Lilly was particularly upset about the inkblots shown her by the defense psychologist. She covered her eyes in terror as she described the "blood splashes with the horrible witches and everything" that she saw on the cards.

Sometimes Lilly played broad farce, and her attempts to con me seemed childish and laughable. At other times, I strained to catch the revelations and flashes of insight that might be cloaked in her gibberish. Always, more than I cared to admit, Lilly was seductive. A woman indeed of a thousand faces, many of them reminding me of people I knew and even loved — a favorite European aunt, the Bulgarian obstetrician who delivered my baby. Sometimes, eerily, the faces were not even human, as when I looked into her soft brown eyes and saw the loyal pet collie we had to put down the year before. I had no doubt that Lilly had almost surreal powers to influence people. How sad, I felt, that she had chosen to waste them. She was a natural charismatic leader.

It was hard for me to pry myself away at the conclusion of the interview. I had the feeling that Lilly had the energy and determination to keep talking all night. As I was packing up my pen and pad, Lilly reached out to grasp my hand, her eyes darting like those of a cornered animal. "Fear rules everything!" she whispered. "Words don't mean anything. Wouldn't you say anything to save yourself?"

The anguish and urgency in her voice were most convincing. "Besides," she added, her mood suddenly shifting to studied casualness, "I was only kidding about the killing!"

Whether or not Lilly was malingering, her case was no laughing matter. Lili Madjarova had been evaluated for competency four years earlier under another of her aliases, Elizabeth James, by the psychiatrist who was now retained by her defense. At that time he had seen no evidence of psychosis and pronounced her competent to proceed. Now, as Lilly faced federal sentencing, his opinion had changed. Describing her peculiarly in his report as "neat, clean, poorly-kempt," he diagnosed her as schizophrenic with elements of undifferentiated and paranoid types. According to this defense expert, when the government set up its sting operation it colluded with her "unconscious fantasies about a perfect world outside jail," and she, while seemingly rational, "incorporated unrealities as necessary without any rational coherence or reflection on the whole." He likened Lilly's scheme to rub out two agents to the "fantasy thoughts and play of a child." To me, this psychobabble belonged more in a B-movie script than a court of law. But the defense was banking on the grizzled Freudian beard and professional demeanor of its mediagenic expert.

I struggled through more than five hours of this doctor's videotaped examination of Lilly Schmidt. I found it a veritable smorgasbord of faked psychoses. At one point, Lilly, looking straight at the camera while curled on the chair in a fetal position, talked in a reedy voice about her paranoia and the plot she believed the government had against her. The doctor excused himself to go to the bathroom. When he returned, he resumed the examination, asking Lilly, "Now, where were we?" Without missing a beat, Lilly, who had been sitting there poker-faced waiting for him to return, began right where she had left off, tears streaming down her face as if on cue.

It seemed obvious to me that Lilly was faking bad — deliberately skewing interviews and test results so as to appear mentally ill. Only with some objective filter could I cut through Lilly's smoke screen and demonstrate it to the court. Since she seemed to have established a good rapport with the defense psychologist, I requested that he administer to her the Hidden Schizophrenia Attitude Scale, something of an aptitude test for schizophrenia developed by my colleague Jim Audubon. Its multiple-choice text draws on a pool of statements about covert attitudes, thoughts, and beliefs expressed by hospitalized schizophrenics. Because of its subtle and forced-choice format, it is very hard for a faker to figure out which answer a true psychotic will pick. The more the response pattern deviates from that of the schizophrenic, the more improbable it becomes that the person is really suffering from a schizophrenic thought disorder. I have found the scale indispensable in separating normals from psychotics and those on the borderline.

Most people without psychotic illness who take this test are amused by some of the seemingly comical and bizarre items. The fakers, in an attempt at gross exaggeration of mental illness, will tend to endorse statements like: "Every day at noon the devil tells me 'kill someone'"; "A policeman is poisoning my brain with radiation"; "I frequently see my face on NBC"; or, "My soul merges with those of criminals." The probability of all of those disparate and specific delusions occurring in the same individual is practically nil. True schizophrenics genuinely believe their delusions to be real. As such, they are as personal and detailed as a normal person's perception. Once when I administered the test, a hospitalized schizophrenic tried to correct an item. "There's a misprint," he said. "I only see the devil once a week, on Sunday."

Lilly obtained the highest score we had ever obtained for fakers. She had endorsed every pathological and improbable item to the maximum extent. She was the empress of fakers. I was, however, convinced that Lilly did suffer from a broad panoply of serious, pervasive, and longstanding personality problems. For all her manipulations and scheming, Lilly usually became her own worst enemy by consistently irritating and alienating people. Her emotional distress was at times compelling and genuine; her stories of childhood abuse had the ring of truth about them. Lilly was certainly in need of psychological help. However, her real symptoms fell short of disrupting her sense of reality and perception of right and wrong, which is the standard required by an insanity defense. But would my observations and conclusions, combined with her faked schizophrenia test score and common sense, be enough to convince a federal judge to send Lilly off to prison for an extended period?

After six months of motions and countermotions, Judge Kimba Wood ruled that the defense could produce from Bulgaria a doctor said to have treated Lilly two decades before. I doubted that Dr. Marina Boyardgeva could reliably remember Lilly's symptoms, specific diagnosis, and clinical features after twenty years. Nor was I comfortable with testimony not supported by embassy-validated psychiatric records. After all, Lilly had snowed more than one doctor in her life. Even if everything about the doctor was on the up and up, the issue at hand was Lilly's contemporaneous mental health: Was she competent to stand trial and be sentenced? It seemed like an expensive stalling tactic to me.

Finally, arrangements were made to produce the doctor. Lilly persuaded her mother to scrape up the money for a plane ticket and hotel. The hearing was scheduled for February 3, 1995, one year to the day from my first examination of Lilly Schmidt. Mental conditions are unstable; they can change dramatically in a year's time. Thus, I had to request a new court order to reexamine Lilly.

Back in the surprisingly bright and cheerful interview room of New York's Metropolitan Correctional Center, Lilly told me that she had been hearing voices — people she knew, dead people, her mother, male and female voices, coming from the TV. Unlike most genuine delusional schizophrenics, Lilly could not give a detailed account of what the voices or the personalities said. She took control of the interview, in a last-ditch attempt to act as bizarrely as possible. Just when I thought she had exhausted all possible psychiatric symptoms, she explained the existence of her many aliases by confiding that she was "many different people at different times." Lilly explained that she was compelled to give these multiple personalities names; she chose monikers like Elizabeth (Queen Elizabeth), Jackie (Onassis), or Marilyn (Monroe) because she needed to name them after famous people. She said that these persons "take over" and "are totally independent of each other" — they ordered her to do things and she had to obey.

Finally, when I didn't seem to be responding as she desired,

Lilly handed me one of her medical records from Beth Israel Hospital on which she had underlined the words "paranoid schizophrenia." Unlike genuine sufferers of psychosis, malingerers are overly eager to call attention to their symptoms. While they can sometimes manage pretending to hallucinate or have delusions, they cannot truly imitate the *form* of schizophrenic thought disorder. Schizophrenic language has certain distinguishable characteristics that were among the only symptoms not produced by Lilly. She made a common error among malingerers — exaggeration, believing that nothing must be remembered accurately. Like many studied malingerers, Lilly gave the appearance of profound concentration before she produced an absurd answer.

Spectacular fakers like Lilly Schmidt have become for me a clinical sampler of the criteria for detecting faking. In Lilly's case, as with many other fakes, there existed an alternate, rational motive for the crime. She had suspicious hallucinations or delusions, such as the mouse she saw in her cell mocking her and when she was afraid to go to the bathroom. Her crime fit her pattern of prior criminal conduct as a con artist. At no time did she show any subtle signs of psychotic thinking. She was very goal-directed, capable of scheming and carrying out plans. She also employed a double denial of responsibility for her actions ("Besides, I was only kidding about the killing!") and a far-fetched story of psychosis to explain the crime.

The hearing — or, more appropriately, the Lilly Schmidt Show — lasted for over a week. Dr. Boyardgeva, a spry octogenarian Lotte Lenya look-alike with coal-black dyed hair, testified in surprisingly clear English without the aid of an interpreter. I was beginning to develop an admiration for the determination and pluck of Bulgarians based upon my experiences of these two distinguished ladies. Dr. Boyardgeva offered a designer defense with a Balkan flavor, using esoteric terms that didn't translate into American *DSM-IV*-speak. Notwithstanding her unfamiliarity with the American insanity defense, she adamantly maintained that Lilly's exotic mental condition excused her from criminal responsibility.

Presiding over the hearing was Judge Kimba Wood. During my testimony she frequently asked me direct questions regarding some technical point in the psychological testing and had me clarify it until she understood precisely what I meant. She gave the experts "homework," specific instructions regarding legal concepts such as "rational understanding" which she wished to have elucidated in psychological terms as they applied to the statutes. She exercised extreme patience and forbearance with Lilly's disruptive behavior and frequent demands. Lilly had succeeded in turning the federal agent assigned to guard her (coincidentally the same agent she had accused of rape) into her personal valet. The agent was attentive to her frequent requests for coffee, soda, and sandwiches. One day we broke early because Lilly had a stomachache and could not go on.

When all the testimony was in, over three thousand pages of it in transcript, the judge ruled:

> Although Ms. Schmidt might seem to exhibit some of the symptoms of schizophrenia, her behavior is better explained as malingering, that is, faking symptoms in an effort to appear schizophrenic. Dr. Kirwin has done extensive research into malingering on the part of criminal defendants. Her conclusion, based on analyses of psychometric tests administered to Ms. Schmidt, was that Ms. Schmidt's responses fit the classic pattern of a malingerer.

I was not in court on February 13, 1995, when her sentence was handed down, but I'm sure it jolted Lilly to the core: thirty years. Her cunning and subterfuge had failed. I had no doubt Lilly would survive, even thrive, in jail; she always had. Just last September she wrote me from the Shawnee Correctional Center in Florida. "Dear Barbara," she began, "I am sorry I offended you. I am in very bad shape and they stopped my medication. Please call my Mom . . . and help me get transferred because there is no psychologist on duty. I am begging you. . . . I tried to kill myself. Sincerely, Lilly Schmidt."

As a forensic psychologist, I am, in a sense, undercover — a psychological spy, trying to tease out from the defendant the clues I need to determine whether he is mentally ill and not responsible for his crime. The fundamental underpinning of a forensic examination is that of mutual distrust; for a clinician trained in helping people, this role is sometimes hard to accept.

When I work as a treating psychologist I enter a partnership of healing; the lying I contend with in a therapy session generally results from the lack of insight, the denial, or the neurotic self-deception a patient uses to approach life. Such guile is unconscious and ultimately self-sabotaging. Factual veracity is not a major issue in the consulting room; not many people pay over $100 a session to lie deliberately to a therapist. If they do, it becomes part of the psychodynamic to be explored in treatment. In forensics, I become an opponent, a psychological sleuth stalking a defendant for evidence of malingering and deception. In the forensic exam, the defendant's deceit is clearly goal-oriented, a conscious strategy to feign mental illness or lack of responsibility for the purpose of getting away with a crime, or to obtain a cash reward by claiming mental disability in civil litigation cases.

Dr. Lawrence Siegal, a colleague of mine, asks sarcastically, "How do you know a forensic patient is lying? When his lips are moving." If I'm not to get conned, that is the jaded attitude I must possess when I begin a forensic exam. I have read many a report by a well-intentioned, forensically naive therapist who has been completely suckered by a clever psychopath. Sadly, it is the most dedicated help-givers, often those in religious callings, who are the easiest pawns. A savvy forensic psychologist must be not only a careful diagnostician but also a human lie detector.

Such a hypervigilant attitude — waiting to trap a defendant in a lie — is uncomfortable for me, because of its faintly duplicitous nature. As I discovered in cases as varied as those of Lilly Schmidt, Stephanie Wernick, and Joel Rifkin, a forensic exam has to become a game of wits and strategy, where cunning and conning count. Sometimes, as when I listened to Lilly Schmidt spin tales, I have flashbacks to my years as a narcotics parole officer, with junkies swearing to me that they were clean and begging me to waive random urine tests. One time, as a young, green parole officer working toward a psychology Ph.D., I truly believed the bright, attractive woman who convinced me to waive a parole violation and give her what we called a "play," a second chance. An hour later I was identifying her body on a motel bathroom floor — dead from an overdose of heroin. She had looked me straight in the eye and lied, knowing full well that she was going to leave my office and go directly to shoot up. I trusted her, I believed her, and she was dead. Those lessons stick with you.

There is no system, form, or set of standards for conducting a forensic examination, determining what materials to review, or establishing a format for writing up a report. In fact, if a psychologist is retained by the defense, in many jurisdictions she is not even required to submit to the court a written report of her examination. Many experts simply take the guesswork out of the psychological examination and go into an interview with a defendant seeking to garner evidence that supports whichever side is paying them.

No matter what the motives and morals of the examining mental health professional, forensic interviews are very direct. The goal is not to enhance the well-being of the accused; the goal is to pursue the truth and protect the interests of society. The confidentiality of the therapy room does not apply. Even if no written report is prepared, all notes made during a forensic interview must be turned over to the court and opposing counsel. Sometimes both attorneys are present at the interview. The session may be audiotaped or videotaped. The risk in this examiner-

directed approach is that the psychologist can summon up the answers he wants. Since a record exists of the defendant's or plain-
tiff's responses to questions, many experts have developed a
polished technique designed to ask questions that will elicit only
responses favorable to their position, avoiding or evading anything that might be contradictory, so that the interview can be airtight in communicating the examiner's point of view. These are
not interviews but interrogations. When psychologists working
for the prosecution run these sorts of interviews, they remind me
of the way I worked as a parole officer rather than as a psychologist, since they are working to get a defendant to admit guilt about
the facts of the crime rather than to reveal anything about his
mental state.

The focus for the forensic psychologist should be mens rea —
"guilty mind" — the defendant's mental state as it pertains to the
legal statute in question. Juries have a difficult time grappling with
the complex jargon of psychological testimony. They also seem to
have trouble reconciling the idea that the defendant is actually admitting to having committed the crime with the mitigating circumstance of mental disease or defect. Prosecutors play to this.
They overwhelm juries with factual evidence, letting them lose
sight of the issues of mental illness and criminal responsibility and
turning their verdict into a question of guilt or innocence.

I begin my examination by warning a defendant that everything
he might say to me is *not* confidential and can and will be used
against him. When I have been retained by the prosecution, I remind the defendant that he does not have to talk to me if he
doesn't wish to and that he may have counsel present, in which
case the district attorney has the right to have a representative sit
in as well. Given the nature of my warning, I am always amazed
that the defendants will see me so eagerly. I know they have been
informed by their attorneys that they must submit to an exam if
they are pleading insanity, but one would think that the prospect
of a shrink trying to get inside your head to entrap you or railroad
you with your own words would inspire enormous dread, espe-

cially when the stakes are so high. Yet most defendants, even those accused of murders, will talk — freely, in great detail, and with a disarming amount of candor. This might be due to what psychologists call the Hawthorne effect — so named for a psychological study of workers in Hawthorne, New Jersey, which showed how people respond favorably and perform better just by being singled out and given individual attention. It could also arise from the fundamental human need to be noticed, listened to, and taken seriously — or the drive for that fifteen minutes of fame. Sometimes I think they ache to connect with another human being, an opportunity they might not have had before they committed their crimes.

I focus my forensic examination on the defendant's mental state before, during, and after the crime. If there is a question about his competency to stand trial, I look at current mental functioning. Occasionally, however, when a defendant acquitted for reasons of insanity is being considered for release from a psychiatric hospital, I am asked to predict his future dangerousness. That is perhaps the most daunting responsibility of my forensic work. But no matter where in the justice process I do my work, I believe I need to use as many objective methods and administer as many tests as possible as I formulate my psychological opinion. To the surprise of many laypeople, not all psychological examiners use standardized tests in their forensic evaluations. Many examiners rely on what the defendant reports to them and on whatever insights they can gain from his past history. Their reports are, in my view, no more likely to be an accurate indication of a mental condition than what the man in the street could come up with. In the clinical method, an expert examines all available information, integrates it according to his own preferences or subjective standards, and offers a diagnosis or prediction. With their empirical discipline and training, psychologists can accurately interview defendants, review their history, and diagnose them, but their most particular professional contribution is to administer objective psychological tests. Some of these tests, such as the MMPI, have been around for over fifty years, providing significant and ever more refined research data; they represent state-of-the-art diagnostic and predictive measures. Moreover, studies reveal that combining tests with clinical examinations makes for a clearer and more valid diagnosis. Standardized tests also ensure more objectivity and reliability on the part of the examiner — always a vital concern. They apply corrective filters to detect faking; they can give us information about a person's mental state faster and more efficiently than we could ever do on our own; and they help us explore the covert attitudes, thoughts, and beliefs that the person may be able to conceal during an interview. I am frequently called into a forensic case, as with Lilly Schmidt's, to be a fake-buster when psychiatrists are stumped or suspect that the person is dissimulating in some way they can't put a finger on. Apart from my own detective smarts, the tool I use that they don't is tests. Judge Kimba Wood was most persuaded by the results of the objective testing of Lilly Schmidt; it gave her a firmer basis to arrive at a decision to sentence Lilly severely.

In the past decade, more Ph.D. psychologists have begun to enter the forensic field, which remains dominated by M.D. psychiatrists. Medical doctors work from the disease model and draw intuitive conclusions; psychologists more often employ empirical science and psychological tests. One might expect that an increase in psychologists would result in greater use and advancement of testing techniques in the forensic field. Ironically, I have seen the opposite occur. Because the tests are boring and arduous to administer, many psychologists back away from giving them at all. And many of those who formerly administered tests in forensic evaluations are now waiving them because their reports must then include those objective findings — not a good thing if the test results threaten to point the evaluation in a direction inconvenient to the side they are working for.

Some psychologists therefore prefer to use methods with less objective answers: Rorschach inkblots; sentence fill-ins, in which the examinee is given stems of sentences to conclude; drawings of houses and trees for interpretation; and gloomy 1930s-style photographs to respond to. The theory behind these so-called projective techniques is that such tests will reveal a person's inner character. But the results can be neither proved nor disproved. They are subjectively interpreted and can therefore be molded to the desired shape of the testimony. Still, as one particularly sophisticated but cynical assistant district attorney once said to me, "When are you ever going to dispense with your objective measures? Just give them an inkblot and tell the jury what you want." The most heinous of these projective techniques is the use of anatomical dolls in investigating allegations of childhood sexual abuse. Innocent people have had their lives shattered and spent years in prison because of a so-called expert's testimony gleaned from a child pointing to a doll. There is absolutely no evidence for the validity of these techniques in ascertaining the truth of a charge of child sexual abuse.

Certainly the utility of objective psychological tests is limited. They are simply tools, and pretty crude ones at that. Yet they are a valuable and integral part of the mosaic of information that a forensic psychologist considers in formulating an opinion. And they help keep us psychologists honest when we agree to take the witness stand in an adversarial system. I have always taken to heart the admonition of my internship supervisor, who warned me to know my test data and stick closely to it: "Don't let some overeager DA push you into saying things you're not comfortable with."

Psychological testing can be especially effective in screening for types of mental illness or retardation — and it is vital in detecting those who are faking mental illness for some secondary gain. Lilly Schmidt's case was a gross exaggeration of a strategy for faking. But Lilly's faking cost the taxpayers a bundle in expert witnesses fees, court time, and so forth. It took years of competency hearings and mental examinations before she came to justice. Sometimes the faking is more subtle. A defendant can simply stonewall, saying "I don't remember," when asked about the facts of a crime. And, of course, designer defenses conjure up a pastiche of syndromes, from dissociative phenomena and amnesia to a brief reactive psychosis (the fancy psychiatric term for "just snapping"). When it comes to detecting fakery in a designer defense, the tests may be so invalid, or the defendant may have stonewalled to such a degree, that I may have nothing to go on but my own intuition.

Gustavo Nina was charged with second-degree murder when he shot his friend Ruben Gonzales to death in an argument over damage to Gustavo's motorcycle. He was pleading that he suffered from psychological amnesia and psychotic dissociation. When I first met him at the lockup on the second floor of the Brooklyn courthouse, his attorney was absent and Gustavo was reluctant to meet with me. When the sergeant introduced us, I thrust my arm through the bullpen bars to shake his hand. His demeanor softened as he clasped my hand warmly and gave it a squeeze. "Since it's the little lady doctor, I'll go ahead," he said, relenting. He signed a waiver. The sergeant opened the holding pen grate and Gustavo came immediately to my side, escorting me to the examining area as if he were my champion, directing the other inmates in their cells along the corridor, "Say good morning to the lady doctor!" I was followed by a schoolboy chorus of greetings. Gustavo must have been very persuasive to command such respect from the other prisoners.

He was a slim, well-proportioned, fastidiously groomed young man. His manners were impeccable, and I could see that he must have had enormous success with women. Despite a poor academic history, he had high intelligence and a heightened psychological awareness and sensitivity. In short, Gustavo possessed many of the right qualities for success as a citizen, not just as a criminal. How had he come to this? Gustavo assured me, as I perused his lengthy rap sheet, that he had been a highly successful drug dealer and had lived the high life. He told me about his cars, his custom-made clothes, his girlfriends, and how he took care of his mother. His machismo was getting the better of him as he bragged about going around with over $20,000 in his pocket for spending money. Still, every time I got around to talking about the shooting, he drew a blank or changed the subject, averting his face from me and staring at the wall. Gustavo was a career criminal — bright, cunning, and fully aware that an insanity defense was his only shot. He was charming, he was flirtatious, and he was giving me nothing.

After our first session, I scored the paper-and-pencil tests and analyzed the results. Gustavo was experiencing major emotional problems, mostly due to the stresses of his current situation. The key to his personality was pride and arrogance, especially with regard to the impression he conveyed to women. I knew his pride would win out in the end. He would not want me — a woman he perceived as confident and attractive — to see him as crazy, even though this might be in his best interest. I planned for our next session.

Gustavo was already in the holding pen waiting for me, eager to begin our encounter. He told me that after being locked up for so many months it was a real pleasure to see a nicely dressed lady who "smelled so clean." Gustavo was animated and expressive, joking and talking about his life and exploits. I steered him into a conversation about guns. He revealed that he always had a fascination for guns. He bragged that he had stolen a loaded .38 from his uncle's house when he was a five-year-old. The murder weapon was a Colt Python .357 magnum. "I own a Colt Python three-fifty-seven," I told him, "and I love it too." I began to rhapsodize about the gun — about the vented barrel, the striated grips, the feel of firing it.

Gustavo joined in enthusiastically. "You know," he declared, a swagger in his voice, "I went to my house to get a gun to go after Gonzales. First I picked up an automag, but then I went back to get the three-fifty-seven — it was more accurate."

I sat back triumphant. Gustavo was busted. With those few words, he had revealed a motive of revenge and showed consideration, planning, and a full awareness of his acts.

A faint smile of resignation grew on his face as he realized his blunder. But like a gentleman he accepted his fate, as if he had been outsmarted in a game of wits, fair and square, or caught with his hand in the cookie jar. "My mother was helping to get me back to the Dominican Republic," he told me. "Another couple hours and I would have been on the plane and free. She's a lot like you. A very special woman, and she stands by me." He waved his hand. "God bless you." His benediction sounded sincere.

In my fake-busting arsenal, I store bits and pieces of a lifetime of trivia, hobbies, and interests. It is usually easier to break through a defendant's defenses when he is not on guard. Generally, a defendant's story has been well rehearsed with the defense attorney before our examination, and he knows enough to try to stick to it. If I can lull him into a sense of security by seemingly trivial conversation, I can often find the chink in his armor; the defendant's true mental state and motives will frequently reveal themselves in the most inconsequential areas of his life. Since I am also on the lookout for covert attitudes that may have to do with the defendant's personality and the crime, I know better than to go in and bombard him with interrogation-style questions — that's the job of the district attorney. Whether it's Lilly Schmidt, Gustavo Nina, or Richard Taus, I get people to tell on themselves in a less direct way.

Ann Green, the baby-smothering nurse, was a puzzle to me. Nothing abnormal showed in her test results, yet clearly her behavior was outside the norm. Most mothers, however much provoked, don't murder their kids. Her designer defense of postpartum psychosis was not supported by any observations or medical records, even though her bevy of experts swore she experienced this extremely rare disorder after all three of her births. Ann herself just stonewalled it; she said she didn't remember anything about how the deaths occurred. The jury bought her defense, and she was acquitted. I will never really know why it was that Ann killed two of her infants and attempted to smother the third. But I will always remain convinced that she did not suffer from any mental illness and knew fully well what she was doing.

After I began to interview Ann Green, I elicited information that, for me, explained many aspects of her behavior — and assigned blame to her. Much of our examination centered around Ann's religious convictions and the theology of the Catholic Church regarding her actions. She told me she felt at peace because she had been absolved in confessions of her sins — God had forgiven her. Why would Ann herself have sought absolution if she did not believe that she had done wrong? She also made sure that each child was baptized by the hospital chaplain before she took them home. Ann explained to me the church's position on baptism. She took her infants' lives, but she was able to draw the line at cutting off what she believed to be their immortal salvation. "They were baptized — they are in heaven," she affirmed to me, as she lowered her head and made the sign of the cross.

Oftentimes when a defendant is on guard, I must cast around to get the information I need. I feel like the bumbling Lieutenant Colombo, asking silly questions and bantering on innocuous topics until I get the defendant to reveal himself. But usually I know what I'm casting for, even if others don't. Once during my examination of a defendant I used this technique and the exasperated defense attorney jumped up from his seat and exclaimed to me, "I can't take any more of this nonsense about recipes and Greek cooking!" He was representing Niki Rossakis, an attractive and well-to-do young woman who had shot her husband in the head while he slept. She was claiming battered woman syndrome, even though the only evidence was her call to 911 during an argument two days before the killing. Niki, through downcast eyes with devastatingly long lashes, was sticking to her story of abuse. My brief distraction about cooking broke her train of thought. When I returned to the story of her battering, she began to contradict herself and fabricate new details. She said her husband had taken her down in the basement and made her kneel while he fired into the floor and walls around her. Ballistics found no evidence of gunshots in the basement.

Niki's test results showed psychopathic tendencies and a penchant for drug abuse. During our next session, she redoubled her effort to present details of torture and battering at the hands of her husband. To the silent consternation of her defense attorney, she was incriminatingly candid about her early experimentation with drugs. She had done pills, cocaine, heroin. She talked almost nostalgically about how each high made her feel. I was starting to get the impression that the real problem here was drugs and that the slaying probably had more to do with that than battering. I went on to diagnose her as having a narcissistic antisocial personality disorder and warned the court in my report that she was prone to criminal behavior. A few months after the exam, while out on bail, she was arrested for trying to purchase barbiturates with phony ID and a forged prescription. Bail was repealed and she was sent to Rikers Island to await trial on the murder charge. Back in jail, Niki was diagnosed with Hodgkin's disease, and a long course of chemotherapy followed. If ever there was a sympathy case, this was it — a beautiful young woman, mother of two small boys, battling with cancer, with a wealthy family and an army of BWS advocates behind her. But there was a flaw in this picture: Niki's drug arrest while out on bail. The jury was able to see through her facade. In May 1996, Niki Rossakis was convicted of second-degree murder and criminal possession of a weapon. She was sentenced to twenty-three years to life.

Just because a defendant is faking bad does not mean that he is not mentally ill, as was true of Jose Angeles, accused of shooting his common-law wife to death. Jose's paramour, Maria, had cheated on him consistently throughout the two years of their relationship. She finally left him at the request of her former husband, who felt that Jose was not a good influence on his children. Jose loved Maria desperately but feared that her ex-husband would come after him. He began to carry a gun. He also claimed to have been drinking, using angel dust, and snorting cocaine after the breakup.

Jose shot Maria in 1984, when he found her in bed with another man. He claimed that he did not remember the shooting or his arrest. At other times he told doctors that he had fired a shot, "but not [at] Maria. I shot the devil because of what I see in my eyes at the time." For the ensuing five years he had refused to discuss the crime and acted psychotic and delusional every time he was evaluated to proceed. Consequently, Jose Angeles had succeeded in never being tried for Maria's murder. He had been considered unfit to proceed. He had been sent to Mid-Hudson Forensic Psychiatric Center in upstate New York, where he got into fights and generally created disturbances. Although staff psychiatrists felt he did suffer from schizophrenia, they noted that he seemed to be able to turn it off and on depending on his court schedule. The DA grew impatient, and the doctors were fed up. It was time to get to the bottom of Mr. Angeles's little charade. Jose shuffled into the exam room at the Manhattan court lockup looking for all the world like an extra from *One Flew Over the Cuckoo's Nest*. He was unshaven, disheveled, and drooling. I was shocked at first at seeing someone so deteriorated. He refused to look at me and kept mumbling under his breath. When I began the interview, he said he couldn't understand English, although he had been in the United States for more than ten years. Leaving nothing to chance, I made arrangements through the Manhattan DA to send a Dominican Spanish interpreter right away. While we were waiting for the interpreter to arrive, Jose sat across the table from me, staring vacantly at the wall and rocking rhythmically back and forth. His hands and lips were trembling in the palsied involuntary way indicative of tardive dyskinesia. Tardive dyskinesia, or TD, is a result of heavy tranquilizer use that damages cells in the extrapyramidal tract of the brain. Once a person develops TD, it is irreversible and if left untreated progresses until the patient can no longer keep his tongue in his mouth or even feed himself.

The interpreter arrived and the interview and testing proceeded. Jose's test scores revealed that he had made a concerted effort to appear as crazy as possible. He was faking bad on all instruments. Jose was receiving heavy doses of antipsychotic medication. His neurological symptoms were genuine. But that was as far as his dysfunction went. Beyond that, Jose was a master of improvisation; this simple, uneducated man made the histrionic and melodramatic Lilly Schmidt seem amateurish by comparison.

By our second meeting, Jose's English seemed to have improved dramatically. He was eager to begin even before the interpreter got there. When I asked him to draw a face for me, he picked up the pencil tentatively. After making a few faint lines on the paper, he began to scribble all over it furiously. Throwing down the pencil, he wailed, "It's the face of the devil — I can't go on," in English. I stopped the task and he immediately calmed down. I continued, showing him a card with a drawing of a hand on it and asking him to describe it. He became agitated, shouting wildly, "It's the devil's hand! There is blood on the hand! It's going to grab me!" Immediately when I would change the task, he would calm down from these outbursts and become well oriented and lucid. At one point, lunch was served to us. Jose ate his meatball hero with gusto, while chatting cordially with me about boxing and other sports. He drew a whimsical cartoon of a boat — "the Santa Barbara," he said to me slyly. When we resumed the exam, Jose suddenly began to roll his eyes upward. "I'm hearing voices," he said, transfixed. Without any prompting, he added, "The devil and God and voices of spirits and saints. Santa Barbara," he threw in for good measure.

Jose had gone too far. After my report, he got the justice he deserved.

Mental illness is not the only component of an insanity defense, although it is the one most widely utilized. Mental defect — that is, mental retardation or organic brain damage — can also mitigate a person's criminal responsibility. Mental retardation can be even easier to fake than psychosis, and there are no provisions made in IQ tests to detect malingering.

Horatio Cox, with an accomplice, robbed a taxi driver, shooting him once in the side of his face. The victim, a twenty-year-old college student who drove a cab part-time, died upon reaching Nassau County Medical Center.

Cox, who now faced charges of second-degree murder, offered his history of attending special education classes in elementary school as proof he was so retarded that he was unfit to proceed to trial. Cox wanted the refuge of a mental institution; he was desperately afraid of prison. His codefendant, whom he had ratted out on these murder charges, had threatened to retaliate against him from behind bars. Cox knew he would make good on his threat. To his way of thinking, life in a mental hospital was better than no life at all.

School records did in fact substantiate that Horatio Cox had an IQ in the borderline retarded range. However, every psychologist had made a notation attesting to reservations about the validity of this number as an indication of Cox's intelligence. He seemed to possess uncanny common sense, good judgment, and astute social intelligence. They felt that he was streetwise and had the ability to adapt more successfully than predicted by what seemed to be inordinately low IQ scores. Cox certainly was not motivated to perform in school. By age fourteen he was suspended from classes because he was "defiant of authority, threatening and bullying those smaller," according to records I referred to. At age sixteen, he dropped out of school and turned to crime. By age twenty-two he had graduated to armed robbery and murder.

Nassau County's own mental health experts had evaluated Cox and pronounced him incompetent — this was the same team that would later allow paranoid schizophrenic Colin Ferguson, the Long Island Railroad gunman, to pass on to trial with flying colors. In his report, the psychiatrist gave specific examples of Cox's retardation. He was unable to recall three objects after a short time; he added 5 plus 1 as 9; he stated that "they said I killed somebody" and then went on to ask, "Why is killing against the law?" The doctor concluded that Cox was not malingering because he appeared to be cooperating and answering the questions to the best of his ability. "Regarding the psychiatric evaluation, any minimal attempts at malingering were greatly overshadowed by the patient's gross mental retardation." He concluded that since mental retardation was permanent, it was likely that Cox would never become competent and would remain in a "long term protective treatment facility" forever. At another examination Cox score an IQ of 51. He added 2 and 2 and came up with 5; he gave a wrong date of birth, and insisted that Jesse Jackson was the president before Ronald Reagan. He admitted that he killed someone but said he believed the maximum sentence was "four or five months" for murder. At one point in the examination, the psychologist noted, Cox spontaneously used the word "paranoid" to describe his feelings about jail. He was able to correctly define it. "The possibility that Mr. Cox might be malingering occurred to this examiner," he noted, "but in light of the IQ findings, this possibility does not appear to be likely."

IQ testing has long been controversial; intelligence is defined as what intelligence tests measure. In the psychological community, there is much disagreement about what IQ scores actually mean or predict, and much confusion about their susceptibility to racial, social, and environmental factors. In my book, there is nothing sacred about an IQ number — intelligence is as intelligence does. And while Cox might not be able to prove himself smarter than he was, he certainly could make himself seem stupider.

When the state's own experts found the defendant incompetent, the district attorney called on me as a fake-buster to observe him during a psychiatric exam and see what I thought about the possibility of his malingering. During the exam, Cox evidenced a very simplistic strategy of faking. When he was asked a question directly related to his competence for trial, Cox would give a patently ridiculous answer or shrug. He couldn't remember a sequence of numbers, the day of the week, month, year. The psychiatrist was getting nowhere. When I decided to administer intelligence tests to Cox, he continued the same act. He couldn't even put four blocks into a pattern, put puzzle pieces together, define words like "table" or "boat," or repeat two numbers in sequence.

With an expression of concern on my face, I stopped the testing and began to pack up my materials. Cox relaxed; I began to engage him in conversation. He started to flirt a little, talking about his many girlfriends. "With so many ladies," I teased, "how do you keep them all straight? Aren't you afraid you'll call one up and mistake her for another?" "No," he said and shook his head, delighting in the game. "I got their numbers all down in my head."

I laughed as if challenging him. Cox began to show off, rattling off a string of seven-digit phone numbers.

"I bet you won't remember my number," I said playfully, then recited it to him.

Pleasant and affable, Cox began discussing the particulars of his case — the plea the DA had offered, the maximum sentence he could get. It was apparent that Horatio Cox was competent to stand trial. We spoke for over an hour more about many other topics. Cox had a good fund of information on current events. As I was leaving, I chided him, "Bet you don't remember my number."

"You lose," he joked: "555-4789."

Criminal defendants are not the only ones who have a critical stake in feigning mental illness. Some of the most outrageous and inventive fakers I have encountered have been people engaged in litigation over civil damages. The criminal defendants are faking for freedom; the civil litigants are faking for dollars.

Max Schleiman was a member of the Hasidic Jewish sect and had amassed a fortune in the gold business. He had vast real estate holdings in Brooklyn, some of which were in high-crime areas.

One afternoon in December 1990, when Max was closing up his metal findings factory, he was allegedly held up by two armed black perpetrators who shot him in the shoulder and made off with a fortune in gold bars from the safe. Max filed a claim with Lloyd's of London, his insurer, for over $2 million. He also claimed that he had been so traumatized by the robbery that he was no longer able to work; he was suffering, he said, from the severe and incapacitating symptoms of post-traumatic stress disorder.

I was called in by the psychiatrists retained by attorneys for Lloyd's of London. Based on his antics during his psychiatric exams, they felt that something was drastically wrong emotionally with Max, but they didn't think it all originated from the robbery. For purposes of his lawsuit, this was the key point. If we could determine that Max's mental problems predated the alleged robbery, we could dispute Max's claim. Meanwhile, Lloyd's had hired a private investigator to check out every detail of the robbery.

Max came to my office accompanied by his young and expensively dressed wife. They made an incongruous pair. He was fat, vulgar, and crude; she had every hair in place on her high-fashion *sheitel* — the wig worn for religious reasons by Orthodox Jewish women in public. Once he was alone inside my office, Max twitched and squirmed and cried while he related the horrors of the robbery and how it had ruined his life. At one point, he said he couldn't go on and ran down the hall to the bathroom. Raucous and stagy sounds of vomiting emanated from behind the locked door. After a few moments, Max emerged and announced, "I got so upset I threw up." I could detect no smell of vomitus as he sputtered these words right into my face.

He returned to my office, plopped down on the couch, and pulled out a flask. "This is vodka," he proclaimed, opening it and waving it under my nose. I smelled nothing. "Don't tell my wife, but I stay home and drink all day." For the next hour, Max acted out with great exaggeration every symptom given by the diagnostic manual for PTSD.

Nevertheless, when I scrutinized some of his test scales, I saw that in addition to psychopathic tendencies, they revealed some covert signs of the fuzzy thinking that veers toward schizophrenia. Max was indeed disturbed — but not as a result of the robbery. His problems in areas of social and emotional functioning seemed longstanding. I firmly suspected that Max Schleiman manifested what is called in psychological terms a severe borderline personality disorder with serious cognitive disturbances and psychopathic tendencies.

At our next meeting, I decided to interview Mrs. Schleiman. She seemed only too happy to get away from him for a while. Max was overbearing to the point of exhaustion. Once inside the sanctuary of my office, she began to unburden herself with the story of her difficult arranged marriage to Max when she was fifteen. She was grateful that he was a good provider, but she often feared his temper, the gun he carried, and the crazy nightmares and fits of anger he would experience. All these had been occurring since she first had met Max; the only thing that had gotten worse since the robbery was the fact that he no longer went to work and was around the house more. She could tolerate him better when he spent more time away.

Before I could submit the report of my findings on Mr. Schleiman, the attorneys for Lloyd's called. The private eye had incontrovertible evidence that Max had staged the robbery, including shooting himself in the shoulder. The gold was recovered in another of his warehouses. For all his dramatic malingering, Max had no choice but to confess.

Whether the human being is a normal and law-abiding person or someone as peculiar as Max Schleiman, one fact remains. Personality — that collection of enduring and pervasive traits and styles of acting, thinking, and feeling that characterize an individual over a lifetime — is as unique as a fingerprint. It is almost as hard to fake. Even when an individual is trying to cover up or to feign mental illness or emotional distress to collect on a damages case, this indelible signature will surface.

A father's distinctive personality and motivations set the stage for a particularly pathetic case of malingering involving a retarded young man and allegations of sexual abuse. In February 1994, twenty-four-year-old Arnold Kolber was suing a major religious philanthropy for $7 million in damages allegedly inflicted on him by the sexual molestation he suffered while he was a camper at a program for the retarded that the philanthropy sponsored. On the last day of camp, as the buses were loading to return to the city, Arnold approached the camp director and asked to speak to her. She got distracted and never checked back with him. When Arnold returned to his sheltered workshop program, he spontaneously told a counselor that his friend at camp, Sean, had kissed him and touched him "down there." Arnold became distraught when the program notified his family.

Arnold's father, a burly and quick-tempered man, was a retired New York City police detective out on a full-pay disability. He was outraged by the allegations his son had made and quickly mobilized a legal team. Arnold was directed to a sexual abuse clinic for evaluation and treatment. The sexual abuse counselor immediately confirmed that Arnold in fact showed the signs of having been sexually abused, although her notes in his official records do not reveal any physical evidence nor any sign of severe psychological trauma: Arnold, she noted, had "some dreams, depression, minimal behavior changes at work, but this seems currently OK. His father wants to be sure Arnold is OK." His father also filed a criminal complaint against the camp counselor, an Irish exchange student.

With his father's support and coaching, Arnold was able to testify before a grand jury. "I did real good at the grand jury," he told me later. "My father said I did real good, I was a champion! I stood up in front of a bunch of people and told them what happened at camp." Arnold beamed at getting his father's approval. Mr. Kolber told the therapist how proud he was of his son's performance.

Arnold told his therapist that he wanted to "go on TV and talk about what happened."

The grand jury did not find sufficient evidence of abuse to indict Sean, the counselor. The criminal matter was closed. Undaunted, Mr. Kolber mounted a civil case against the charity that managed the camp, suing them for $7 million. I was retained by the law firm representing this large and well-respected philanthropy. These considerate and low-key attorneys expressed a genuine desire to be clinically enlightened about Arnold Kolber's mental condition and wanted me to look into the possibility that some sexual abuse had in fact taken place. The Kolber case was occurring in the climate of the McMartin preschool trial, when big payoffs were being awarded by sympathetic juries in damages cases. The charity, of course, wished to avoid any scandal. I was personally relieved that they were not encouraging me to discredit this young retarded man's case even if I indeed found some clinical evidence for abuse.

I carefully studied all Arnold's past records before I met him, because in this particular case I felt I needed a complete picture of his problems, deficits, and level of functioning. This was essential in conducting this exam, because Arnold's cognitive limitations would have to be carefully compensated for in constructing a test battery and interview. Arnold was his parents' only child, and by kindergarten had been diagnosed as retarded, with nonspecific congenital neurological and organic damage. Mr. Kolber was especially resistant to viewing Arnold as handicapped. Soon Arnold began to manifest emotional and behavioral problems. He was angry and aggressive toward other children; his constant inappropriate attention-seeking behavior made him difficult to manage. His record chronicled the attempts of the rehabilitation program staff to engage the family in treatment for Arnold, but Mr. Kolber often responded as aggressively as his son. Once he yelled at a counselor so menacingly that she had to summon security to her office to escort him out.

Despite his emotional problems, Arnold was educable and

made vocational progress. By age twenty he was involved full-time in a sheltered workshop program. During the summers, he went away to camp, where he seemed to get along pretty well. He enjoyed a friendship over several seasons with Sean, the counselor he later accused of molesting him.

Arnold arrived at my office, accompanied by his father. Before I could greet them in the waiting room, Mr. Kolber, built like a linebacker, ambushed me in the hallway. "Can I have a word with you alone before we start?" he ordered more than asked. Ensconcing himself at my desk, he began to fire questions at me concerning the tests I was going to administer to his son. "I know all about testing," he informed me. "I'm a polygraph expert." He began to brag about his consulting business and how he really knew how to get the truth out of people. I probably should have been annoyed at Mr. Kolber's pushiness, but instead I saw his bluster as the attempt of a proud man to cope with the intense emotions and vulnerabilities stirred in him by his son's disabilities. When I called Arnold in to begin the exam, Mr. Kolber refused to leave. "He does better when I'm here," he insisted. Even though I explained to him that the presence of a third party during a psychological examination usually presented a problem because it could strongly affect the person's performance, Mr. Kolber would not budge. Arnold, sitting hunched over on the sofa, looked apprehensively back and forth between his father and me.

I decided that I would begin asking Arnold some simple questions about himself and observe what happened. As I anticipated, Arnold looked to his father for the answer to every question, including basic ones like his date of birth. He was reluctant to volunteer any information on his own. "Mr. Kolber," I finally said, "I feel very strongly that Arnold is not performing up to his capacity because you are here. He is depending on you to answer all the questions. I don't think I can get an accurate assessment with you present. I must ask you to leave."

Mr. Kolber was antagonistic; he started to argue with me and tell me what he thought of psychological tests. Meanwhile, the time allotted to examine Arnold was being frittered away. Perhaps that was Mr. Kolber's strategy. Finally I insisted that he call his attorney and consult with him about proceeding. We were at an impasse. It was a waste to continue with Mr. Kolber present, and he knew that his son had to be evaluated if his suit was to proceed. I left the room to allow Mr. Kolber some privacy. Through the office door I could hear his heated argument with his lawyer. After fifteen minutes Mr. Kolber emerged from the office, resigned. "Go ahead and examine him. I'll wait outside."

When the door closed behind his father and we were alone in the office, Arnold's whole body relaxed. He began to make eye contact with me for the first time. He came alive — he was alert and responsive to questions; his speech and vocabulary improved. My initial tests quickly proved that Arnold's retardation was not so great as to cast doubt on the credibility of his story. Something else was going on for him. As we talked in general terms about the events at camp, I realized that his story was full of contradictions. Moreover, his emotions did not match up to the alleged events, and he tried to change the subject whenever he could. We had lunch brought in: his favorite, a meatball hero and Arizona iced tea. He was able to read the menu and make his selection without any assistance.

Arnold began to really enjoy himself; he liked the attention. "This is fun," he told me. "Can I come back and see you again?"

I drew him into a conversation about Sean and the incident at the camp. He became fearful. "My father will be mad. He told me not to talk about this." Nevertheless, I sensed that at some level he wanted to unburden himself. Arnold talked about Sean: "He had a black girlfriend who was always yelling at him. I used to get in the middle of it. I used to get angry with her, and I told him not to go with her. He didn't listen. I used to get pretty angry and pretty upset, too!" Arnold was intensely emotional as he recounted Sean's involvement with the girl. He said he was "jealous" because Sean was ignoring him and spending all his time with his new girlfriend. "I knew that Sean did something nasty at night with her and he would get in trouble for it." Arnold's lips tightened in rage.

"Why?" I asked.

"Bingo!" Arnold leaped from his seat excitedly. "No sex with a counselor or camper." He recited the rule by rote. "He knew he would get in trouble for it, and he told me to shut up!"

Arnold wanted to talk about sex. When I turned the topic to the alleged incident at the camp, Arnold was uninterested. Instead, pointing at an item from the Hidden Schizophrenia Attitude Scale, he insisted that the statement "I have dreams of raping people all the time" applied to him. "I have these dreams all the time. Just ask my father, he'll tell you." The more I expressed concern about and interest in his "dreams," the more emotional and elaborate Arnold became, producing more and more details about the alleged dreams. I was discovering just how much he was susceptible to leading questions; he could produce accounts of almost anything if he felt it got him attention or approval.

Especially about sex. Arnold was a robust twenty-four-year-old man with a normal physiological sex drive. He knew about the facts of sex but still had an overwhelming sexual curiosity. He told me he had a girlfriend from his rehab program but that his mother said he shouldn't see her anymore. He said he was afraid to talk to his father about sex because his father would get angry.

Arnold was clearly titillated by the discussion. He asked me to sit next to him on the sofa. He became very upset and confused, complaining that he was feeling sick and having chills. He stretched out his hands to show me how they were sweaty and shaking. "Can I kiss you and hug you?" he suddenly asked.

"No, Arnold," I answered, firmly but kindly. "I am married and I am too old to be your girlfriend."

Red with shame, he described what he felt in his penis. "That's what you're supposed to feel with a woman you like. It's okay," I said reassuringly.

Arnold said he felt those same feelings in his body that night when he asked Sean to give him a goodnight hug. "I got scared, I was jealous, I was angry," he stammered, in one of the clearest psychodynamic explanations that anyone could give for his allegations. For a while, the tale worked for Arnold because it garnered his father's attention and approval. I believed that Arnold never intended for it to hurt Sean so badly, but he got swept up into something he could not control.

I was shaken by what I had uncovered. It was larger than a lie to get back at a friend, or an enterprising father's desire to score big on his handicapped son. We may think of developmentally disabled adults as if they were children, but they have sexual urges and sexual rights. Arnold may have acted childishly at times, but he had the powerful sexual urges of a healthy young man. He was confused, frightened, and ashamed of these urges, which he was unprepared to manage; Arnold's personality problems, his developmental disabilities, and his lack of social skills limited appropriate sexual outlets for him. Apparently, his parents and caretakers were likewise unable to address them.

The thirty-five-page report I submitted made an airtight case against the credibility of Arnold's allegations. The Kolbers agreed to settle for $70,000 out of court. The philanthropy's reputation was safe; the law firm was relieved. I felt I owed it to Arnold to temper my exposure of his faking with some recommendations for treatment and rehabilitation. He was a young man in a difficult family situation, with potential for development that was not being tapped. Maybe some of that $70,000 will go toward better treatment for Arnold.

Augie Mancuso was a wiseguy. By age fifteen he had moved out of his mother's home because he couldn't get along with her endless parade of husbands and boyfriends. He moved in with an uncle in Howard Beach, mobster John Gotti's neighborhood, where he supported himself with "off the books" work. Augie also developed a $50-a-day cocaine habit and a knack for hot-wiring cars. He was arrested for possession of a stolen car and sentenced to probation. Augie did not take the conditions of his probation seriously. He stole a motorcycle and, while he was speeding away from the scene, was broadsided by a station wagon. Augie was pretty banged up. He remained in a coma for three months. After regaining consciousness he was sent to a very expensive private sanitarium for the treatment of head injuries. The medical bills were paid by one of his mother's boyfriends.

Augie was young and strong and made a miraculous recovery. Now his lawyers were petitioning the courts to dismiss the motorcycle theft charges against him "in the interest of justice." They claimed that he was a seriously disabled person and that any form of incarceration would critically jeopardize his emotional well-being and chances of recovery. They forwarded impressive documentation from all manner of rehabilitation experts at the swanky treatment center describing the amount of brain damage and deficits in functioning sustained by Augie.

This was an unusual form of psychological defense. There was no question about Augie's criminal responsibility for the crime. The issue was whether he suffered from a mental disease or defect that rendered him disabled and unfit to be sentenced to jail — somewhat the same circumstances as those in the Lilly Schmidt case. Psychological defenses can be hydra-headed.

The Queens DA asked me to review the records, talk with the treating doctors, meet with the family, and examine Augie to see if his claim was legitimate. When I called the family home to arrange the interview, Augie himself answered the phone. He was alert, coherent, and quite friendly and cooperative. Not at all what I had expected from reading his medical records.

On the day of his interview, a black Lincoln Town Car pulled up outside my office and Augie, his mother, and a large man wearing a black leather trench coat got out. Chickie Mancuso was barely five feet tall, even in her five-inch spiked-heel mules and towering beehive. She introduced me to her son and her ex-husband, Carmine, Augie's father. Mrs. Mancuso talked nonstop; tears flooded her eyes as she spoke authoritatively of her son's injuries. It was clear she was the brains of the operation. She hovered over her son and wouldn't let me get near him. Finally I gave her a questionnaire to fill out and whisked Augie into another office.

Once away from his mother, he seemed relieved. He was a robust and roguishly handsome young man. There was evidence of cerebral damage in his somewhat slurred speech and his occasional stammering and groping for words. But all in all, he was remarkably garrulous and sociable. However, when I began to administer certain psychological tests, Augie's level of performance took a nosedive. His MMPI was faked bad — he admitted to all possible types of problems and symptoms, even those that had nothing to do with organic brain injuries. His HSAS was likewise faked. The only interpretation that could be made of his results was that he was employing a conscious strategy of malingering. He performed equally poorly on the memory tasks and IQ tests. Although he used words in conversation, he was unable to define them when they appeared on a test.

The questionnaire Mrs. Mancuso completed for me was designed to assess the level of functioning of organically impaired patients at home. According to her, Augie was a vegetable, so profoundly incapacitated that he required around-the-clock nursing care. During our private interview, Augie said he was able to prepare food, dress himself, and take care of his personal hygiene. He complained bitterly about being treated like a baby by his mother. He also resented her numerous relationships with men, particularly her renewed affair with his father. He pointed out that Carmine was still married and cheating on his wife. He said he felt useless, lonely, and isolated from his friends in Howard Beach. He seemed grateful to be able to talk to an understanding adult.

I made my report to the court, indicating that I felt Augie was malingering and that he had made a sufficient recovery to stand trial for his crime and to be sentenced to jail time if convicted. Six months went by, during which the Mancusos and their attorney brought in more rehabilitation experts and began a civil damages suit. When Augie's hearing was finally scheduled for August, I requested permission to reexamine him to assess his current condition and level of functioning. This time, Augie came with his father and Chickie stayed home. He appeared in terrific spirits, healthier and even more robust than he had been at our last meeting. He reported that things were better since he moved out of his mother's home and into a rehabilitation program.

Augie took off his leather jacket, leaned back on the sofa, and lit a cigarette. "Look," he said, leveling with me, "I'm getting tired of two and a half years of aggravation that I've gone through with the legal system." He revealed that his mother and her lawyer put him up to this because they didn't want him in jail and they wanted to "collect big" in the civil lawsuit. "The DA wants me to do time — I think it would be better to get it over with like a man." Augie paid attention and worked hard on the tests this time. He scored in the average range on all tasks.

That day in court, as I was giving my testimony about Augie's fitness to be sentenced, Chickie Mancuso was giving me the *mal occhio* — the evil eye. I could've sworn I saw Augie smile at me and wink.

Telling the fakers from the real thing is still more of an art than a science for most forensic examiners, especially if they don't have the statistical and actuarial methods of psychological tests to go on. One prosecution witness, often criticized for being a hired gun and overly simplistic in his approach to psychological issues, gave his litmus test for faking: "You have to look at what they did after the crime. If a person called 911 after killing someone and said he just rid the world of demons, he is probably ill." From my experience, I would tend to say just the opposite — such a person is probably a shrewd psychopath playing the only card he's got. If he was so psychotic that he believed he rid the world of demons and didn't know it was wrong, why would he report it to 911? If he regained his sanity so quickly after the crime as to have full awareness of his criminality and turn himself in to the police, I would be doubly suspect.

Gowain Tremont took a page from that last script, literally. A butcher by training, over six feet four inches tall, and weighing close to 270 pounds, Tremont prided himself on his custom-made wardrobe and size 15 cowboy boots. The product of an abusive upbringing in his native Trinidad, Tremont came to America illegally at age twenty-three to romance older women. "I got my survival needs," he would tell me, speaking of his relationships with these women.

Tremont thought he hit pay dirt when he moved in with Velda, a financially solvent widow. Velda doted on him, bought him fancy clothes, and promised to finance a truck for him to set up his own tractor-trailer business. When the romance started to cool, however, Velda held on to her dollars and refused to put up the down payment for the truck. Gowain was enraged; the two drank and quarreled continually. Velda's family disliked Tremont and thought that he was taking her for a ride.

One night, Tremont claimed, after he read the Bible, Velda started to look like the devil to him. He grabbed a knife and, as he said later, "fear gripped me," and he thought to himself, "Kill her or she'll lose her soul." He hacked Velda to death and left her bleeding on the kitchen floor. In the struggle, he severed an artery in his hand and was losing a lot of blood. Tremont called 911 and said, "I've killed my wife."

Later, at police headquarters, Tremont gave a statement to police. "I had been fasting myself for the last 14 days and I was trying to cleanse my body and soul," he told them, "because I believed that Velda was now possessed by the Demon Devils, and those same demons would get into my soul. I tried to get Velda to fast with me but she wouldn't. I knew that her soul was lost to the Devil."

The night of the killing, Tremont said, he placed a long-distance telephone call to his sister in London. Velda told him that he would have to pay for the call. They began to argue. "By this time, I was in a turmoil," Tremont continued to tell police.

I saw that Velda was wearing a lot of jewelry on her wrists and around her neck. I then tried to rip the gold jewelry off her body, but she fought me and she refused to take it off. I then slapped and hit her about the face but she kept fighting me. I then ran in to the kitchen and I grabbed a butcher knife that was lying on the counter near the sink. It had a big wide blade with a wooden handle. I knew then that I had to kill this woman because she wouldn't stop holding on to me and God had now told me that I should kill Velda in order to save my own soul. I was in a fucking rage!

The defense used a modified Twinkie defense strategy. Tremont had poorly controlled diabetes, his attorneys claimed; he was not eating, he was drinking excessively. A few days before, he had presented himself in the emergency room and was treated for low blood sugar and electrolyte imbalances. His physical condition, they said, had caused him to hallucinate that Velda was the devil; he killed her in deluded self-defense.

I spent a total of thirteen hours with Tremont at the request of the district attorney, talking to him and administering the standard psychological tests. He was gracious and charming, one of the brightest people I had ever tested. Among his many jobs, he had worked for five years as an attendant in the admissions unit of a state hospital. I soon suspected that he was drawing on that experience now as he constructed his delusional tale of the stabbing of his common-law wife.

Tremont tried to fake good on the psychological tests, denying any shortcomings or personal flaws. He was holding his cards close to his vest. This man showed no psychotic tendencies at all, not even in items that referred to his experiences in the past. Even when he called 911, he knew it was Velda he had stabbed and no longer thought she was the devil. It was as if his "organic psychosis" had materialized out of thin air, only to evaporate immediately after the stabbing. It puzzled me how he could recompensate from a physiological delirium so quickly without any medical interventions and be able to give a lucid and coherent statement to detectives just an hour after killing Velda. Then and now, Tremont was busy bolstering his own self-confidence by seducing and manipulating everyone in sight, including me, just as he had with Velda.

The same psychological tests had been administered to Tremont by the county's psychologist. Tremont had used the same defensive strategy and tested the same way as he had with me. This psychologist felt Tremont was a faker and a shrewd psychopath and candidly expressed to me his chagrin that so many professionals at the county hospital were suckered in by him. This doctor related many instances of how Tremont had garnered the sympathy of seasoned staff members on the psychiatric observation ward. The nurses would bring him gifts of street clothes. Attendants brought home-baked pies. Doctors signed orders for off-ward passes and other special privileges.

At our concluding session, Tremont oozed self-pity. He complained tearfully that Velda's family would not release his personal articles and that he was "being forced to wear someone else's clothes." "I've had very bad luck," he told me, shaking his head balefully. "My only wish is that I will get a break from someone and get a second chance."

Gowain Tremont got his wish in the person of a psychiatrist who was generally "soft" on physiological defenses of mental illness — the same doctor who had testified to the presence of postpartum psychosis in Ann Green three years before. Though he was retained this time by the prosecution, as I was, the doctor spent much of his report criticizing my findings and affirming that Tremont, in fact, was not an antisocial personality but an organically deluded unfortunate suffering from low sugar and low salt. The DA's hands were tied; he couldn't very well mount a strong case with one of his experts claiming that the defendant was not responsible. Without a trial, Gowain Tremont was adjudicated insane and remanded to a maximum-security mental hospital.

After this outcome, Velda's distraught daughter called and set up an appointment to speak with me privately. For over an hour in my office, I did what amounted to crisis intervention therapy with this dignified and insightful lady. Karen's grief was intense, but it was more than matched by her outrage at a legal system that seemed to look the other way in cases of domestic violence. She also believed that the outcome would have been different if Tremont had murdered a white woman.

Tremont settled into institutional life with his customary aplomb. It wasn't long before he was released back downstate to a civil hospital. Once he was in a less restrictive environment, he began to drink and assault other patients. He has become a problem for both the hospital staff, who keep pressing his case for discharge on the grounds that he is not mentally ill, and the district attorney, who wants to keep him locked up at all costs. Ironically, my original report of his alcoholism, psychopathy, and violence keeps being mentioned as he tries to prove he is not psychotic. Hardly five years have passed since Tremont slashed Velda to death. The hospital where he is housed is slated for closing. Perhaps Gowain Tremont will get his second chance after all. That's more than Velda got.

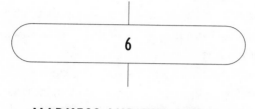

6

MADNESS AND THE MEDIA

When I took the stand as an expert witness for the prosecution in the Stephanie Wernick trial, the first thing I noticed was the imposing antlerlike rack of floodlights stationed just to the right of the witness box. A video camera fixed its unrelenting lens alternately on the witnesses, Judge Abbey Boklan, the prosecutor, the defense counsel, and Stephanie Wernick herself, the C. W. Post coed accused of strangling her secretly delivered newborn with toilet paper and discarding him in a dormitory trash can. Throughout the trial she sobbed almost continuously and very dramatically, her head resting on the shoulder of the wife of her attorney, Steve Scaring.

Scaring, a former Nassau County prosecutor considered by many to be the best criminal lawyer on Long Island, felt that the camera's presence — indeed, all the media coverage of the trial —

harmed his client. She had become so fearful and emotional that she was unable to take the stand on her own behalf, he said. Consequently, the jury heard only the testimony of experts, the police, the emergency medical technicians, and other witnesses. They never heard Stephanie Wernick tell her own story.

As I testified, it was as if the video camera were choreographing my testimony. When I said something dramatic, the camera would swivel itself to shine its light on me — cuing the jurors to pay attention. Sometimes when I was subjected to the floodlights, I almost expected the jurors to applaud my performance. At those times, indeed, spurred on by the camera's approval, they perked up and took note. The camera would train its eye on defense counsel Scaring only when he became acrimonious. The more he harangued and waved his arms and pointed accusingly, regardless of the import or content of his questions, the more the camera stared at him. The more Stephanie Wernick cried, the more airtime she got. It was clear that we were all actors in a drama not of our own creation. Even though Scaring would stick to points of law, even though I would try to answer questions with a reasonable degree of psychological certainty, the camera had its own story to tell.

George Peck, the prosecutor who later handled the case of Colin Ferguson, the Long Island Railroad killer, deftly used the cameras to get across his point about the deliberateness of Stephanie Wernick's actions in the death of her baby boy. "Dr. Kirwin, could you describe for us," he asked abruptly, "how the infant would have reacted at the time of strangulation?"

I was shocked; Peck had not discussed this with me before. But over the frantic objections of the defense, Judge Bocklin allowed me to respond, based on what I had learned from the autopsies performed on the children that Ann Green had smothered years before. Sensing drama, the camera zoomed in, staring wide-eyed up into my face. I responded:

My experiences in cases where children were killed indicates that the children struggle. The infant struggles. There

is an instinct to preserve our life. One of the primary instincts is the instinct to take in air and breathe. Children,
immediately after birth, have gag reflexes, they have involuntary, very violent responses to push anything out of the
airway so that they might live and breathe. So there would
be gagging and choking sounds. The arms and legs would
flail out, and the body would arch itself, almost as you see
when someone is having a seizure, for the purpose of pro-
pelling whatever is blocking the airway out, so that the child
could instinctively preserve its life.

Hour after hour on cable television, my emotional testimony
was broadcast and rebroadcast. I scrambled to keep my six-year-
old from seeing it; I wondered about the effect it would have on a
child to see his mother filling the TV screen, gesturing to describe
the strangulation of an infant. What would the children who were
my patients think as they flipped through channels, as one of their
parents prepared dinner in the next room?

I remain uneasy about that part of my testimony in the Wernick
trial. Clearly, what I viewed as most scientifically compelling
about my testimony — the personality testing results that under-
scored Stephanie's self-absorption and lack of mental illness —
was not what swayed the jury. Letters from jurors, received unso-
licited by George Peck after the trial, referred to my testimony
about the infant's death as most persuasive regarding my credibility and Stephanie's intent.

Stephanie Wernick was convicted of criminally negligent
homicide and sentenced to one and a half to four years in prison.
Judge Bocklin did not subscribe to the newly minted designer defense of "neonaticide syndrome," which her attorney tried to advance. Neither did the jury accept the argument that Stephanie
deluded herself into believing that she was not pregnant, killing
her son in a brief psychotic episode that was the final act of her
denial. After her 1993 conviction, Stephanie Wernick, aged
twenty-three, remained free on appeal, living at her parents' home
and working as a waitress at a local restaurant. Finally, in 1996, six

years after she rammed toilet paper down her newborn's throat, the court of appeals upheld her conviction. The Wernick case was a landmark decision against the leniency the courts had customarily granted in cases of infanticide; at that time, it was unexpected that she would be convicted at all. The verdict also struck a significant blow against the validity of designer defenses based on untested and scientifically invalidated insanity syndromes.

The court's ruling on Stephanie Wernick's appeal was announced the same day as the press broke the eerily similar story of Amy Grossberg and Brian Peterson, the eighteen-year-old college students who delivered a baby boy in a Delaware motel room, allegedly killed him with a blow to the head, and tossed him into a Dumpster. The state of Delaware is seeking the death penalty in this case, which has received a great deal of sensationalist media coverage and evidences the backlash against perceived leniency against crime.

In televised trials like Stephanie Wernick's, the cameras change not just the emphasis of the testimony but the testimony itself. I was on the stand for three days, one and a half days for direct testimony and the same for cross-examination. This was the most extended and acrimonious cross-examination I had ever experienced. In the past, without the presence of the media, my testimony had generally required a day: the morning to present the direct case, the afternoon for cross and possible redirect. The camera not only intruded into the private tragedy of the Wernick family but also exposed the grief and complex emotions of all those who were participants in this courtroom drama. When my testimony was televised that day, the muted sadness I felt about Stephanie's crime became public property.

Throughout the trial, I was worried about my practice. My patients' sessions were being preempted day after day. They were not able to see me in the consulting room, yet they could watch me hour after hour on the local news. I began to wonder if I could responsibly continue to treat my private patients while I was involved with the courts. And what bothered me that week has since become the wave of the future, now that the media have redis-covered the insanity defense.

During the Wernick trial, the parents of several twelve-year-old girls I was seeing in group therapy called frantically, asking me how to handle their daughters' reactions to seeing my testimony televised. One of the girls, quiet and sensitive, was extremely up-set; her mother was pregnant. Another, who was coping with her parents' bitter divorce by acting jaded and tough, shocked her mother by saying she felt that what a girl did with an unwanted baby was her own business; she was angry at me for being so hard on Stephanie for her "mistake." A third girl, abused and aban-doned by her father, was worried I was going to desert her too, for a career in TV. The most concerning to me was the depressed daughter of rigid and controlling parents; she found something appealing in Stephanie's act of rebellion toward her parents and all the media attention it was garnering for her. I called an emer-gency group meeting with the girls on a Saturday morning during the trial, to reassure them and help them manage their anxious feelings around the media's abduction of their therapist.

With the proliferation of cable news stations hungry for sensa-tional local news, all trials not just on Long Island but throughout America have become dog and pony shows for the media. I do not question the importance of allowing reporters to cover a trial. Clearly, it is every citizen's right to be present in the courtroom and observe the legal process. Some have argued that the camera in this regard is just a high-tech observer that allows us to partici-pate in our legal system without even leaving our living rooms. But even if the substance of the broadcasts is just the unedited televising of the trial, with no reporting, editorial comment, or dramatic camera angles, I still maintain that the presence of the camera in the courtroom contaminates the proceedings of justice. I borrow the term "contamination" in this context from experi-mental social psychology, to describe how a factor added to a social situation alters the outcome and can make people act in ways that are vastly different from and sometimes even contradictory to their normal predictable behavior.

So far there have been no systematic studies on how the presence of television cameras actually affects the outcome of a trial. It is not likely that such expensive and extensive studies could ever be undertaken. Currently, New York's state legislature has extended for thirty months the trial period for considering whether to continue to permit cameras in the courtroom. Ideally this would be the perfect time to commission definitive studies and to perform a systematic survey of how court systems and judges have managed — or mismanaged — media coverage, state by state, from imposing gag orders on all participants, to sequestering juries, reacting to press coverage of a trial, and allowing or disallowing cameras to rove the courtrooms. However, I fear these important issues will instead be settled along political lines. After all, the media are extremely important to the election and the continued power of any politician, and there are ratings to be won, stardom to be had, and money to be made in broadcasting courtroom dramas such as Lorena Bobbitt's trial for assault and the Menendez trials.

The lack of solid formal research notwithstanding, everyone involved with the court systems will agree that the basic courtroom atmosphere alters the minute the camera begins to roll; nobody will even attempt to maintain that it has no effect on the proceedings. What is hotly and emotionally debated is whether that effect is good or bad — for the defendant, the prosecution, the overall meting out of justice, and the rest of us in American society who are willing or unwilling witnesses to the circus of televised justice. Many bar associations welcome the addition of the camera to the courtroom; they believe it keeps the proceedings more honest when the participants know their behavior is open to public scrutiny. As the justice system continues to reel from the aftermath of the interminably televised criminal trial of O. J. Simpson — the most media-saturated case ever — it is debatable how salutary the effect of the media was on Judge Lance Ito's courtroom, not to mention American notions of race and justice. One critic of the sensationalized televised proceedings in this case worried that we as a society had opened a "peephole" rather than a window into our judicial system.

Some lawyers have suggested that trials should be broadcast, but not until thirty days after a final decision has been rendered by the court. They believe that if the media were to observe this moratorium, the voyeuristic market might decline but the public's right to know, the right to free speech, and the citizen's right to a fair trial would be preserved. The tendency to sensationalize the proceedings would very likely lose its thrust with this cooling-off period. Those who are promedia argue that the very purpose of televising trials is to show the public what is occurring in our courts when the public is more interested, not less so, and is more likely to watch. They worry that limiting speech about trials at the precise times when the public interest is highest would interfere with our constitutional rights because citizens would not have access to important news at precisely the time they are most eager to know it.

Yet to me, a television broadcast from the courtroom is very different from a report in a newspaper or other print medium. The TV camera doesn't just reflect and report; it shapes the story it tells and becomes a full participant in the courtroom proceedings at the moment they occur. It tends to gravitate and pander to the lowest common denominator of the testimony. Attorneys and experts pitch their questions and answers to that denominator, thus reducing the standard of courtroom procedure. The posturing of attorneys in front of the camera becomes caustically adversarial, sometimes beyond the dignity of what should ever be permitted in a civilized courtroom — irrelevant, obstructionist, sometimes even lewd. In short, the media coverage seems to give license to the more angry and aggressive of the legal profession to act out shamelessly. It is common knowledge that this type of acting out is exacerbated for effect in jury trials. When such vicious, exhibitionistic types get to perform before the TV camera, this acting out is exaggerated tenfold.

In February 1995, during the federal court hearing on the sentencing of con artist Lilly Schmidt, which occurred while the New York federal courthouse was under enormous security restrictions due to the trial of the accused World Trade Center bombers, I walked past the police barricades and through the metal detector and scanner to encounter simple signs stating, "No cameras are permitted within this courthouse." That prohibition exists for all federal court trials. I felt reassured that during this federal proceeding justice would actually be done. And I was right. In spite of the drama of Lilly's crime — she had, after all, attempted to escape Rikers Island prison and arranged to kill two federal agents in the process — and notwithstanding the colorful characters involved in the hearing, such as the ancient Bulgarian defense psychiatrist Dr. Marina Boyardgeva, the case, by media standards, was extremely boring. Judge Kimba Wood grappled with the complicated issues presented in the experts' testimony. Each attorney's questions were penetrating and extremely relevant; there was no strutting, posturing, and badgering. Good psychology does not make good entertainment. Designer defenses and vivid psychopaths are far more mediagenic.

Neither does true psychosis make salacious television. In no case was this more apparent to me than in the Nassau County trial of serial killer Joel Rifkin, for whom I was the sole defense witness. Television and newspapers immediately tried, convicted, and sentenced him within days after he was picked up by the state troopers that steamy June night with the decomposing corpse of Tiffany Bresciani in his truck. When Jack Lawrence, Rifkin's attorney, contacted me to examine Rifkin, I had already been subtly affected by the media bombardment I could not elude. My gut reaction was that he was a ghoul, a sexual psychopath — sadistic, warped, but clearly responsible for his acts. It took more than fifty-six hours face to face in intense conversation with this killer; extensive interviews with his family, former therapist, and others who knew him; poring through four boxes of police materials, school, jail, and medical records, and reports of other experts; reading Rifkin's voluminous poetry and writings; and encountering the most psychotic test scores I had ever obtained, before I overrode my media-induced prejudice and changed my opinion.

Clearly, such a process is not something that the average juror has the opportunity or inclination to do — not to mention consumers of news, who have no chance to research the facts before the media hand them an opinion. I was unable to find substantiation for many of the "facts" reported in news articles about Rifkin. For example, it was frequently repeated that Rifkin pulled the teeth and fingernails out of some of the victims. Prosecutor Fred Klein asserted this throughout the proceedings as if it were a fact. Rifkin told the nine doctors who examined him many things that were inconsistent, improbable, and contradictory. To me he denied removing his victims' teeth and fingernails. Such was the chameleon-like nature of Rifkin's disordered personality; he played to his audience. I concluded early on that I could not accept the truth of anything Rifkin said he did or did not do. Until the coroner produced a corpse with missing teeth and fingernails, I would not give Rifkin's statement the credence that the media and the prosecution did. However, reported "facts" such as this were used to heighten the shock effect of Rifkin's crimes to the public.

As soon as word went out that Rifkin was utilizing an insanity defense and that I was the defense expert, I was inundated with calls from the tabloid TV shows, all of which I avoided. Jack Lawrence and I had made a strict pact between ourselves and with the Rifkin family that none of us would talk to the media before the trial. We felt that nothing could be gained other than to further contaminate his trial.

The trial, of course, was a circus. The reporters and the TV equipment with its tangle of wiring made the entrance to the courtroom look quite literally like the door to a snake pit. Not only was the ubiquitous in-court camcorder with its rack of blazing lights constantly at my elbow through the four solid days I was on the stand, but a second photographer using a handheld Nikon with a motorized shutter and strobe knelt at my feet, shooting up at my face with mechanized regularity. During direct examination, while I was trying to concentrate on the clarity and comprehensiveness of my testimony, *zap! zap!* — the blinding strobe would go off, leaving me to view Jack Lawrence and the courtroom through dancing spots of blue and yellow.

I believe that the legal proponents of cameras in the courtroom have a more practical reason for their position: it is enormously good for business. For myself, in the aftermath of all the free advertising and promotion I received in the Wernick case, my phone would not stop ringing. I was contacted by prestigious private law firms and noteworthy defense attorneys. Suddenly I had been discovered as the kind of expert who could possibly succeed at pulling off a designer defense — even though I'd been the one to challenge Stephanie's spurious claim of mental illness. And all because I'd been on TV.

The public's craving for news about crime and punishment is not a recent development. Attendance at public executions — the more exalted the prisoner, the better the turnout — is well documented in the bloody annals of places like the Tower of London. There is something undeniable in the human psyche that gravitates to the spectacle of gore and the bizarre. In 1888, when Jack the Ripper was killing prostitutes in the Whitechapel district of London's East End, the local and international press carried thousands of words about the case. The crimes of the Ripper were one of the first media events. In "Jack the Ripper and the Myth of Male Violence" (*Feminist Studies*, 1982), historian Judith Walkowitz has noted: "One cannot emphasize too much the role of the popular press, itself a creation of the 1880s, in establishing Jack the Ripper as a media hero . . . and in elaborating and interpreting the meaning of the Ripper murders to a 'mass audience.'"

In Fall River, Massachusetts, in the summer of 1892, the presses churned with sensational stories about the spinster Lizzie Borden, who allegedly "took an axe / and gave her mother forty whacks; / when she saw what she had done / she gave her father forty-one." The proper New England village was invaded by journalists and reporters. The notoriety ushered in a period of boom and prosperity for local merchants, as townspeople made tidy profits renting out spare rooms to the hordes drawn to witness the trial. Locals stretched and fabricated stories of their involvement with the Borden family and knowledge of the crime for the press. Moreover, without the present-day specter of legal action for libel and defamation, the press had carte blanche to print anything without checking sources or corroborating the truth of these tall tales.

The Borden jurors were not sequestered; nor was there any attempt to shield them from reading the newspaper accounts, which uniformly attested to Lizzie's guilt. Prevalent at the trial was a form of media representation that was less controlled than television is today, one even more potentially damaging to the defendant: the artist's rendering. Many papers of the times showed realistic drawings of Lizzie wielding the fabled axe, burying it in the forehead of her napping father or approaching her stepmother from behind with the weapon raised menacingly. The artists' unbridled imagination could construct the reality for the readers without the least obeisance to facts. Yet in spite of all this hyperbolic press coverage, Lizzie Borden was acquitted based on the circumstantiality of the evidence.

Though tabloid TV shows and confessional, setup talk show jousts like the *Jenny Jones Show* might make it seem otherwise, Lizzie Borden in fact suffered from sensationalist press coverage even more than we do today. When it comes to the basic veracity and responsibility of the print media — newspapers, magazines — a century's worth of laws have insured more creditable journalism. The exception to this, of course, is the tabloid paper whose stock-in-trade is the paparazzo photo and the lurid headline.

One of the most tragic and bizarre confoundings of life and media took place in 1995, when a young man named Jonathan Schmitz was invited by the *Jenny Jones Show* to tape a segment on "secret crushes." During the taping, Schmitz learned that his secret admirer was his gay neighbor, Scott Amedure, a casual acquaintance and drinking buddy. Although he seemed to take Amedure's revelation in stride at the taping, Schmitz later confessed that he was actually angry and humiliated at being the object of the other man's affection on the talk show. After he received an anonymous, suggestive note several days after the taping, Schmitz bought a 12-gauge shotgun, went to Amedure's mobile home, and shot him twice in the chest. Several hours later, Schmitz called the police and confessed to the murder, claiming that the public humiliation and exposure on the talk show had driven him to it.

By the time Schmitz came to trial, his attorneys had concocted an elaborate kitchen-sink designer defense. They claimed he was suffering from depression, alcoholism, and Graves' disease, a thyroid condition that can cause erratic and violent behavior. Humiliation, along with an "ambush" by the talk show's producers, caused Schmitz to snap. Part of the blame, they suggested, should be borne by the *Jenny Jones Show* and other irresponsible outlets of tabloid television, which pushed him over the edge. Their Beverly Hills defense expert, psychologist Dr. Carole Lieberman, testified even more precisely to the cause and moment when Schmitz's "mind totally snapped." She theorized from the stand that Schmitz killed Amedure because a wicker chair gave him a flashback to when he had been humiliated in the sixth grade. Allegedly, years of emotional abuse by Schmitz's parents and siblings, who had teased him about his size and femininity, flooded his fragile psyche at the moment Amedure picked up a wicker chair to protect himself.

Prosecutors tried to discredit Dr. Lieberman by citing her frequent appearances on talk shows discussing such subjects as "Princess Di and One-Night Stands," "First Anniversary: Michael Jackson and Lisa Marie Presley," and "Beavis and Butthead."

"I take that work very seriously," Lieberman responded. "Through the media I can reach more people than I can reach in a lifetime in my office."

Since then, I have seen nearly twenty shows dealing with some twist on the plot that led Jonathan Schmitz to the home of Scott Amedure. The more recent of those shows, a Canadian import called *Forever Knight*, features a rehabilitated vampire turned cop cracking the case of a talk show producer who shows murders on the air to boost ratings. Contemporary U.S. society has no monopoly on media madness.

Despite Dr. Lieberman's mediagenic performance, the Pontiac, Michigan, jury convicted Jonathan Schmitz of second-degree murder. Some jurors felt that enough of the blame belonged to the *Jenny Jones Show* to serve as a sort of diminished-capacity defense, which lowered the conviction from first-degree murder. The Amedure family has filed a $25 million lawsuit against Schmitz and the show.

If the "secret crushes" show had ever been broadcast, it might have topped the chart in ratings. Crime and domestic disasters make for compelling media, no matter how tragic they may be — or how much in bad taste it is to broadcast them so lovingly and lingeringly. Consider the attempted murder of the wife of Joey Buttafuoco by his teenage mistress, Amy Fisher, whom newspapers dubbed the Long Island Lolita. On one of the occasions when I was examining Joel Rifkin at the Nassau County jail there was a flurry of activity outside the interview room, coming from the visitors area. Rifkin grew agitated and started cracking his knuckles loudly. "Is there something wrong?" I inquired.

"Yeah," Rifkin muttered bitterly. "He's what's wrong with America!" I looked up to see Joey Buttafuoco, the Italian stallion, in all his glory, surrounded by a retinue of reporters and TV cameras.

The public can move from egregious bad taste, as in the Buttafuoco case, to egregious amorality when it makes cultural icons of depraved predators such as Ted Bundy. Jane Caputi, in the

Journal of American Culture, describes a flyer distributed at the University of New Mexico in Albuquerque, advertising a program for students on pornography. Under the killer's likeness appeared the logo, *A Man with Vision. A Man with Direction. A Prophet of Our Times. . . . Bundy: The Man, the Myth, the Legend.*

It is as easy to make Jonathan Schmitz a media victim as it is to make Ted Bundy a media hero. There is no doubt that antiheroes of media iconography are seductive. We may flatter ourselves that we see past media hyperbole and sensationalism, but those phenomena exist because we want them to. At their best, people may be wise enough to see through all the fantasy and hype — reasonably normal people, that is.

I have witnessed the bizarre and tragic effect that media images can have on that segment of society whose fragile minds and psyches are not so immune to the media's message. The television series *Kojak*, featuring a tough cop on the streets of New York, became part of the twisted interior drama of Joel Rifkin, who had episodes of *Kojak* on videotape. He detailed to me a scene from a Hitchcock thriller in which a man lures his fiancée to a secluded spot, presents her with a silk scarf, and strangles her with it as he lovingly ties it around her neck. Such fragments, always in disjointed flashes, presented themselves to Rifkin's disordered mind. But they were from mainstream movies and TV shows — not from porno films or underground S and M art. Rifkin remembered a snatch of dialogue from a *Kojak* show in which the victim was dismembered, with parts of her body put in a fifty-five-gallon drum and the rest scattered on both the Jersey and New York sides of the Hudson River: "She's floating from here to Jersey!" Rifkin had disposed of the body of one of his victims in the same way. "His mind is like a videotape in that it fast-forwards, then suddenly rewinds," I testified at his trial in Nassau County. Indeed, Rifkin's mind had become a grisly collage of erotic images of violence to women, a cracked mirror reflecting what the mainstream media gave him. Unfortunately, Rifkin could no longer tell where fantasy left off and reality began, until the two merged in the deaths of seventeen young women.

Even the phrase "serial killer," the most glamorized and sensationalized term for a sequential murderer, owes itself to the movies. Robert Ressler, retired head of the FBI's Behavioral Science Unit in Quantico, Virginia, states that he coined the term because he had in mind the serial adventures that kids used to see at the movies during the 1940s on Saturday afternoons.

It is not only the sensationalism of television drama and news that can spur and shape the actions of serial killers and other violent criminals. In 1978 David Berkowitz, the Son of Sam killer, using a .44 magnum, killed six young people and seriously injured several more who were parked in cars and necking, on streets throughout the boroughs of New York City. Berkowitz's crimes were defined by his urge for media fame. Craving attention and notoriety, he left notes at the scenes of his shootings and communicated directly with the newspapers. The fact that he held New York City in a grip of terror so strong that many people did not venture out at night, and long-haired brunettes in their twenties — his preferred victims — started wearing wigs, titillated this withdrawn and nerdy postal worker and bolstered him against his extreme feelings of inadequacy.

Berkowitz began to design and improvise a veritable publicity campaign of murder. He borrowed the notion of leaving cryptic notes at the murder scene from a book he had read about Jack the Ripper, the patron saint of serial killers. The "son of Sam" phrase would come later as a passing reference in a note he sent to newspapers. When the press latched on to this appellation, he took it over and began signing his notes that way. In this folie à deux with the media, he was symbiotically constructing the persona of the Son of Sam.

Newspaper columnist Jimmy Breslin seemed to have the inside track on this killer. The attention that he lavished on him in his columns inspired Berkowitz to write to him directly:

Hello, from the cracks in the sidewalks of New York City and from the ants that dwell in these cracks and feed on the dried blood of the dead that has settled into the cracks. . . . Don't think that because you haven't heard from me that I went to sleep. No, rather, I am still here, like a spirit roaming the night. Thirsty, hungry, seldom stopping to rest; anxious to please Sam.

The first day that just a part of that letter was printed, the *Daily News* sold a record-breaking 1,116,000 copies. The *New York Post* and the *News* were at that time — as they so often have been — embroiled in a circulation war, trying to outdo each other with sensational and lurid details of the case. The *New Yorker* criticized Breslin for baiting Berkowitz and spurring him on to commit more murders while he had the spotlight. Years later, Berkowitz confirmed that the *New Yorker* may have been right. After his fourth shooting, he remembered,

I didn't much care anymore, for I finally had convinced myself that it was good to do it, necessary to do it, and that the public wanted me to do it. I believe that many were rooting for me. This was the point at which the papers began to pick up vibes and information that something big was happening out in the streets. Real big!

The irresponsible reporting and mythologizing of violent killers in the media also encourages copycat crimes. A recent movie that is in fact called *Copycat* depicts the hunt for a peculiarly modern monster, the murder groupie who has studied the MOs of past serial killers and replicates them for the pleasure of tormenting a star (female) criminologist. The Boston and Hillside stranglers, Ted Bundy, the Son of Sam, and Jeffery Dahmer are among the killer's role models. The film's graphic murder scenes are modeled after the real ones in excruciating detail. I suspect that somewhere America's next serial killer sits before a videotape of this movie in his living room, mesmerized by the action and carefully taking mental notes.

The media's romance with murderers affects all of us. Children can purchase serial killer trading cards with packs of bubble gum. Legislators in Nassau and Suffolk counties in New York tried to outlaw the sales of these cards to minors, but a recent state court decision struck down the ban as violating minors' First Amendment rights.

While serial killers, sane or insane, are celebrated as media anti-heroes, one group in society remains far more stigmatized: the mentally ill. Studies show that 80 percent of the time that the mentally ill are depicted on TV and in the movies they are portrayed in connection with violent crimes. They usually come to some horrible and gory demise. The fact is that the mentally ill commit heinous crimes with far less frequency than so-called normals. Because the mentally ill tend not to have many wealthy and concerned family members and don't vote, their rights to fair and accurate representation are not protected. As a practicing therapist, I am always shocked at the comments even educated and seemingly sophisticated people let slip regarding the "nuts," "crazies," and "psychos" who in their estimation need therapy. Certainly such ideas trickle down from the populace to the popular media — and to people who themselves have mental or emotional problems. This stigma militates against people getting timely treatment and diagnosis early in the onset of their illness. The media, such a powerful force for attitudinal changes in society, have shirked their responsibility and exploited a group of people suffering from schizophrenia, a group who make up almost 1 percent of the population, or nearly 3 million Americans.

When someone kills, we assume he is psychotic — we perceive the killer as a real-life Hannibal Lecter, Norman Bates, or Freddy Kruger. But in spite of what the news media and the entertainment companies would have us believe, few people with schizophrenia or other psychotic disorders are at all violent. In my forensic examinations of more than three hundred murderers — a preselected population of cases, in which psychosis seemed to be an issue — fewer than a tenth were genuinely mentally ill. Not even one came close to resembling these neatly dramatic, unnervingly attractive fictionalized versions.

Madness as presented by the media is often the artistic creation of organized and creative professionals who are so balanced, articulate, and disciplined that they cannot even begin to comprehend the horror and disintegration of true madness. Psychosis is the antithesis of creativity and organization. Very simply, it is chaos. When mentally ill individuals kill, they are not clever fiends with foul and twisted minds. They are no less tragic figures than their victims.

Reporters and media journalists covering trials that have to do with an application of the insanity defense often find themselves in strange and alien territory. Mental illness is complex and confusing even to professionals who have dedicated their lives to its treatment; those subtle hairsplitting decisions upon which an individual's future treatment and prognosis depend so critically are often agonizing for the clinician. Some journalists get assistance from mental health consultants and try to educate themselves; some just wing it. When I read some of the newspaper coverage of trials I've been on, I am often astounded at the misunderstandings and inaccuracies reported. More news stations and newspapers should consider hiring crackerjack psychological specialists as technical consultants to make sure that the information they are presenting to the public on the issue of insanity and mental illness is accurate. For example, in their year-end roundup of the first Rifkin trial, *Newsday* announced, "His defense is temporary insanity." In my four days of testimony, I never used the term "temporary insanity" — nor do I ever use it. Very simply, it is clinically and psycholegally meaningless. Organic psychoses and states of delirium or substance intoxication perhaps come closest to that phrase so often uttered by the public. However, Rifkin's insanity defense was a classic psychological issue of paranoid schizophrenia, long-term psychotic thinking, defects in logic, time, and sequences of events, serious emotional deficits in relating to people, disturbance in reality testing, and poorly articulated auditory command hallucinations.

Ignoring the facts by carelessly dubbing Rifkin's defense as temporary insanity is abuse of the public's right to know, abuse of the rights of due process of the defendant, and prejudice against the mentally ill. In my experience, one notable exception to such slipshod journalism is John McQuiston of the Long Island bureau of the *New York Times*. Throughout the coverage of the Rifkin trial, McQuiston would ask for clarification of terms, concepts, and statements made during my psychological testimony in the trial. He was the only reporter to correctly state about Rifkin that "the jury is being asked to determine only whether he will spend the rest of his life in prison or in a state hospital for the criminally insane." This very core of the insanity defense process is something that prosecutors want to keep the jury and the public unaware of. Prosecutors like to add more oxygen to the public's fiery prejudice that the mentally ill who commit homicide are always loathsome creatures lurking in the alleyways of life, human vermin to be flushed out and eradicated at all costs. Because it sells newspapers and can convict defendants, both journalists and district attorneys have a vested interest in letting the public believe that a killer found not guilty by reason of insanity is given cab fare and let out the courtroom door to prowl the streets again, looking for fresh victims.

In the Rifkin case, the prosecution capitalized on fear. The Nassau County district attorney began peppering the local newspapers and cable networks with gruesome stories and personality profiles of the confessed serial killer almost as soon as he was arrested. By nine o'clock on the morning after Rifkin was apprehended, news of his confession to the stranglings of seventeen young women was faxed to nearly forty media outlets across New York State. Every day during the trial I was mobbed by reporters outside the courtroom. "Did you know that Rifkin told another doctor that he had sex with a corpse?" a *Newsday* reporter fired at me, while someone else shoved a microphone in my face. "Can you give us some examples of Rifkin's delusions and hallucinations, his sexual perversions?" As they all thronged me, another reporter implored. "What about his masturbating on articles of his victims' clothing? Did he give you details about how he mutilated them?" I ducked into the ladies' room, hoping to elude them. Out of the next stall came a voice, "And, Dr. Kirwin, was he ever sexually explicit with you?"

That night, I arrived home to find that an obscene death threat had come to my office. Several threats followed throughout the four days of my testimony. Some calls were obscene, delivered in slurred and breathless tones, graphically threatening to "dismember" or "dissect" me in the same way Rifkin treated the corpses of some of his victims. But the scariest were the ones who had calm, educated, and deliberate voices. They sounded like my neighbors. "How could you pervert all your education and training to help a serial killer get away with murder?" one professional-sounding middle-aged man questioned accusingly. "I hope something like this happens to you and your child and then we'll see how you feel."

Several callers mentioned my child. I duly reported this information to my local police department. The police were concerned about the threat of kidnapping and the mention of my child in the threatening calls. My profession sometimes took me into the sewers of the criminal justice system, so I was no stranger to this side of life; but I was flooded with guilt and self-recriminations that the way I chose to earn my living might endanger my child. I had always been careful, especially after reading the harrowing experiences of Kathie Lee Gifford and the kidnapping attempts on her children, to avoid revealing private details in my forensic work. The need for safety, anonymity, and discretion had impelled me, for example, to take on the major overhead of an outside office rather than practice from my home.

As a result of the publicity surrounding the Rifkin case, I was advised by the local police to keep my son out of his first grade class for the entire week of my testimony. Months later, when I was reviewing a videotape of the cable broadcast of my testimony under cross-examination, I realized I had revealed that I had a son when the DA was nitpicking about discrepancies in my retirement dates from Creedmoor Psychiatric Center. I had mentioned the time I was on maternity leave giving birth to my son. I shuddered. An innocuous statement, which had nothing to do with the issues involved in a serial killer trial, had been reacted to by more than one warped-minded and irate television viewer.

The threatening and harassing phone calls I received clearly indicate to me the level of public fear and prejudice about mental illness, not to mention our society's general ignorance about the legal meaning of insanity and the role of the expert witness. When the media do not take seriously their responsibility to educate and inform the public on important concepts and facts and seek either to pander to sensationalism or be a propaganda agent of the district attorney, they serve to create a lynch mob mentality that subverts justice. Media irresponsibility also functions to deter highly skilled and reputable mental health experts from tendering their services in forensics. How can experts justify putting themselves and their families in danger, becoming objects of harassment inside and outside the courtroom, especially when their work is perceived as being of no account to society?

Based on the incendiary publicity and emotional fallout from the Rifkin and Nathan cases — out of three hundred cases the only two in which I was able to support the defense — I have become extremely wary of getting involved either in the defense or in high-profile cases in the future. My sort of reluctance, which is shared by many other experts, represents still another serious disadvantage to the defendant on an already skewed playing field. Considering that the prosecutors pay their experts better, defendants have to be as wealthy as O. J. Simpson or the Menendez brothers to avail themselves of suitable professional expertise.

Moreover, scholars, scientists, and academics, who often make the most objective witnesses, are notoriously media-shy.

Further still, cases that stir wanton media interest encourage the involvement of a certain type of witness, the kind who craves media attention and is able to promote and tailor a mediagenic personality, and maybe even spurs a designer defense to go with it. As I have found out from firsthand experience, cases as salacious as Rifkin's and those of other sex killers often attract ambulance-chasing experts who tender their often questionable skills to the defense in exchange for an exclusive on the story rights or a quick grab at their quarter-hour of fame.

Ron Fox, Ph.D., past president of the American Psychological Association, has become outraged by "colleagues on television who elevate the trial, glibly generalize from unique or bizarre particulars to broadly applicable principles, or spew forth nonsensical psychobabble that confuses issues and encourages thinking that may be toxic." Talk radio, with its hugely popular Dr. Laura, the "just do it shrink," is perhaps an even more heinous example of what seems to me nothing short of an attempt to dupe a vast segment of decent but unsophisticated listeners into swallowing psychopap in the guise of reputable psychology. Although the professional psychological associations declare that her advice is not the kind that any psychologist would give, the general public, including callers in genuine distress, doesn't know that. Dr. Laura is not a psychologist with a license to protect; therefore she lies outside the purview of the professional ethics she violates. In short, Dr. Laura, and dozens like her nationwide, is not a psychologist beholden to a code of ethics but a media personality bound only to ratings. David Bartlett, president of the Radio-Television News Directors Association, retorts, "The best way to insure failure on a radio therapy show is to concentrate on psychology." The public wants easy answers and doesn't want to wrangle with complex and ambivalent issues. Psychology has no easy answers about why people do the things they do, especially when they commit horrible crimes. It seems that the best way to kill an insanity defense is also to concentrate on psychology.

During the early media feeding frenzy in the O. J. Simpson case, I was courted by local TV news outlets and newspapers to comment on the defendant's state of mind and possible motivation. I candidly told the program directors that I could offer no information on his mental state because I had never met him, examined him, tested him, reviewed his history, or interviewed his family or friends. They seemed annoyed, as if I were being difficult, a nitpicker. Fox 5 News offered to send a limo to whisk me to its studio. In another instance, the *Montel Williams Show*, while always polite and courteous with its offers, was confounded that I would not jump at the chance to "analyze" on the air a woman who had murdered her child. After all, it would take only fifteen minutes.

Sometimes I fantasize about producing a documentary-style TV show in which the viewer could observe actual forensic examinations of defendants or psychotherapy sessions with patients, followed by elucidating commentary by a panel of mental health professionals — all supplemented by viewer call-ins. It would be sort of a media version of grand rounds, as such teaching presentations are traditionally called in psychiatric hospitals. The real human drama of such intense encounters would be far more profound and poignant than anything that media scriptwriters or media shrinks could summon up.

My two sole appearances for the defense and their incidental press coverage adversely affected not only my sense of safety and security but my livelihood. After the Rifkin case, even Nicholas Marino, the defense counsel in the case of Oliver Petrovich — the young man who had murdered his parents — told the press he was surprised that the Nassau County district attorney's office would so viciously attack a "witness that they themselves have relied upon as expert in this very field in the past." Nevertheless, when prosecutor Fred Klein branded me a hack, a whore, and a liar, trashed my methodology, and threatened to hold me in contempt for the same professional behavior that I had consistently applied to the many cases I had done for the prosecution, he created a court transcript that would forever haunt both of us.

The day I took the stand for the defense for the first time in my life, I was testing my own mettle and banishing the rumors that I had become a prosecution-only hired gun. I was also sealing my fate with the Nassau DA. If I ever took the stand again for the prosecution in Nassau County, Klein's scathing attempts to discredit me would be hurled into my face and the prosecutor's: "Dr. Kirwin, is it not true that in the case of Joel Rifkin, you were accused by the prosecutor of . . ." Despite my fifteen years of work with the Nassau County district attorney's office, I suddenly became persona non grata. After the prosecutors had bashed their own former star witness so viciously, how could they rehire her in future cases? Certain assistant district attorneys who still felt some loyalty to me would call to chat or request advice, but circumspectly, from their own homes.

On the contrary, the Wernick case, less than a year before, when I appeared for the prosecution and was televised directly on cable news, generated a veritable boom of business for me. The proficiency of my presentations in Wernick, Rifkin, and Nathan was, I believe, equivalent; after spending years in the hot seat of the witness stand, one achieves a marked consistency of performance. However, my testimony in Wernick was more dramatic and media-friendly than anything I could have honorably managed in the other two trials. Nonetheless, I will always believe that my testimony on schizophrenia and psychological testing in the Rifkin case was the most lucid and scientifically compelling I have given in my forensic career.

An inspiring example of the responsible handling of the media occurred in the tragic case of Susan Smith, the young mother who rolled her car down a boat launch into a lake with her two sons strapped securely in their car safety seats. Cameras were banned from the small-town courtroom, and a South Carolina law prevented attorneys from discussing details of the case with the media before or during the trial, keeping lurid speculation to a minimum. Despite a designer defense that included a history of incest corroborated by her stepfather, depression, and emotional instability, the jury gave her a substantial penalty compared with the generally lenient dispositions afforded most women, especially attractive and sympathetic ones, who kill their children.

I believe Susan Smith's mistake was in courting the media herself. Had she not, in a bizarre and cold-blooded attempt to garner sympathy and deflect suspicion, concocted the story of a carjacking by a black male and conned a nation for nine days, she might even have remained sympathetic to a jury and the media and been acquitted. After all, baby killer Ann Green fatally smothered two children and walked, without even something like incest to arouse the jury's pity, in a case that occurred in a simpler, less media-driven era (the 1970s) and was not publicized at all. The media demand human sacrifice. In Susan Smith's case the media may have ironically proven her downfall and contributed to the workings of justice.

The kind of adversarial approach we see in press coverage of trials should exist only in the courtroom, where it is governed by the appropriate legal rules and regulations and balanced by the defense's side of the story. Even then adversary justice-making has its problems. There should also be an increased emphasis on informative and educational programs about mental illness, violent crime, and the insanity defense. Programming such as that produced by Court TV can be a powerful force in upgrading the knowledge of potential jurors. Clear reporting can do a lot to debunk the myths that abound in the area of mental illness and the law. The more the public understands about the true nature of mental illness, the better position we are in to prevent and treat it. If America is going to continue to uphold the principles of free speech, we need to exercise these constitutional rights responsibly and to view them as privileges that could be lost through apathy and abuse. This goes far beyond the profit motives of a few scions of the media, or the penchant of people to be titillated by salacious details. If we agree that the media are inevitably a powerful creator of social attitudes toward crime and the mind, then let's harness that power for positive and informative ends.

The work we have to do begins at home. One of my young patients, Vin Parks, was stocky and precociously developed for his eleven years. He had been referred to me for evaluation and treatment by the private school that had suspended him after he tried to set fire to a classmate with a cigarette lighter. At our first meeting, Vin was surly, hostile, and almost impossible to reach. Clenching a stack of cards in his jackhammer fist, he baited me. "You want to see my collection of serial killer cards?"

"No thanks," I replied, as indifferently as I could. I didn't want to reinforce his apparent obsession with violence, but neither did I want him to think he could shock me into backing off from him. He was angry, confused, and in pain — definitely someone to be wary of — but he was still only a boy.

By the time of our second meeting his attitude had totally changed. He seemed thrilled to see me. It turned out that Vin had ardently followed the newspaper and television coverage of the trial of Joel Rifkin. "I saw you on TV," he said to me, his face beaming. "Wow! What's it like to shake hands with a real hero?"

7

AFTER THE VERDICT:

TREATMENT, QUARANTINE, OR REVENGE ?

*R*ichard Winkler's blue eyes twinkled when he spoke, and every white hair on his head was carefully brushed into place. His khaki work clothes were immaculate, even though he had come to meet me straight from work in the hospital's electric power plant. His tone of voice soothing, his demeanor folksy, he seemed more like the neighbor you might be chatting with over the back fence than a murderer. Richard Winkler was sitting in the armchair across from me in the small examining office at New York's Kings Park Psychiatric Center. The breeze wafted cherry blossom pollen through the open, screenless window. I had an unnerving question to answer: Was this man mad and dangerous?

For nearly twenty years Richard Winkler had been locked in wards for the criminally insane. Had he not been acquitted on the basis of insanity, he would have been sentenced to eight and a third years in jail. Richard Winkler wanted increased freedom and privileges, including periodic unescorted furloughs. The doctors at Kings Park did not believe that he continued to suffer from a dangerous mental illness. The district attorney, pressured by the family of his victim, was hoping that I would be able to penetrate Winkler's smooth and inscrutable facade. If there was any vestige of paranoid schizophrenia still lurking in him, it was my job to unearth it and convince a judge that Winkler's release on unescorted furloughs was "inconsistent with the public safety and the community welfare."

"Have you ever heard of having to take your shoes off when you go to a minister's house?" Winkler asked matter-of-factly. "It's kind of like Hindu. When you go into the house he had music on, sometimes psychedelic music. He had books on ESP, on dreams." Twenty years ago, Winkler had become very involved in religion. He joined a Lutheran congregation led by the Reverend Schonberg Setzer, a minister involved with parapsychology and Eastern mysticism. In Setzer's charismatic prayer groups and quasi-therapy sessions, Winkler began to have hallucinations, trance states, and out-of-body experiences. He saw special signs and codes in Setzer's foot gestures.

On the night before Thanksgiving, 1976, Winkler began to feel that he was being possessed by the minister in the form of a satyr. He looked at the pamphlets Setzer had given him. "They were clearly blasphemy," he told me, "and I burned them. That night I didn't want to go to sleep. I tried to stay awake by reading the Bible, but I fell asleep and in so doing, I lost the battle. When I woke up I knew what I had to do." Early Thanksgiving morning, Winkler had a vision of the gates of hell with masses of humanity writhing within. Agitated and preoccupied, he asked his wife, Gertrude, to call Setzer and set up a meeting. Mrs. Winkler was frightened and confused; she had heard her husband speak of the minister as an "evil person" in the past, even though he also attended his "spiritual enhancement" classes and seemed to take great comfort in them. But since Setzer was a practicing psycho-therapist, she felt he could help her desperate husband.

On the drive over, Winkler muttered about "evil" and cried out several times, "I have lost the battle!" Setzer greeted the Winklers in his sitting room. They all sat on large cushions strewn around the floor and began to pray. With her eyes closed in silent prayer, Gertrude heard Setzer plead, "Richard, don't!" She jumped to her feet to see her husband stab him in the chest with a butcher knife. Setzer broke loose and, calling out for his wife, staggered up the stairs pursued by Winkler and Gertrude, screaming and pleading with her husband to stop. In the upstairs hallway she spied the knife on the floor and kicked it out of sight underneath a table. But Winkler dove for the knife and attacked Setzer again, stabbing him repeatedly. Setzer's wife screamed at seeing her husband pinned against the wall while Winkler stabbed him wildly. Mrs. Setzer tried to pull Winkler off her husband, but she was not strong enough. She ran outside, screaming for her neighbors. Winkler greeted them in the foyer. "Setzer's not here anymore. He's dead. Praise the Lord!" he said. "We got rid of the demon." Setzer's wife raced upstairs to find her mother bending over her husband. "Is he dead?" she cried. "Yes," said her mother, in shock. "His heart is outside his body. His neck is slashed."

Richard Winkler, a robust forty-nine-year-old at the time, was indicted for murder. Though insanity was his only possible de-fense, he was reluctant to be considered "crazy" because he be-lieved that he was justified by God in killing an agent of the devil. At a psychiatric examination a month and a half after the stabbing, he told Dr. Daniel Schwartz — who would examine the Son of Sam, David Berkowitz, the following year — that "if one half of the information I've given you is correct, Reverend Setzer was re-sponsible for his own death, and they should just open the doors and let me out." Then, tantalizingly flirting with sanity and culpa-bility, Winkler added, "I don't know if God will forgive me. I should have left my family for a short while and this would never have happened."

Richard Winkler received a smorgasbord of diagnoses: adjustment reaction of adult life, atypical psychosis, atypical paranoia,
delusional disorder. His archival psychiatric record spoke more to
me about his crime and his mental state twenty years ago than he
did. I had to stretch my imagination to see this kindly old elf of a
man, toothless and hard of hearing, much loved among ward staf-
fers, as someone capable of cutting out a man's heart. However,
another Richard Winkler lurked behind the pages of his hospital
history. He had been a hard-drinking, brawling, narcotic-abusing,
womanizing soldier of fortune who had led a footloose and reckless life in his twenties and thirties.

Born to a middle-class family in Brooklyn, Richard Winkler
was something of a hell-raiser and never went beyond grammar
school. In 1944 he joined the navy, but he never saw combat. In
1947 he was married to Gertrude and together they had three
children. At age twenty-eight Richard began an affair with a
woman and divorced Gertrude. His second, tumultuous marriage
ended when his wife took their two children and fled to Idaho. In
court papers blocking Winkler's visitation with the two boys, his
wife claimed that he was physically abusive to both her and the
children; he never saw his children again. He returned to his first
wife, Gertrude, on a platonic basis. Although they never remarried, they were living together at the time of the crime.

In 1966, at age thirty-nine, Winkler, a master electrician,
worked as a civilian in Vietnam. When he lost an illness-related
disability suit, he felt victimized, embittered, and depressed.
Three years later, when his son was killed in combat in Vietnam,
Winkler began to fragment. He claimed his dental plate contained electronic transmitters and started to believe that thoughts
were implanted in his mind through microchips in his brain, his
right ear, and his left eye. Suffering from paranoid outbursts exacerbated by recurrent bouts of abdominal pain, he made major
use of Dilaudid, Demerol, and Percodan. By 1975 he was anxious,
suspicious, argumentative, and addicted. He worked only sporadi-

cally, at a menial job in a vinyl factory. Sometimes he withdrew for days in a profound depression. His interest in religious issues burgeoned to the point of obsession. He seemed to have found a haven in Schonberg Setzer's parapsychological prayer group.

Once at the maximum-security Mid-Hudson Forensic Psychiatric Center, Winkler seemed to recover his sanity immediately. He cultivated a quiet, soft-spoken manner, was always helpful and pleasant, and quickly ingratiated himself with hospital staff. In less than a year he was recommended for transfer to a regular civil hospital, Central Islip Psychiatric Center, as no longer dangerous. Fearful and outraged at the prospect of Winkler's returning to a civil hospital in the community just months after the murder, Setzer's family took legal action. But within the context of the legal statutes governing the criminally insane in New York State at that time, there was nothing they could do. Even though he refused to take medication or attend individual psychotherapy sessions or group therapy, the doctors were saying that Richard Winkler was in remission from his mental illness and no longer dangerous.

Richard Winkler and I arrived at Central Islip on the same day in 1978. I was beginning my postdoctoral internship in clinical psychology with a specialty in forensics. He was seeking to prove his sanity and gain his freedom. Our careers would intersect more than once as we negotiated the twists and turns of insanity defense reform over the next seventeen years, until we were sitting face to face at Kings Park Psychiatric Center in May of 1995.

What matters most about the insanity defense is what happens after the verdict. The court's disposition of defendants deemed insane is as maddeningly arbitrary and unpredictable as the insanity defense verdicts themselves. But what happens to the criminally insane after they leave the courtroom is a serious matter of social policy, with tremendous practical consequences. When we decide we will not convict the mentally ill for crimes because they are not criminally responsible, we then have to take responsibility for their fates. Not only must we be prepared to design a humane alternative to punishment and imprisonment, we must finance and maintain it. We must take similar care of those mentally ill people who, rightly or wrongly, end up in prisons. And when a patient like Richard Winkler petitions for release from the locked psych ward, we have to be extremely careful once again to exercise justice.

All the moral, political, and philosophical commotion over the insanity defense is a smoke screen for avoiding the larger issue of what we do with the mentally ill who commit violent crimes. Society has yet to come up with a humane and workable treatment for even the nonviolent and noncriminal mentally ill in its care, as we can see from the many mentally ill people released, during the Reagan years, from institutions into homelessness. And we are worse in managing the care of violently psychotic criminals. Searching for secure mental health care, we are confronted with a crazy quilt of statutes and insanity defense decisions, psychopaths like Gowain Tremont who work the system, inadequate numbers of undertrained staff, crumbling physical plants, almost nonexistent security measures, cutbacks in funding, and hospital closings — a recipe for disaster.

Nineteenth-century insane asylums were basically prisons where doctors and attendants replaced guards and inmates were sentenced for life. Insanity was a permanent condition; the madman was presumed ill and irrational when he committed his crime, at the time of trial, and forever after. By the 1960s in America, society had come full circle in its conceptions of insanity. We rejected the idea that insanity was incurable in favor of a more fluid concept of "temporary insanity." Insanity could wax and wane in intensity. The popular notion took hold that a person could "just snap" into insanity and thus could just snap back. It remains a tenet of modern psychiatry that sooner or later the "disease" of mental illness will abate and the defendant will regain his sanity. By the 1970s several U.S. Supreme Court decisions upheld the rights of the criminally insane to be released from mental institutions when they were no longer dangerously mentally ill. In 1973, in a landmark case, *Dixon v. Cahill*, the Supreme Court gave mentally ill people hospitalized through the criminal courts the right to a hearing to determine whether they were still in need of hospitalization. Of the 230 patients examined in a maximum-security hospital in New Jersey, the courts determined that 180 of them were no longer in need of a maximum-security setting. Five men who had spent a combined 250 years hospitalized were released either to freedom or to regular civil psychiatric hospitals. This decision affirmed the patients' right to treatment in the least restrictive setting. The cumulative effects of such rulings made the commitment and release procedures of insanity acquittees more closely resemble those of noncriminal civil patients.

But even as the courts recognized the rights of patients, they also encouraged a harmful denial and naive sentimentality about the management of the dangerously mentally ill. Balancing the rights of the violent mentally ill with the public safety has always involved extreme swings of the pendulum. Someone always seems to get hurt in the process.

Young, pretty psychologist Judith Becker truly believed in the broodingly handsome young man assigned as her patient. Ricardo Caputo had been sent to the maximum-security Matteawan State Hospital in New York for the 1971 killing of Natalie Brown, his girlfriend. Claiming that he was hearing voices and behaving in bizarre ways — talking to the deceased Natalie from his jail cell, for instance — Caputo had been examined psychiatrically and declared incompetent to proceed to trial.

Once Caputo was incarcerated, his psychosis miraculously lifted. He was sent to a less secure facility within a year. At Wards Island he continued to be a model forensic patient, worked in the snack bar, and was allowed to roam the grounds freely. Once he won the right to unescorted weekend furloughs, he often visited Judith Becker and stayed with her in her apartment in Yonkers.

He even accompanied Judith to visit her parents in Connecticut, where he impressed her family as being very "charming, intelligent, and personable." Eventually, Becker seemed to tire of his attention and his tendency to show up at her apartment at odd times. Caputo's freedom to come and go at the hospital unquestioned was, in that era, not a matter of law. Hospital authorities were not even aware of his absence until days after he had gone to Judith Becker's apartment, battered her with his fists, and strangled her with a nylon stocking. He fled in her car.

On the run, he spent three months in San Francisco. Adopting an alias, the first of many, he took up with Barbara Ann Taylor, twenty-eight, an educational film consultant. After her friends persuaded Taylor that he was sponging off her, she bought him a plane ticket to Honolulu to get him out of her hair. Caputo returned two weeks later and beat her to death. He fled to Mexico, where he was detained by immigration officers. He was able to break out of the prisonlike barracks and scale a chain-link fence to freedom and anonymity in Mexico. When his romance with Laura Gomez, a twenty-year-old student from a prominent family, began to sour, she was found bludgeoned to death in the apartment they shared. For the next seventeen years Caputo moved back and forth between the United States and South America, using false names and passports. He married twice, fathered six children, and succeeded at supporting his family by working at different times as a waiter, martial arts instructor, English teacher, and restaurant manager.

In 1994, now in Argentina, Caputo confessed to his family. As a brilliant legal strategy, Caputo's attorney staged a formal press conference before his client even spoke to Argentine police. He wove a tapestry of all the current designer defenses: repressed memories of childhood physical and sexual abuse at the hands of a stepfather; three distinct personalities, one of which urged him to kill; the presence of demons and voices; a onetime diagnosis of schizophrenia. Caputo stumped the psychiatrist who examined him after his surrender to U.S. authorities. He could not reconcile

Caputo's periods of extremely violent, seemingly psychotic behavior with his later years of stability. This doctor gave Caputo a provisional diagnosis of schizophrenia and discounted the more glamorous but less mainstream one of multiple personality order. He explained that he could not rule out the possibility that Caputo was a "psychopathic personality pretending to be crazy." Public attitudes had changed radically since the 1970s, when Caputo had been considered unfit to stand trial. The insanity defense, that edifice of social compassion and individual responsibility in American jurisprudence, is built on shifting ground. Reversing a twenty-three-year-old court decision, a judge found Ricardo Caputo fit to stand trial in the murder of Natalie Brown, the first of the women he had killed.

The spring of 1994 was a boom time for killers on Long Island. I was at the Nassau County jail listening to serial killer Joel Rifkin complain about his brawl with Colin Ferguson, when Caputo was brought in, restrained by shackles and leg irons. He was stocky, still darkly handsome at forty-four, with a predator's eagle eyes. Exasperated with trying to bring coherence to Rifkin's ramblings, for a moment I thought that it would have been refreshing to find out what made Caputo tick. But by now I knew the true sum of all these cases — the emptiness of psychosis, the banality of evil.

Whether he was simply tired and burned out from running, taking the best possible path to eventual freedom, or genuinely suffering remorse, Caputo abandoned his original defense of not guilty by reason of insanity. "I stabbed Natalie to death, and I was very emotionally disturbed at the time," he told the court. Caputo, like the Son of Sam killer, David Berkowitz, cut a deal for manslaughter in the first degree and was sentenced to eight and a half to twenty-five years. If he had gone to trial and been convicted of the original murder charge, he could have been sentenced to twenty-five years to life. Even if Caputo had succeeded in his insanity plea, he would have put himself back into the hospital, probably until he died, or until he escaped again.

New York State authorities, stinging under the obvious embarrassment that the repentant Caputo represented, were quick to counter that it would be impossible for Caputo to "elope" once again from a mental institution. If that fact is true, it is not due to Caputo's crimes or increased hospital security but to two other high-profile New York tragedies that brought changes to the law nationwide.

Adam Berwid was a Polish-born engineer who was originally jailed for violating a family court order to stay away from his wife, Ewa, and his two young children. A rigid and unforgiving man, Berwid drafted a detailed letter to his estranged wife in which he painstakingly described how he was going to kill her for trying to take his children from him. Berwid was charged with aggravated harassment and the judge committed him to a state hospital for ninety days for evaluation. His court-ordered commitment ended in August of 1978, but the hospital was able to retain him under involuntary civil commitment procedures. During this time, Berwid managed to escape from the locked ward at Pilgrim State Hospital twice. Each time he sought out Ewa, threatening both her and the children. After the second elopement, he was transferred to Mid-Hudson, a maximum-security mental hospital, where, as brilliantly obsessive as ever, he began to use the system to his advantage. He filed complaint after legal complaint about the treatment of inmates and the abuse of their rights. Although he had become a thorn in the side of the treatment staff, he himself was a model patient. As mandated by the statutes, he was transferred back to the less restrictive civil hospital of Pilgrim State; his doctors had declared him no longer dangerously mentally ill and not in need of a secure setting.

Two weeks after his transfer downstate, Berwid was given a day pass on the orders of the ward psychiatrist, over the feeble objections of another doctor and the protests of the head nurse. Berwid purchased a knife and went straight to his ex-wife's home. A police 911 operator listened helplessly to the screams of a young woman that December afternoon in 1979. "Oh my God, he's killing me. I'm . . . I'm dying." The operator tried in vain to get the caller's name or address; without that information, help could not be dispatched.

The police learned of Ewa's murder twenty-four hours later, when Berwid called to turn himself in. The black loose-leaf binder in the chart room at Pilgrim State foretold the tragedy. Taped to its cover were two warnings alerting staff that police and Ewa Berwid should be called immediately if Berwid escaped. Inside the file, for anyone who cared to take the time to read it, was a strong letter from the district attorney and the committing judge. "We have no doubt that if he is released, we will be reading about the murder of Ewa Berwid in the news at some time in the future."

Curiously, Adam Berwid was not acquitted of his wife's murder by reason of insanity. He was convicted and is serving thirty-five years to life at New York's notorious Attica Prison. Berwid remains a loner who does not participate in prison programs or have a prison job; he sometimes behaves erratically, complains to prison staff, and writes incoherent letters to public officials. His correctional counselors maintain that he has a good disciplinary record, and he will be eligible for parole in seventeen years.

On the same Thanksgiving morning in 1976 that Richard Winkler was responding to his vision of the gates of hell, New York City police officer Robert Torsney reacted to what he thought was a perpetrator pulling a gun. Torsney shot to death a fifteen-year-old black youth on a Brooklyn street. Torsney was charged with murder, but his case became a cause célèbre to the Patrolmen's Benevolent Association, the police union and advocacy group. He was acquitted by reason of insanity, based on one doctor's testimony that he had a rare form of psychomotor epilepsy — automation of Penfield — that no other medical examiner or neurological test had uncovered. Some cops muttered off the record that Torsney was an expert marksman who used to like to practice his quick draw when he was drinking.

I met Robert Torsney at Creedmoor Psychiatric Center when he became one of the subjects in my Ph.D. dissertation research on the criminally insane. He was quiet, self-contained, very controlled, and socially precise. He was not receiving medication or therapy or in any way participating in the therapeutic regime. Torsney was marking time. Extensive psychological and neurological testing revealed no psychosis, epilepsy, or psychopathic tendencies. After a year, the hospital applied for Torsney's conditional release. Following an outcry from professionals, politicians, community leaders, and the public, the appellate court overturned the lower court decision to release Torsney. With backing and support from the PBA, the court of appeals then reversed the appellate ruling and upheld his release, on the conditions that he no longer work as a police officer or carry a gun and that he continue receiving psychiatric treatment — for what disease or condition was never clear, since none could be found after his acquittal.

In shocked response to both the Berwid and Torsney incidents, New York State revamped its procedures governing the granting of passes, privileges, and release of dangerous and criminal mental patients. Other states followed suit, swinging the pendulum toward protecting the public safety and the welfare of the community. Under the Criminal Procedural Law (CPL) in New York State — typical of other procedures nationwide — a defendant acquitted by reason of insanity must immediately undergo a thirty-day psychiatric evaluation period to determine whether he or she is dangerously mentally ill, mentally ill but not dangerous, or is not mentally ill. The final logical option — that the defendant is dangerous but not mentally ill — does not apply, since institutionalizing someone on the basis of a suspicion that he might be dangerous in the future constitutes "preventive detention" and is unconstitutional. Ironically, in my experience with this procedure, this has often been the most correct diagnosis.

Defendants found to be dangerously mentally ill are then committed to a maximum-security psychiatric facility for a minimum of six months. Retention hearings — after the first six months, one year later, and thereafter every two years — explore whether the defendant should continue to be "retained" involuntarily in the secure setting. At these legal proceedings, generally held in special courtrooms at the hospitals, the Office of Mental Health must prove that the defendant remains dangerously mentally ill and should be retained in a secure facility, or that the defendant is no longer dangerously mentally ill and will not pose a threat to the public safety if transferred to a civil hospital. The district attorney must always be notified.

On paper, the successive hurdles toward freedom — which ultimately include a hearing in front of a judge between the district attorney and the state attorney general before release — sounds like cautious and foolproof justice. In practice, the system often fails. It fails not only because the nation's mental health system is in serious decline due to cutbacks in funding, hospital closings, and increased pressures toward deinstitutionalization, but more fundamentally because no expert or judge can predict who might kill again. The psychiatric expert is viewed as a seer, divining what went on in the mind of a killer at the time of the crime, evaluating his competency to stand trial, and peering into the future to see if he will murder once more. But expert psychiatric and psychological predictions of violence at best reach the level of chance. That is, with Richard Winkler and with so many other cases, it would be far more practical and economical, and just as effective, if we simply tossed a coin and said, "Heads, he's dangerous; tails, he's not."

The public believes that the criminally insane can be successfully treated. With some exceptions, that is a myth. Richard Winkler's progress through the psycholegal system is a microcosm of the twists and turns in social mental health policy resulting from the new laws. At first, he seemed to function in an exemplary way — more as one of the staff than a patient. A skilled handyman, he made extra money doing favors and odd jobs for the Central Islip staff, and for over two years he had a full-time paid position at the local golf course. Every couple of years, Winkler pressed his petition to be released but was always turned down. He had the run of the hospital, until New York State tightened the reins on all criminal patients in the wake of Adam Berwid's murder of his wife. Winkler felt his rights had been violated. He was betrayed and enraged. The twinkle in his eyes was replaced by a steely coldness as he angrily confronted hospital staff regarding the loss of freedom of movement. He began to get into fights with other patients and once threatened to kill one of them.

When Winkler realized that the process of regaining his freedoms would be long and arduous, he took a more expedient course of action. In February 1986, he walked away from the hospital while on a grounds pass. He headed for Tulsa, Oklahoma, the home of Oral Roberts University, where he set himself up in a small apartment and looked for work. Because he used his real name, Winkler was easily traced by police and funneled back to the Mid-Hudson Psychiatric Center. Again, Winkler cleaned up his act. He became polite and ingratiating. Within a year, staff doctors petitioned to transfer him to a civil hospital because they deemed him no longer dangerous. "He has been praised as a sociable, helpful, energetic, and industrious man who has been accorded employment privileges," read the forensic committee's report. Although during the interview Winkler refused to discuss disemboweling the Reverend Schonberg Setzer, the doctors wrote, "He was, all in all, a friendly person." Winkler himself had no desire to leave Mid-Hudson and be returned to Central Islip, which he considered an intolerable prison after the changes in the law had restricted his freedoms. The civil hospital had no amenities and made it harder for him to win points toward eventual release. Moreover, there were more seriously damaged mentally ill people in residence there — people too ill even to be able to commit a crime. When speaking of this to me on one occasion, he echoed the sentiments of most criminal patients about "just laying up in a civil hospital. I have no desire to go back to that horror."

Winkler was right to complain about the miserable conditions of the mental hospitals he'd been confined to. Little has changed since the days of the snake-pit asylum, when mentally ill persons were not considered fully human. It is an inescapable irony that confining mental patients in surroundings that make most prisons seem like vacation resorts is considered more merciful than "punishing" them. Although their conditions are better than those of civil hospitals, most maximum-security mental hospitals are essentially penitentiaries run by doctors, nurses, and attendants, and lack the funding and the amenities of real prisons. Ask any experienced criminal where he would rather serve time, and he'll choose jail over a psychiatric hospital. Although the politicians and prosecutors would like the public, the media, and the juries to forget this fact, after the verdict the truly insane do not just walk. What they usually get is a one-way ticket to a decaying, substandard, poorly staffed Devil's Island.

In 1980, with a fresh Ph.D. in clinical psychology and a background in law enforcement, I was appointed director of the Social Skills Unit at Creedmoor Psychiatric Center. Creedmoor, at the outer limits of New York City, was once one of the largest asylums in the United States, warehousing more than 6,500 mentally ill persons. Now it was facing a shrinking budget and expanding population of criminally insane and dangerously violent patients, while at the same time grappling to meet the state's new procedures. The scandalous proceedings I encountered there were, I discovered, true not just of my facility and of New York State but of mental hospitals nationwide. I would alter forever my idea of what it meant — and should mean — to rehabilitate the criminally insane.

Euphemistically dubbed the Social Skills Unit, the treatment program at the fifty-bed lockup at Creedmoor was designed solely to prevent patients from assaulting and killing each other. It became the downstate holding pen funneling the criminally insane who had been deemed less dangerous from the maximum-security hospital at Mid-Hudson into New York's downstate civil mental hospitals. I had been promised a generous budget to hire qualified staff, upgrade existing staff skills and salaries, provide safe restraint training, make capital improvements, and bolster security.

Within the necrotic mental health bureaucracy, this seemed too good to be true. It was. The increased funding appeared on paper but never left the director's office and certainly never made its way to the ward. The extra staff, mandated by the state, proved as phantasmagoric as the other support services we were promised. The secure unit, as it was soon called, was a tragic misnomer. No one, neither patients nor staff, enjoyed even a normal measure of security over his possessions or physical safety. As more and more employees went out on leave as a result of injuries sustained in re-straining violent patients, we generally ran with a ratio of eight violent patients to one staff member. Eventually, only the female staff members remained fit for duty; the males had a higher casu-alty rate from patient incidents. If a patient got hurt, the staff member would face suspension pending an investigation of pa-tient abuse. In the prisons I had seen, there was nothing to match the uncontrolled danger and violence of this ward.

The unit became the dumping ground for all kinds of difficult patients — the severely regressed, the organically brain-damaged, psychopathic killers, criminals, and drug addicts. Among our criminal patients was Billy, who had stolen a car and killed three elderly women when he lost control of the vehicle and jumped the curb. One day he tore down the curtains in the day hall and poked out another patient's eye with the metal rod because he was "bothering" Billy for a cigarette. Nothing happened. How could Billy be further reprimanded or restrained? Billy was already in hell, and there was nobody looking out for the other patient. Years later, after the unit had been disbanded, I met Billy at a diner in the hospital neighborhood. "Hi, Dr. Kirwin," he said, beaming, greeting me in his gruff voice. "I got grounds privileges now. I'm cured." His eyes were glazed and he walked with that pe-culiar gait known throughout mental hospitals as the Thorazine shuffle.

Sixty-two-year-old Arthur had never committed a criminal act in his life, the last forty-five years of which had transpired within the walls of a mental hospital. Arthur was mute and atavistic, the type of regressed schizophrenic whose behavior seems more animal than human. He ate with his hands, did not respond to people, and defecated and urinated on himself. No amount of psychotropic medication was ever able to budge Arthur from his primitive state. We had inherited Arthur on this forgotten back ward because he was dirty and ugly and because no one else wanted to bother with him anymore. Mostly he went his silent way, dunking tea bags in the urinal and sucking on them all day. One day, a nurse pulled the string dangling out of Arthur's mouth to remove the tea bag. It wriggled to the floor — a mouse. Clearly, Arthur belonged where he could be protected from harm. On this ward, Arthur became a punching bag. I feared for the old man's life.

Ali, a usually docile, hugely muscular young man nicknamed for his resemblance to the champion boxer, frequently went on unpredictable rampages. It would take eight men to restrain him and tie him in a "camisole" — the hospital euphemism for a straitjacket. Finally, Ali ripped the canvas straitjacket to shreds and smashed out of the padded seclusion room, ripping a foot-thick steel door off the hinges. Another patient, an intravenous drug abuser, deliberately cut himself in a fit of rage and menaced patients and staff with his blood, smearing it on doorknobs and eating utensils. Those who had actually been judged criminally insane were usually the most manageable of the lot. Generally, they were extremely intent on obtaining more privileges and eventual release and were more than a little frightened by the violent, lost souls who surrounded them.

All my attempts to obtain relief for the dangerous and inhumane situation were in vain. The hospital director, who was later dismissed for Medicaid fraud and faced deportation, informed me that the funding promised was not available. Suspicions abounded that it was siphoned off by the director for his personal needs. Corrections officer Frank Muccio, a Sylvester Stallone look-alike and a veteran of prison riots at Rikers Island and Attica, offered to help train the staff in safe and humane restraint techniques. While he was demonstrating nonviolent holds, a rampaging patient sent a row of metal lockers crashing through the walls and down on the employees. The patient, George, a punch-drunk ex-prizefighter, continued hurling broken pieces of dayroom furniture through the TV screen and windows. After only two hours on the unit, Muccio left, aghast, muttering, "You guys should be armed. Anything less is suicide."

"Just because they call me crazy doesn't mean that I'm stupid," Jim Hatchett would tell me, with a jovial grin. A bullnecked and amazingly strong man, Hatchett was much in demand; he provided the staff with protection from the assaults of other patients. His goon squad kept even the most violent and unpredictable patient in line — for a price. No one really knew why Hatchett had wound up in Creedmoor. He had a minor criminal record and had done some light time, mostly for barroom assaults. Hatchett had a short fuse when he was drinking; now he seemed to have retreated to the secure unit to dry out and rest for a while. Yet Hatchett, for all his charm, was one of those impulsively hostile and dangerous antisocial types who work a dysfunctional mental health system to their own advantage and, in the long term, cause the most damage to the community. Once his psychiatric condition had been somehow established, he had virtual carte blanche to commit additional crimes with the assurance that if he was caught his acts would also be excused by mental illness.

Only someone who has spent day after day in the shadow of madness in a psychiatric hospital can understand the symbiosis that occurs between the staff members and the patients they manage, from the Jim Hatchetts to the Arthurs with a mouse in their mouth. At its best, the bond suggests the kind of care that can exist between human beings. More typically, as in the secure unit, the staff and patients rely on each other simply for survival. As conditions deteriorated, Hatchett became increasingly disgruntled. The influx of street types from Mid-Hudson started to cut into the operations he was running on the unit. He had competition for king of the hill. Drugs and alcohol began to appear on the wards; there were fights about money and cigarettes; female patients were smuggled into the dorms. One patient, Cookie, a six foot five inch hermaphrodite, began having sex with both patients and staff. She was flamboyantly histrionic and would play patients off against each other in jealous triangles. One day Hatchett and Cookie got into a spat over some cans of soda in the token store. Hatchett was livid; he slammed Cookie against a stack of soda crates. All of his frustrations were channeled into rage so blind that he began to lash out at everyone in his path. He jumped the psychologist and began banging his head on the tile floor. He flung a recreation worker against an iron grate with such force that the metal ripped through his cheek. It took eight security officers to restrain Hatchett. The psychologist was beaten unconscious; the recreation worker required almost thirty stitches to close the gaping wound in his face.

Both patients and staff, white with fear, looked to me to do something. Hatchett, calm now, and remorseful, sat in my office, begging to be taken away and sent to jail. The director was adamant: Hatchett was a mental patient under his supervision and he would not have the police nosing about on the hospital grounds. Such incidents were internal matters. The recreation worker and the psychologist, who was still hospitalized with head injuries, pressed charges of assault. Still, the police would not execute the warrant if the director would not permit them on the hospital grounds. I called Al Annenberg, the director of the forensic bureau for the Queens district attorney's office, and assured him that Hatchett was competent; I had convened a hasty forensic committee composed of the two ward psychiatrists and a psychologist to evaluate Hatchett's current mental state and his understanding of the situation. Al got the warrant for Hatchett's arrest, but he warned that Hatchett would have to show up at the precinct and turn himself in.

Over a cup of coffee, psychiatrist Clarice Donaldson and I mapped out for Hatchett his options and the procedure. His hands were trembling and sweat was streaming down his face, but he began to feel relieved. Packing a few personal belongings and saying an emotional good-bye to his dormmates and staff, he

walked out to the loading dock of the building, where I was waiting for him in my car. I knew that among all my other seat-of-the-
pants interventions the unauthorized transport of a patient
off-grounds in my personal vehicle was the least of my problems,
although technically it could have cost me my job. In the state of
permanent siege under which the unit operated, a job seemed
nothing compared with someone's life.

Hatchett was a perfect gentleman. He laughed and smiled on
the ride to the station house, jumped out to open the car door for
me, and spoke clearly and cooperatively with the detectives. He
later wrote me glowingly from prison. "Thanks for what you did
for me. I am much happier here. And thanks for the ride in your
red Mustang. It was fun."

It was only a matter of time before someone would be killed on
this unit. Broken and defeated, I and the entire professional staff
tendered our resignation from the unit en masse. Now, reassigned
to work as assistant director of administration, I chaired the hospital's Patient Abuse Committee. This became the center of a
controversy when a straitjacketed patient named Roberto Vanegas was strangled to death by an attendant trying to restrain
him. The attendant first sat on his chest, then struck him in the
throat with a blackjack, crushing his larynx. Even though nurses
and ward staff knew that Vanegas's heart had stopped, they made
no effort to administer CPR. The secure unit was closed. A massive investigation was instituted. The hospital director and deputy
directors were dismissed. I was asked to remain in the new administration but couldn't countenance what I saw as continuing
abuses. It was beyond me to make a difference. Vanegas was not
the first, nor, sadly, the last patient to be beaten to death in a mental hospital. Nor was Creedmoor the worst hospital in the New
York State system or unusual in any way.

In my research and during my years at secure units like Creedmoor's, I have examined hundreds of highly defensive, overcon-

trolled, and rigid forensic patients. Personalities like that of Richard Winkler are quite guarded and defensive. Even before their violent crimes, they play their emotional cards close to the vest, their hostility and rage kept tightly under wraps. After they kill, they redouble their vigilance, cultivating pleasing and ingratiating personas and blatantly "faking good" on psychological tests. Once killers of this type are incarcerated as mental patients, they remain walking time bombs; yet, along with the dangerous psychopaths, they are often the ones most likely to be released from maximum-security hospitals.

In 1989 I was retained by the district attorney to examine Richard Winkler with regard to his dangerous mental illness and his application for supervised, off-grounds visits to his sister who lived a few blocks away from the Kings Park Psychiatric Center. Winkler was as charming and avuncular as I remembered him from my internship days at Central Islip. His test profile also had not changed. He remained constricted and guarded, even after more than eleven years of treatment. Winkler did not attend most of the so-called insight-oriented individual and group psychotherapy that was part of the therapeutic regime on the ward. Neither did he take psychotropic medication. He went his own way, worked at the power plant, and took meals in his room away from the other patients. Yet his hospital record was still replete with positive staff notations, all consistent with his desire to present himself as trusting, adaptive, and accommodating. Winkler was hard to get to know. His preoccupation with religion and his transcendent experience of being "born again" served as a smoke screen under which he could conceal his anger and distrust. So scrupulous was Winkler in editing his responses for objectionable content that he declined to answer the true-false MMPI test question "I would rather win than lose a game." "I am not competitive," Winkler, a former golf pro, told me. He smiled. "It doesn't matter whether I win or lose." Any golfer will tell you how suspect that answer is.

Though this hostile, overcontrolled, defensive man was resistant to any meaningful therapeutic change, he was capable of making one calculated strategic alteration in his behavior: he had learned when it was appropriate to talk about his religious beliefs and when it worked to his detriment. Since most of the psychiatrists on his release committee were either Hindus, Moslems, or other non-Christians, they could not easily frame the scripturally based questions that would push Winkler's buttons. He did not bring up religion until he cautiously asked if I was a "Christian" and had "read the scriptures." I told him that my mother was a Southern Baptist and even though I had been raised a Catholic I had read the Bible. He quizzed me. Did I know about Jesus casting out devils? Did I believe in Satan? Had I been tempted by false prophets? Richard Winkler was clearly more comfortable asking me the questions than answering them himself. I had decided to take the therapeutic tack of "joining" him, so I tried to make my answers consistent with the elements of Winkler's religious delusions. Almost immediately, he became so euphoric, expansive, and manically pressured in his speech that he could no longer keep his mind on the test questions. He cried tears of joy, shouted "Praise the Lord," and grabbed me and hugged me impulsively. After he was reassured of my faith, Winkler seemed less reluctant to discuss the particulars and motivations of the crime he had committed so long ago. He confided that God, as the highest authority, did not obey the rules of society. "Sometimes," Winkler explained, "as with the biblical story of Abraham, who was commanded to sacrifice his beloved son, Isaac, God asks of his servants things that cannot be comprehended by man." Satan, Winkler believed, was a powerful and real personage who prowled the earth in search of souls. He expressed no remorse for his crime, because he still truly believed he was obeying God's command. Winkler offered as proof positive of the minister's pact with the devil the fact that Setzer's wife remarried in January 1977, just two months after his death.

After thirteen years, Winkler was able to clearly describe his Thanksgiving Day vision of the gates of hell and his instructions to kill the minister. He believed he was again called by God when he escaped and went to Oral Roberts University in 1986. Recently, he reported, he had been hearing signs from the sky that might be indicating God's readiness to call him again. Winkler's speech grew solemn and hushed. He leaned over and practically whispered in my ear. "I heard the wind rustle through the tree leaves the other day, and I looked up into the sun and heard a voice call my name, 'Richard.'"

At the conclusion of the examination, Winkler reached out to clasp both my hands in his. "God bless you," he intoned. "I know you will be guided to do the right thing."

At the hearing I did do the right thing. I testified that nothing really had changed for Winkler; he still suffered from the same religious delusions that had triggered the original crime. I expressed concern that, once in the community, he would seek out fundamentalist religious groups, or be sought out by proselytizing groups like Jehovah's Witnesses, against whom he had evolved paranoid beliefs.

As I left the courtroom, Winkler was standing outside with his sister and brother-in-law. I averted my glance as I passed by him, almost ashamed at what I had said about him on the witness stand. He was, after all, such a sympathetic old man. His steel-blue eyes shot out sparks like flint. "Mighty fanciful of you, Doc!" he said, laughing sardonically, shaking his head. "Mighty fanciful!" I shuddered at the sudden revelation of the other Richard Winkler. The Office of Mental Health withdrew its application for extended privileges for Winkler. But the kindly old man would be back.

On March 14, 1980, Dennis Sweeney, a courageous 1960s civil rights activist, walked into the Associated Press Building on Rockefeller Plaza in New York City, took the elevator to the ninth-floor law offices of Laden & Sherman, and shot Representative Allard Lowenstein dead. He then walked out to the waiting room, put the gun down on a desk, and announced what he had done. Sweeney was carted off to Bellevue Psychiatric Hospital for evaluation. Political commentators and journalists thrashed around for the murderer's motives. Some framed the killing in purely political terms: Sweeney had almost worshiped Lowenstein until they had a falling out over the ideology of the civil rights movement. There was a fearful symmetry in Sweeney's desperate act ending the career of a onetime radical like Lowenstein. Some feared that Sweeney was a hired assassin eliminating one of the prime proponents of American liberalism. Everyone remembered Dennis Sweeney as what *Village Voice* journalist Teresa Carpenter called a "perennial youth endowed with mythic qualities of bravery and idealism." They wondered what had transpired in the ensuing twenty years to so twist Sweeney's mind.

After his arrest, Sweeney never opened up to his doctors. Yet unlike the more difficult-to-diagnose murderers like Winkler and Caputo — whose psychoses seemed to evaporate upon acquittal — Dennis Sweeney was a classic paranoid schizophrenic. After his quick rise in the civil rights movement, Sweeney soon began a downward drift, until, by the end of the 1960s, his wife of one year had divorced him and he was experimenting with LSD. By 1971, suffering from delusions and hallucinations, he was admitted to an Oregon psychiatric hospital. In the ten years between his psychotic breakdown and the Lowenstein murder, Sweeney experienced increased social isolation, paranoid ideas that people were plotting against him, and voices inside his head that constantly tormented and harassed him. In a routine delusion shared by thousands of other paranoids, he believed that transmitters had been placed in his teeth by which the voices communicated to him. In 1979 Sweeney suffered a serious head injury from a pump jack accident at the construction site where he was working. While he was recuperating, he was shaken by the news of his stepfather's sudden death. For the next two weeks, Sweeney became obsessed by the belief that Allard Lowenstein, his onetime mentor, was responsible for many recent world tragedies, including plane crashes — and, more personally, his stepfather's death. It was this delusion that drove Sweeney to purchase the gun and confront Lowenstein in his office. His main intention was to convince Lowenstein to cease these destructive activities; the gun was a backup in case the congressman refused.

Since his insanity acquittal, nobody much had bothered about Dennis Sweeney at the maximum-security mental hospital where he was confined. Unlike Winkler, he had accrued no fan club among the staff. While psychopaths and some seriously disordered individuals can be disarmingly friendly and charming, the hallmark of schizophrenia is deficiency in relating to people. Paranoids such as Sweeney are characteristically withdrawn, reclusive, distrustful, irritable, and sometimes just downright nasty. They are simply not fun to be around, even for other psychiatric patients.

No one from the hospital treatment team had suggested that Sweeney should be evaluated for increased privileges or transfer to a nonsecure setting. Sweeney had not even gotten to first base in the system after nine years. His hospital record was peppered with the handwritten entries of staff: "Socialization has not improved." "Spontaneous interaction is poor." "Interaction with people continues to be limited." The progress notes described Sweeney as rigid, sarcastic, and possessed of a "desire to feel that he is superior." Many hospital "progress notes" documented his arguments or misunderstandings with other patients and staff: "Altercation with employee." "Sweeney will bully other patients — he always has to be right." "Strong desire to control others' actions." "Has a tendency to taunt patients." Sweeney would not win a popularity contest — and that was often the single most important component in initiating a bid for freedom — but in all fairness, neither did he indicate active psychosis, hallucinations, or delusions. His psychosis had managed to stabilize without the benefit of psychotropic medication. He was possessed only of the mild suspicion that a fellow patient was eating all the chunks out of the soup and leaving the liquid behind.

In February 1989 Sweeney petitioned for transfer to a nonsecure facility. But his case, even after all these years, still had a high political profile. Before and after killing Representative Lowenstein, he had made threats to another ex–civil rights worker who was fearful of his safety if Sweeney were ever to be released. This put pressure on the authorities to keep Sweeney locked in a psych ward, far upstate. I was retained by the Manhattan district attorney's office to evaluate Dennis Sweeney.

It is a pleasant ride from New York City to Mid-Hudson Forensic Psychiatric Center, which is situated in a bucolic valley away from any urban sprawl and, except for the halo of razor-wire fencing, looks like any other WPA-era redbrick and sandstone mental hospital. Despite Mid-Hudson's "maximum-security" designation, security and regimentation were nowhere near as tight as I had experienced at county jails or even minimum-security correctional centers. I could imagine that it would not be a very difficult feat to escape from this place, except for one problem: Walking down a desolate, two-lane blacktop highway through abandoned farmland, where would a runaway patient go? Who among the mostly local people who traveled the road would stop to pick up a hitchhiker outside this place? In its own way, Mid-Hudson was an agrarian Devil's Island.

Sweeney was trim, well groomed, and incredibly boyish for his forty-six years, with the same clean-cut Ivy League look he sported in the hippyish 1960s. Although he was extremely courteous and cooperative, there was something uneasy, even evasive, in Sweeney's demeanor. He avoided looking me in the eye, generally staring straight ahead at the blank wall, and seemed relieved whenever he did not have to interact with me directly. Throughout the nearly four hours I spent with him in that stuffy little room, Sweeney seemed more like some 1960s icon than a real, functioning person. On the tests I gave him, Sweeney was so defensive, so reluctant to admit to even the most minor flaw, that he succeeded in "faking good" — blocking out all vestiges of pathology. Although he might have had a conscious strategy to advance his case for release by throwing the tests, I sensed the results might also be attributable to his highly rigid, emotionally flat, and uninsightful personality.

Despite his blanket attempt to deny any personal inadequacies, tendencies toward mental disorder, or trouble controlling his temper, Sweeney still presented the test results of a highly defended paranoid personality who — even with his psychosis in remission — was still severely limited in his ability to cope with life. He was no longer experiencing delusions or hallucinations, but he was extremely fragile psychologically, with a poor tolerance for even the normal stresses and pressures of daily life. During our interview, Sweeney, as if reciting a prepared script, described himself as being "out of touch with the human community," "intolerant," and "not having patience or real compassion for people." Although these self-observations were accurate, they did not appear to come from any process of reflection or insight, nor were they infused with any remorse. It was almost as if he were parroting what was written over and over again in the doctors' entries in his chart.

I organized my forensic interview of Sweeney around three questions, to assess his self-knowledge and ability to manage his stress and symptoms: What are your ultimate future plans? How have you changed for the better — what's different about you now from the time of the crime? What do you see, in terms of your adjustment, as a dangerous or problematic situation you should avoid? Sweeney's responses all started out as logical, coherent, and relevant. However, the more he talked the more he rambled, tripping over details until he lost the thread of the question. Eventually, his answers manifested that overelaborate, digressive, highly metaphorical, and idiosyncratic style characteristic of schizophrenic language and thought.

Sweeney remained the clinical picture of a chronic paranoid

schizophrenic in what psychologists call the residual, or final-stage, phase of the disease. He no longer experienced the break with reality that marked the active phase of his psychosis and his murder of Lowenstein. Although he was not cured and could not even pass as normal, Sweeney was at least "burned out," which tends to be the case with schizophrenics as they approach middle age. There was no denying that Sweeney still suffered from a mental illness and that he needed to be kept in a hospital. But would it be risky to transfer him to a locked ward in a regular civil hospital without guards and razor wire? Neither I nor any of the other experts who examined Sweeney could find a trace of the delusions that prompted him to murder his former mentor. Nor had they surfaced in over nine years. After so much time, it was extremely improbable, given the general course of his type of schizophrenia, that they would boil upward again. The extreme stressors of his pump jack head injury and the sudden death of his stepfather, which also triggered his attack, were not the sort of confluence of events that would happen again for Sweeney — at least not in a civil hospital, which was as far as he would get. Besides, no one was suggesting that Sweeney would ever hit the streets on his own again.

Despite the agreement of the experts, the original sentencing judge would not approve a status change for Sweeney. This paranoid killer remains a political hot potato, though he does remain intent on gaining more freedoms. I suspect, however, that he will be counting the chunks in his soup at a maximum-security hospital for a long time to come.

Certainly many criminally insane psychotics try to "fake good" on their exams. But currently, about 25 percent of those pleading insanity can be thought of as having malingered or faked psychosis on psychiatric examinations. The courts must try to decide who is dissembling before the verdict is reached; afterward, a mental institution's doctors and staff must insure that a fair and just distinction is made between the truly mad and the truly bad.

In most fields of medicine, pathology can be objectively observed and measured; but the psychopathology of mental patients depends largely on the patients' self-reported symptoms. It is much harder to fake a disease like tuberculosis than it is to fake hearing voices. Psychopaths who have feigned mental illness and won acquittal are especially prone to the psychological two-step — initially putting their worst foot forward (faking bad) to escape criminal prosecution, and then putting their best foot forward (faking good) to obtain release from hospital confinement. This is the most terrifying glitch in the system. Those who work it best are the very people who truly warrant criminal conviction and jail. Once they manage to infiltrate the mental health system, they become wolves among sheep — working the doctors, other patients, and ward staff like so many nefarious Sergeant Bilkos, and eventually securing release. They are also the criminals who are more likely to commit violent crimes again.

Louis Kahan, the former marine cook who won an insanity acquittal based on a designer defense of post-traumatic stress disorder in the rape and murder of a young Vietnamese girl, progressed through the forensic mental health maze in a record four years and three months from the time of his crime. Kahan was bright, articulate, and seemingly sensitive and introspective. In the forensic unit at Creedmoor, filled with a rogue's gallery of the brutish, the loutish, and the violent, Kahan stood out as being reachable and worth saving. Dr. Richard Quinn, the psychiatrist on the ward, took Kahan under his wing and to his heart. A proponent of the intense and controversial Rosen method of psychotherapy, in which the doctor colludes with the patient's delusions, Dr. Quinn devoted long and arduous hours to rehabilitating his charge. He practically adopted Kahan, becoming the unconditionally loving and supportive father figure Kahan never had. Soon Kahan obtained off-grounds privileges. Earnest and altruistic to a fault, Dr.

Quinn would take him to movies, to restaurants, shopping in the community. He introduced Kahan to his sister-in-law, a recovered mental patient. Kahan became friendly with her; they would talk on the phone and occasionally go out together. Soon, however, Kahan grew more persistent in his attentions to her. One day, Kahan visited her at her home, and an ugly quarrel broke out. She claimed that he shoved her and roughed her up, breaking a music box that had been given to her by her boyfriend. Assault charges were pressed and Kahan's privileges were lifted. He wound up assigned to the locked secure unit, where I was the chief of service.

Kahan became the darling of the staff. It was so rare that they got to deal with a lucid patient. He began an affair with a shift supervisor, a rather statuesque transsexual with a torch singer voice. She had been an outstanding employee and the mainstay of the direct care team, but once she fell for Kahan things started to slip on the ward: there were fights, accusations of favoritism, rumors about drugs being smuggled in, sexual trysts. A female patient on Kahan's old ward named him as the father of her baby boy. The daughter of a prominent psychiatrist, she had tried repeatedly to kill her father, once by scalding him with boiling water, finally by lunging at him with a bread knife. She was found not guilty by reason of insanity and sent to Creedmoor, where she grew morbidly obese, claiming for nearly six years that she was pregnant. After a while, the staff did not even bother to investigate her allegations. When she complained that Kahan had raped her from behind as she bent over a slop sink in the maintenance room, no one took heed — until she went into labor. Kahan was indignant. He denied having anything to do with this patient and certainly did not want responsibility for any baby. He refused to speak to the adoption authorities when they came to the ward.

Surrounded by the truly violent and mad, Kahan, whose reality testing was acute, sensed the danger and wanted out. At his hearing, I testified that he no longer suffered from a mental illness requiring hospitalization and treatment. In my heart I believed him to be one of the most cunning psychopaths I had ever met — but Louis Kahan, acquitted rapist and murderer, could not be detained in a psychiatric hospital in the absence of mental illness. Kahan sat in the court, dignified and subdued, sporting a gray polyester suit with flashy red stitching that fit his bulky frame a little too snugly. I recognized it as a 1970s castoff of my husband's, which I had donated to the hospital thrift shop. In this theater of the absurd, I was not only writing the lines for Kahan's release; I was also supplying the wardrobe.

Psychopaths can work the mental health system to their advantage, but the system on its own can be careless toward the psychotic inmates in its care. After she found her husband had a girlfriend, Ameenah Abdus-Salaam heard the voice of Allah ordering her to sacrifice her children by throwing them from the window of their tenth-floor apartment. Her bizarre and psychotic behavior after her arrest and the fact that she quickly recompensated after being medicated with psychotropic medication had led both prosecution and defense experts to agree that Ameenah was suffering from a schizophreniform disorder interfering with her capacity to perceive reality and know right from wrong at the time of the crime. Six months later, exactly a year after the death of her daughter and the critical injuries to her son (who was still undergoing extensive orthopedic surgery and rehabilitation), the hospital staff at Kirby Forensic Psychiatric Center petitioned the courts for Ameenah's release on the grounds that she no longer suffered from a dangerous mental illness. I was called to examine Ameenah again. Would she continue to take her medication unsupervised? Would she relapse? Would she be dangerous.

The treatment team, led by a South African psychologist, had an intense, almost emotional attachment to Ameenah. They were vociferous in lobbying for her release, believing her to be in total remission from her psychotic episode. Yet notes by other hospital staff described Ameenah as lacking in insight and manifesting poor judgment. That was certainly apparent to me when she cheerfully discussed her plans to get out of the hospital and return with her children to the same apartment where the tragedy occurred. She had strong denial about the trauma that might be involved for her surviving children. Her family brought food and gifts to Ameenah, but no relative had ever chosen to be present at a treatment team meeting where Ameenah's problems, progress, and treatment were discussed. It was as if everyone, including the treatment team, was trying to forget that Ameenah had killed one of her children and maimed another just twelve months before.

Ameenah, with her round, cherubic face, diffident manner, and nunlike Muslim garb, was dramatically different from the low-functioning, actively psychotic, often violent and antisocial types frequently treated at Kirby. The hospital approvingly cited her lack of violence and aggressiveness and her overall good behavior as psychological progress. But that opinion struck me as exactly wrong. Never in her entire life had Ameenah acted out violently or aggressively. Even her crime was not an act of aggression but a psychotically deluded attempt to save her beloved children. Ameenah Abdus-Salaam may have been outwardly demure, obsequious, and compliant, but inwardly she was seething with hostile, resentful impulses she could not express. Her rigid overcontrol gave her no inner thermostat with which she could regulate her emotions. With no ability to discharge tension, Ameenah remained significantly at risk for again being overwhelmed by the stresses that awaited her in her daily life.

In our interview, Ameenah glossed over her future plans for reunion with her children, her education, and her career. With the demeanor of a lovesick teenager, she told me she had been reading the autobiography of rock singer Tina Turner. "I got a lot of inspiration about her life with Ike. . . . I hate my husband, but he is very handsome." She continued dreamily. "I will divorce him in the mosque. I can, after forty days of sexual abstinence." Ameenah fell silent. She seemed transfixed. "I wish I knew what he was thinking."

I was startled by the depth of her ambivalence toward her husband. "Would you ever want to get back together?"

"Oh, yes," she affirmed, without hesitation. "But we would have to start dating again from the beginning and try to get romance back. Here" — she scribbled on a piece of paper — "his girlfriend's name, address, and phone number. Call her and talk with her."

This was another Ameenah I was seeing, suddenly strong, in control, defiant.

According to the plans she had worked out with the treatment team, Ameenah was going to complete her college education and pursue a full-time career in health care while at the same time assuming full responsibility, financial and otherwise, for her children. She would also go about the business of formally divorcing her husband. I was stunned by the tragedy such grandiose intentions invited. The team was sending Ameenah straight back into the situation that had broken her a year before.

My comparison of Ameenah's recent, very normal MMPI profile with one from five months before revealed a difference so remarkable as to be almost impossible. Ameenah had not admitted to even the slightest psychological problem. As always with attempts to throw the test results by faking good or faking bad, Ameenah had overplayed her hand. She had retracted the admissions she had made even five months earlier, changing some very basic factual answers from true to false, such as, "I have not been well during the past few years"; "I had nightmares"; "I have done many things which I regretted"; "I had periods of time in which I couldn't take care of things." Ameenah, extremely defensive and eager to get out, had reinvented her history.

Although she was not successful in her attempt at release, I knew that it would only be a matter of time before the treatment team would prevail. She was sympathetic and gentle — and nobody had bothered to ask her the questions that would elicit the chilling answers I had received. I am comforted only in knowing that with every day of their mother's confinement, Ameenah's children are growing older and more able to protect themselves.

In the five years since I had testified against his receiving off-grounds privileges, Richard Winkler found himself moved from ward to ward at Kings Park Psychiatric Center as the hospital shrank under the cutbacks in funding. But he had also succeeded in obtaining escorted furlough privileges. Accompanied by a hospital attendant, he made a weekly visit to his sister and brother-in-law, who lived a few blocks from the hospital. Now, in 1995, Winkler wanted unescorted furloughs and weekly overnight visits to his sister's home. Once again our paths would cross.

I was shocked at how desolate and deteriorated the grounds had grown since I last examined Winkler. Situated on a beautifully wooded tract overlooking Long Island Sound, the hospital once even had its own yacht club for doctors and other staff. But New York, like most states, was cutting funds and staffing for the care of the mentally ill and working to deinstitutionalize as many patients as possible. The policy of deinstitutionalization in the Reagan years had sent thousands of homeless schizophrenics into the street in the name of community care. No one wants to see a mental hospital booming, but this ghost town was even more ominous. With psychotropic drugs no panacea, and no new miracle cures on the horizon, the number of severely mentally ill has remained the same. In lower New York State alone, some fourteen thousand mentally ill people have been released onto the streets in the last twenty years. Their unsupervised public presence has increased the crime rate dramatically — mostly because they have been victims of crime, although they can become the perpetrators of bizarre and violent acts that leave all of us feeling terrified and helpless.

I walked into the lobby. There were patients milling around but no staff at the reception desk. I made my way to a locked ward and rang the bell. Patients crowded to the viewing window, pressing their faces to the glass to glimpse the visitor. Finally I persuaded one of the more lucid ones to go rouse a staff member to direct me to Richard Winkler's ward. He gave me a big smile and handshake, even though he knew full well that five years ago I had set him back in his quest for privileges. When I asked him about it, he smiled and rambled on about my opinion being "the Lord's will." He told me he had given up "name it and claim it" religion and did not expect God to do his bidding exactly according to his wishes. Listening to him, I found it still so characteristic of Winkler to say whatever was expedient to wriggle out of difficult face-to-face situations and avoid disapproval and criticism.

In 1991 Winkler was treated for an outbreak of herpes at the hospital infirmary. He became loud, assaultive, and very paranoid, but he was calmed down without serious incident. Otherwise, he hadn't acted out since his escape a decade before. And now, at age sixty-seven, he had honed his act. Missing was his habit of inserting religious exclamations into his conversation. Nevertheless, Winkler's pervasive style of defensiveness, his perpetual "faking good," continued to manifest itself on his MMPI. In eighteen years of treatment in a state mental hospital, Winkler had managed to change very little. MMPI profiles of the average person show marked changes as the person is followed through the stages of a lifetime. What was remarkable about Winkler was his stubborn resistance to therapeutic change. Basically, Winkler had been warehoused all those years — in psychological quarantine.

Suddenly, in the spring of 1992, Winkler had agreed to take psychotropic medication. Although no medicine can change underlying personality structure, the prescription seemed to take the edge off Winkler's anxiety and reduce his need for overcontrol. He no longer really seemed to care whether he ever got discharged or not. When his mother and stepfather died, Winkler seemed to lose his desire for eventual release. Being in the hospital for so long can "make the outside social structure very stressful," he said, surprising me with his insight. "Living conditions here are great! I feel like one of the guys at the power plant. I'm living like a normal person." The system had finally worn old Winkler down. I almost felt sorry for him. Had he not been successful in his insanity defense, he most likely would have been paroled from prison nearly ten years before. At last, Winkler was content to stay in the hospital. Like the Prisoner of Chillon, he had learned to love his captivity and was afraid of freedom. In mental health jargon, his very personality had become institutionalized.

This time I saw enough improvement to change my opinion about the risk of Richard Winkler. Outlining six conditions of this status change, including close monitoring of medication and the involvement of his sister in treatment planning, I did not feel that he continued to suffer from a dangerous mental illness. The assistant district attorney didn't resist my conclusion; the county was under severe budget constraints, and she didn't feel that this case was political enough to waste a lot of resources on. Winkler's case had never gotten much media coverage.

Winkler's petition sat for another year, at which point I insisted on seeing him again before reiterating my previous opinion about his leaving the hospital unescorted. But soon there would be no hospital. Kings Park Psychiatric Center would close in November 1996. After the interview, I needed to review his recent hospital records. Although there were many severely regressed, even physically disabled patients wandering around the ward, I saw not a single staff member. I found my way to the chart room and located the records I needed. Suddenly I heard the clang of a bit key turning in the lock. I raced across the room to try the door, crying out, "I'm inside!" but there was no answer. I heard the steel ward door slam shut.

I was locked in. Fortunately there was a phone on the desk. After minutes of interminable ringing, the operator picked up and I explained my quandary; she said she would send staff. Ten minutes elapsed before a pretty and plump woman barely out of her teens cautiously opened the door. "Sorry, Doctor, I didn't know you were inside here," she told me. She was embarrassed, tense, and frightened. It was only her second day on the job. The nurse administrator of the unit soon joined us. She complained that mixed in among the geriatric, severely psychotic patients on this tiny and badly ventilated ward were fifteen criminally insane patients, most of them murderers. Both Winkler and Gowain Tremont were in the building. She and her new employee were the only staff on duty at that time.

I don't know what will become of Richard Winkler, Gowain Tremont, or dozens more as they are shifted from the scuttled ship of Kings Park Psychiatric Center to Pilgrim State, from which Adam Berwid escaped nearly two decades ago, starting the backlash against the rights of the criminally insane. In the twenty years since I first encountered the unkind mind of Richard Winkler, we have come no closer to balancing the needs of mentally ill offenders with the safety of a public who would shut them away for good.

8

CRUEL AND UNUSUAL:
THE BACKLASH THAT BACKFIRED

Spectators thronged to the county courthouse in Mineola, New York, lining up on the steps before dawn, to gain admittance to the freak show that was the trial of Colin Ferguson. They brought portable seats so they could be comfortable as they waited. They looked like ordinary people — your neighbors or mine, if you live in a white neighborhood — but they all wore masks of fear and anger.

On a night six months before, the 1993 holiday season had just gotten under way, and the 5:33 Long Island Railroad train out of New York City's Penn Station screeched into the Merillon Avenue station packed with regular evening commuters and Christmas shoppers. A thirty-five-year-old Jamaica-born man named Colin Ferguson began firing a 9 millimeter handgun, killing seven passengers and wounding eighteen others. Muttering under his breath, Ferguson was reloading another clip when he was wrestled to the floor by three commuters. When he was arrested, Ferguson was found with 150 more rounds of ammunition and notes in his pocket describing his hatred of whites and Asians.

William Kunstler, the firebrand attorney often associated with controversial and unpopular causes and cases, agreed to represent Ferguson. His client had been caught in the act of committing the crime, in full view of a carload of witnesses; short of pleading guilty, his only resource was an insanity defense. I knew George Peck, the prosecutor on the case, to be a fair man, unusually well versed in the area of psychological defenses. But I hoped fervently he would not call on me to be an expert in the case. The climate of rage and terror at Ferguson's trial would make the trial of Joel Rifkin seem like a fellowship service. Even though I tried to avoid much of the media reporting and commentary about the case, it was hard for me not to suspect Ferguson to be a classic delusional paranoid schizophrenic. I had a hunch that if I examined him and administered psychological tests, I would uncover serious psychological pathology. Were I to conclude Ferguson's paranoid delusions were bona fide, I couldn't be of any assistance to the prosecutor. Even more than in the Rifkin case, in which I chose to be on the unpopular side on principle, I would be at risk if I participated in Ferguson's defense. Political agendas, even highly publicized ones, are benign compared to the racial issue in America. Ferguson had violated the white middle-class sanctum: he had brought violence and racial backlash across the divide from the urban ghettos to the suburban backyards. No longer could commuters doze with their heads buried in the newspapers, safe in their complacency.

Instead of claiming that his client was a paranoid schizophrenic and therefore criminally insane, Kunstler announced he would pursue an insanity defense with a designer logo: "black rage." Allegedly, Colin Ferguson had been pushed over the edge of sanity into murder by his justifiable outrage and frustration at endemic American racism. Kunstler, the consummate choreographer of socially provocative dances, was going to leave the psychological establishment on the sidelines by invoking a contrived syndrome as an excuse. Instinctively, he knew what the trial was really about.

Midway through the preparation for trial, Ferguson started to quarrel with Kunstler and his cocounsel Ronald Kuby about the proposed insanity defense. Ferguson steadfastly maintained his innocence. He was not crazy, he said. He saw a white man board the train, take his gun, and shoot at the passengers. All the other passengers saw him too, but they would not admit it; they were all out to get Ferguson because he was black. On ABC's *Nightline*, Kuby referred to Ferguson as a "delusional psychotic," a "deranged man" whose trial was fast becoming "mental health theater of the absurd." Knowing what I know about paranoids, I wasn't surprised when Kunstler and Kuby were dismissed. In his Nassau County trial, paranoid serial killer Joel Rifkin had fired his first two lawyers and severely criticized his third. Rifkin would go through several more lawyers before taking a guilty plea in his Suffolk County case. Paranoid schizophrenics are so vigilant in scanning the world around them for confirmation of trickery, betrayal, and harm that each becomes an isolated community of one, set against the entire system. It is nearly impossible for a paranoid personality like Ferguson to collaborate with a lawyer in his own defense.

As media coverage fueled the public's anger and urge for vengeance, a major issue got lost in the noise: Was Ferguson even competent to stand trial? The assessment of competency in a criminal trial process, probably the most significant mental health issue in criminal law, is largely ignored. Research has shown that for every defendant a jury finds not guilty by reason of insanity, one hundred are found incompetent to stand trial. The courts, the public, and the media have generally ignored such defendants because they are more seriously mentally impaired and they rarely commit high-profile crimes. The basic idea behind the concept of competency to stand trial is that a defendant should have enough of his wits about him to be able to participate — to understand the charges against him, the nature of the court process, and the roles of the judge, jury, prosecutors, and defense attorneys. He should have some realization of the risks he faces, and an ability to make self-protective decisions assisted by his lawyer. The question of competency has to do with fairness. Constitutional law upholds a person's right to face his accusers and mount a defense in his own behalf. A defendant whose disability interferes with this fundamental right cannot receive a fair trial.

At a pretrial hearing in December 1994, a psychiatrist and psychologist, both county employees, testified that Ferguson was "rational, free from delusions," and competent to stand trial. Judge Donald Belfi conducted his own questioning of Ferguson and also concluded that he was competent. I groaned when I read this. I believed that declaring Ferguson incompetent to stand trial — because he was so clearly delusional, paranoid, and unable to work with any lawyers in his own defense — was the outcome that would have served the interests of justice, the victims, the defendant, and the most humane instincts of society. Ferguson then could have been quietly whisked away to a maximum-security hospital to be cured of his incompetency before going to trial. Given the nature and severity of his apparent pathology, this would have taken a long time. It is also doubtful whether Ferguson in his paranoid state would have been compliant with treatment or amenable to taking psychotropic medication. By the time the matter surfaced again, some of the public outrage against his crime would have abated.

But the Ferguson trial was no longer about justice. It was about vengeance. It was about politics. Bringing this paranoid killer into the courtroom intent on punishing him and satisfying a public out for blood, the prosecutors made a travesty of the entire legal system. Because Ferguson had been judged competent to stand trial, he could — and did — exercise his constitutional right to represent himself. The fact that the trial was televised elevated it from farce to electronic freak show. Ferguson, impeccably attired and highly intelligent, opened by telling the jury that he was charged with "ninety-three counts only because it matches the year 1993. Had it been 1925, it would have been twenty-five counts." The illogic and circumstantiality of this statement — reminiscent of Joel Rifkin's illogical rationale for killing exactly seventeen prostitutes — is a first-rank symptom of schizophrenic thinking and language. Ferguson, strutting his stuff in court, eloquently and grandiosely cross-examined witnesses, asking experts such nonsensical questions as whether a bullet had been tested for drug and alcohol abuse. He tried to get the judge to subpoena President Clinton. In Ferguson's case, it might have been more merciful to haul him into the public square and slap him in the stocks while the crowds jeered and threw rotten tomatoes. It certainly would have been more honest.

All the press coverage of the Ferguson trial backfired. As the public beheld this man so clearly unable to distinguish reality from fantasy, their attitudes began to diverge from what had prevailed in other recent insanity trials. When Ferguson himself complained that he had been the victim of a "high-tech lynching" — in his grandiosity appropriating a term first used by Supreme Court nominee Clarence Thomas — the mob paused momentarily to take a look at itself. There were rumblings that the "sham" and "charade" of the Ferguson trial was yet another example of the unconscionably flawed American legal system. Ferguson, in his blundering dismissal of his legal dream team and rejection of an insanity defense, was somehow seen as being more true to his own feelings than his accusers.

Colin Ferguson was convicted on charges of weapons possession, seven counts of murder, and twenty-two counts of attempted murder and sentenced to over three hundred years in prison. At the time of sentencing, he made allusions to the recent murder behind bars of serial killer Jeffrey Dahmer — "setting the precedent for my murder in an upstate prison." Ferguson's reality testing may be flawed, but when it comes to expectations of his own safety he is right on the money. The "legal victory" of Ferguson's conviction left many people feeling hollow. In the words of *New York*

Times legal commentator Jan Hoffman, "As horrific as the crimes are, when people see someone battling for himself and he doesn't know how to do it, they feel this isn't fair."

However, this community examination of conscience was short-lived. Judge Belfi's sentencing statement addressed the implicit social need to punish Ferguson for the terrible thing he'd done and make sure that he never got out. True to the post-Hinckley backlash, the public, terrified by violent crime and fearful of the insanity defense as a way of getting away with murder, needed closure on this crime. The trial gave the public a sense of catharsis that impeded the meting out of justice. As witnessed by the heart-wrenching spectacle of the surviving victims and the families of the dead confronting and vilifying Ferguson during sentencing, it was clear that the body politic demanded a fierce and identifiable enemy. After all his bizarre delusions, Colin Ferguson was ultimately depicted as a sane, calculating, and manipulative person — which is the stereotypical portrait of mentally ill defendants provided in all high-profile insanity defense cases since the acquittal of John Hinckley. This one-size-fits-all prosecution is the backlash to the designer defense.

The fury at Ferguson is not an isolated phenomenon. An irate judge sentenced New York City subway bomber Edward Leary to ninety-four years in prison, lamenting that this maximum was too little. She described Leary as a "vengeful and self-aggrandizing man with an inflated view of his intelligence" who carefully assembled two firebombs from mayonnaise jars, kitchen timers, batteries, and flashbulbs and detonated them on two Manhattan trains. Forty-eight people (including Leary himself) were injured; fourteen were seriously burned. His lawyers had advanced a designer defense comprising a mélange of personal problems plaguing Leary: deaths in the family, the loss of his job, problems with his son, and a veritable Molotov cocktail of medications prescribed by the psychiatrist who had been treating him for depression and anxiety. Although Leary may not have suffered from the type of incapacitating psychotic illness that a M'Naghten insanity defense requires, he certainly manifested symptoms and behavior that indicated severe and perhaps mitigating emotional problems. Did he deserve the maximum sentence, more than most convicted murderers get? Or was the judge, as the defense contended, reacting in sympathy to the victims rather than following the law? Was Leary even more stringently punished because he tried to pull the wool over the public's eyes by using an insanity defense?

When John Hinckley was acquitted by reason of insanity for his attempt on the life of President Reagan, he stirred up a furor that continues to alter the application of the insanity defense. Edwin Meese, Reagan's attorney general, cashed in on the political value of espousing tough federal proposals to clamp down on abuses, real and imagined, in the insanity defense. Throughout the 1980s, almost every state plunged passionately and impulsively into reforming insanity defense statutes, making more changes than at any time since the Criminal Lunatics Act was passed in 1800. The media spurred the public outcry, perpetuating the myths that the American system of justice was being eroded by abuse of the insanity defense — by people "getting away with murder" and by a mental health system that supposedly released homicidal maniacs reflexively into the community. Reforms were designed to alleviate these presumably fearful and exaggerated abuses of the insanity defense. Yet studies show that legislators overestimate the use of the insanity defense and the number of acquittals by a factor of 400; college students overestimate them by a factor of 800, evidencing a set of misperceptions that are matched in the public at large.

Efforts have been made to analyze the realities of the insanity defense and the effect of the reforms of the law-and-order era of the 1980s. Researcher Henry J. Steadman and his colleagues have attempted in a landmark study to collect and analyze factual data on the day-to-day workings of insanity defense reform, piercing all the emotionality and politicization to collect factual data. Steadman tried, he said, to quell the "public cries of indignation about perceived abuses in the insanity defense" and open the door to genuine and informed discussion. His research, published in 1993 and spanning over six and a half years of "countless hours of work in dusty, poorly lit, and cramped record rooms in county courthouses and the basements of state mental hospitals across the United States," was funded by the National Institute of Mental Health. Yet his hard and valuable work, which should have ushered in an age of enlightenment in psycholegal circles, caused barely a ripple. As those bothered by the fate of Colin Ferguson found out, the fiery issues around the insanity defense remain as resistant to reason as ever. As legal scholar R. Moran has written, it "raises to relief and makes graphic the inherently complex and often ambiguous character of criminal responsibility." The politically expedient truth is that Americans are frightened and outraged by violent crime and their frustration at not being able to stop it. Bashing the insanity defense is universally seen as a way of getting tough on crime.

Ironically, as we all seem to abdicate responsibility for our own lives, we seem to assert that everyone else, even the mentally impaired, is responsible for his. Is this yet another symptom of our cultural denial of responsibility and projection of blame on the mentally ill offender?

In sum, insanity is a chameleon, a shape shifter, a diffuse and malleable legal concept given content by the courts, which are in turn shaped and influenced by public opinion. The 1970s was a decade of tolerance and humaneness toward mentally unstable offenders. Unfortunately, most states failed to establish a secure and modern mental health system that truly served both the treatment needs of the mentally ill defendant and the protection and safety of the general public. People were outraged at dangerous insanity defense acquittees who were released or escaped into the community only to kill again. Following John Hinckley's acquittal, the pendulum swung toward the extreme of fear and punitiveness.

Sometimes I do take satisfaction that designer defenses succeed less often than ever in the courts, as judges, media people, and juries take a harder look at them. Many psychopaths who might have beaten the system in the 1970s are getting nowhere with their trendy and insupportable defenses. However, the mindless rush not just to dispense justice but to mete out punishment and retribution to those who are truly mentally ill is a disaster. It's a disaster in the police station, a disaster in the courtroom, a disaster in the prisons, and a disaster in the remaining shreds of our mental health system.

When legislators institute knee-jerk reforms without attempting to obtain scientific information about the effects of those changes, the results can be illusory, inhumane, and downright expensive. When Michigan lawmakers in 1975 sought to reduce the number of insanity acquittals by introducing a third verdict option, guilty but mentally ill (GBMI), they also hoped to prevent the early release of dangerous patients acquitted by reason of insanity. The category of mentally ill offender was created so that a criminal would receive treatment in the prison system rather than in a secure mental institution. Results of this reform ten years later revealed that the number of insanity acquittals remained the same but the number of insanity pleas more than doubled. This new breed of offender required expensive new mental health services within the prisons — most of which existed only on paper. Guilty but mentally ill offenders may not have gotten treatment, but they did get generally higher sentences and served more time than the non–mentally ill defendants who were convicted of the same charges. It seems that under GBMI reform statutes, a defendant received extra punishment for being mentally ill.

Reform statutes have tried to discourage the use of the insanity defense by three basic approaches: (1) adjudication reforms occurring at the plea stage, including substantive standard tests of mental illness; (2) postacquittal reforms that include clarifying procedures for choosing where a criminal shall be placed, establishing guidelines for determining when a dangerous mental illness requires continued detention, tightening rights to release hearings, and assigning final authority over an acquittee's release; (3) combination reforms that focus on both the preverdict and postverdict stages, including hybrids like the guilty but mentally ill option — or the outright abolition of the insanity defense.

In the aftermath of the Hinckley case, thirty-four states enacted changes in the way the insanity defense operated, to reduce its use and ensure the long-term retention of acquitted criminals. Because Hinckley's acquittal was made possible by the fact that the burden of proof in his trial rested with the prosecution, which had to prove beyond a reasonable doubt that he was sane when he shot at President Reagan, thirty-seven states now put the proof of insanity more firmly on the defense. Tinkering with the burden of proof can itself lead to abuses. In jurisdictions where the burden of proof is on the prosecution, psychopaths can beat the system by establishing a reasonable doubt about their sanity. Tilting the playing field in the direction of the prosecutors brings its own set of abuses, as the courts retaliate for threats to public safety that simply do not exist. With our current emphasis on the rights of public protection at the expense of personal freedoms, it could lead to conviction of many truly mentally ill offenders who are unable to legally prove their insanity. The rights to due process for the mentally ill offender are a controversial public policy issue and a matter of constitutional interpretation. Cases like that of Colin Ferguson have again brought these questions to the public attention.

Timing is all in life. W. A. Purdy's timing was off when he entered a psychiatric defense after the Federal Insanity Defense Reform Act of 1984 and landed a pit-bull New York prosecutor who would go on to distinguish herself for bringing down prominent mafiosi. Purdy was six feet six inches tall, weighed 286 pounds, and was pleasant-featured, courteous, and crisply military in his demeanor. At the age of seventeen, he had left behind his dirt-poor roots in Alabama to enter the army, serving two tours of duty in Vietnam as an MP and receiving numerous citations and awards. He was determined to become a respectable and distinguished officer and gentleman — unlike his own father, whom he despised as a shiftless, irresponsible, and violent alcoholic who abandoned his wife and kids. Purdy resolved to be perfect in every way. He married a Japanese woman and raised two children, now college graduates in their twenties. After honorable discharge from the military, he worked as a police officer in South Carolina, where he was highly decorated for bravery.

Tense, high-strung, perfectionistic, W. A. Purdy always worried more than the other guy about doing the right thing. He was diagnosed with diabetes in his early forties. Even with daily use of injectable insulin, his blood sugar was never really under stable control. When the strain of police work started to get to him, he decided to change his career. He studied food service and catering, got a diploma from a prestigious culinary institute, and became the club manager at the Brooklyn Naval Base in New York City. At first Purdy was in his element. He loved pleasing people and being around food and celebrations. The fact that he was in a military environment, with all its hierarchy and structure, made him even more comfortable. Purdy liked his world to be neat and predictable; he also liked to be recognized and acclaimed for his hard work and superior efforts. The officers club soon became the focal point of Purdy's life. He even had an apartment above the club and rarely ventured off the base. By now his kids were grown up and his marriage had dissolved. He was devastated when his mother died; he began to work obsessively long hours and withdrew from his friends.

Things started to heat up between Purdy and his boss, particularly after Purdy had uncovered waste and fiscal misappropriations in the running of the club and had reported it to a supposedly confidential navy hotline. Somehow the information was leaked to his supervisor, who then went on the rampage against Purdy. By all accounts, Bob Wilson, the chief of the officers club, was no picnic to work with. He was a short-tempered taskmaster stingy with praise. Some said he may even have harbored racial antipathy toward Purdy, who was black, in addition to having a score to settle over the anonymous tip.

Purdy started losing his grip — he couldn't sleep or eat, he experienced panic attacks at work, and his diabetes careened dangerously out of control. He sought treatment at the veterans hospital and was referred for a psychological workup. The psychologist noted that Purdy was depressed and suffering from extreme stress and anxiety related to harassment and fifteen-hour shifts at work. Psychotherapy and medication were recommended. Purdy began seeing a psychiatrist privately. The doctor's notes reveal the level of Purdy's distress and his preoccupation to the point of paranoia with Wilson and his difficulties on the job.

In late October 1989 Purdy was decorating the club for a Halloween party when an employee, as a joke, painted a tombstone on the wall with the epitaph, "W.A. Rest in Peace." Stressed to the limit, Purdy went into a superstitious frenzy, fearing that this was an omen. He was unable to eat or sleep. After completing a double shift, he was summoned to Wilson's office first thing one morning — apparently to be formally disciplined. When Purdy arrived, Wilson was not there but left word that he should return at one P.M. For five hours, Purdy stewed over what was awaiting him at the meeting.

That afternoon, November 2, 1989, Purdy walked up the hall to his supervisor's office, past all the military guards. Wilson ushered him in. Purdy pulled a double-barreled sawed-off shotgun from under his jacket and began pointing it at Wilson. "He's gonna kill me!" the guards heard Wilson shriek several times. By the time security arrived, Purdy and Wilson were struggling over the gun in the hall. A shot rang out and Wilson slumped to the floor, a major wound on his left knee. He was bleeding profusely and going into shock. Purdy was standing against the wall in a daze. "Don't notify anyone but TV and the newspaper," he confusingly ordered the MPs. One of the guards later recalled, "I

don't even think he knew who was present." A coworker later recounted, "Purdy said Wilson was a crook, stealing money. He had
heard bad things about him even before he came to work at the
base. This disgruntlement had been going on between them for
about six months. Purdy never told me how he was going to solve
their problem. You could tell he was frustrated, but I never knew
it was to this extent." Wilson recovered after hospitalization.
Purdy was indicted for attempted murder, possession of a weapon,
and several counts of assault.

From his mammoth size to his bouts with uncontrolled diabetes, Purdy shared many of the same features that amounted to an
automatic insanity acquittal in the case of Gowain Tremont, the
truck driver and former mental hospital attendant who stabbed his
common-law wife to death. Purdy's diabetes and psychiatric history were well established. He did not have the checkered past and
marginal social adjustment of Tremont. Never in his life had he
been violent; in fact, people who knew him said he had never even
been angry. Purdy's treating psychiatrist, impressively credentialed (he had served as deputy commissioner of the New York
City Department of Mental Health), testified that Purdy had experienced "an acute dissociative episode as a result of prolonged
stress . . . and the physiological effects of a low blood sugar level
and sleep deprivation." Purdy had a bona fide and well-docu-
mented version of what could be called — too disparagingly, in
this instance — a Twinkie defense. For good measure, his attorney threw in post-traumatic stress disorder as the primary diagnosis, claiming that Purdy fired on his supervisor while he was
experiencing flashbacks of Vietnam combat. This shift to an insupportable designer defense rather than sticking to the real psychological findings proved to be Purdy's undoing.

When I met with Purdy, in the offices of the U.S. attorney, he
was wearing the electronic monitoring bracelet that the government uses for house arrest. At fifty years old, Purdy looked spent,
his bulk bowed down under the weight of his difficulties. His col-
oring was poor, his eyes were bloodshot, and periodically beads of

perspiration sprouted on his cheeks and forehead. His anxiety and discomfort were so palpable that it seemed like cruelty to subject him to six hours of testing and forensic interviewing. But he was able to complete in one session what takes most people at least two. I could see that Purdy wanted to put this whole thing to rest as quickly as possible and that viewing himself as a criminal was an intolerable threat to his carefully constructed self-image. Everything that Purdy stood for — everything he had tried to hold together throughout his entire life — had crumbled in that second in Wilson's office. I believed he was suffering from a major, chronic depression. I was concerned about the possibility of suicide as the case progressed.

I had several meetings with the prosecutor, trying to explain to her that my psychological opinion was going to be a good deal "softer" than what she might wish for from her expert witness. It was unclear whether Purdy was a paranoid instigator and troublemaker or whether he really had suffered harassment by Wilson for being a whistle-blower, as he claimed. Purdy was not a psychopath; he was not faking on the psychological tests; he did suffer from a physical illness that contributes to disturbances of mood; and he had lived an exemplary life till age forty-nine.

The prosecutor decided to attack the defense claim of Purdy's post-traumatic stress disorder and his alleged flashbacks. The psychiatrist on the prosecution team poked holes in Purdy's allegations that he "felt like he was in Vietnam" at the time of the shooting. He came down hard on Purdy, calling him a malingerer, and concluded that his "actions at the time of the shooting are most consistent with his having been angry about his job and his treatment by Mr. Wilson."

I could not be so peremptory about Purdy's guilt. Although I did not believe that he suffered from a mental disease such that it released him totally from criminal responsibility for his acts, I felt that his emotional and physiological state constituted a sort of diminished capacity that affected his criminal intent and should be taken into consideration in terms of his sentencing. After my report, I was not called to testify at the trial. Purdy was convicted, and under the sentencing guidelines there were no options other than time in a federal penitentiary. I doubt his health and pride will survive it.

Sometimes our rush to justice can be untempered by mercy. Such harshness is hardwired into the narrow cognitive standards of insanity defense statutes like M'Naghten. I myself have testified for the prosecution in cases in which the individual was certifiably mentally ill and required inpatient hospitalization, though he knew the nature and consequences of his actions and their wrongfulness. Under the M'Naghten test, such a person is considered sane in the eyes of the law and criminally responsible despite his serious psychosis. On the eve of my testimony in such cases, I often can't sleep. How can I draw the line and evaluate just how much a serious mental illness has affected a human being and contributed to his crime? In the current legal dragnet of the insanity defense, we are snaring a lot of sick fish. An attorney friend and ex-prosecutor scoffed to me, "Does it really matter what we do with someone like Rifkin as long as he is locked up forever?" I believe the answer is a resounding yes. By ascertaining where criminal responsibility lies we are forcing ourselves to come to terms with our own responsibility for caring for the mentally ill and keeping them from committing crimes in the first place. The insanity defense is the exception that proves the rule. Can a society that exacts revenge in the guise of justice against the mentally disabled really believe it is winning the war against violent crime?

If all the insanity defendants in the United States were suddenly vaporized, there would not be a noticeable decline in the rate of violent crime. Yet as part of the backlash against social permissiveness, we are treating the insane worse than we treat criminals. Are we beating the saddle because we can't beat the horse?

In December 1994, John Salvi entered two abortion clinics on a Brookline, Massachusetts, street known as Abortion Row, armed with a .22 caliber assault rifle and hollow-point bullets. Snarling "That's what you get, you should pray the rosary," he opened fire. Two women were killed in the two attacks, and five other people were wounded. In Salvi's deluded mind, he was an avenging angel, saving the Catholic Church from conspiracies against it by Freemasons, the Mafia, and the Ku Klux Klan. After high school, Salvi had been unable to hold a job or take care of his own basic needs. His parents described his apartment as "filthy, stench-ridden, and crawling with maggots."

Dr. Philip Resnick, a renowned forensic expert who had been a consultant to the 1983 National Commission on the Insanity Defense, examined Salvi and testified that he suffered from paranoid schizophrenia with religious delusions. He confronted the prosecutor's arguments — that Salvi was a terrorist methodically planning his crime and later trying to elude capture — by admitting that Salvi knew what he was doing was *legally* wrong but in his delusions believed that it was morally right. To me, Salvi seemed to fit into the ranks of Daniel M'Naghten, Richard Winkler, or Ameenah Abdus-Salaam, and countless others who believe they get their marching orders direct from God. Even by the strict application of the M'Naghten standard, Salvi appeared to have a classic insanity defense.

John Salvi was convicted of murder and sentenced to two consecutive life terms without parole at Cedar Junction Maximum Security Prison outside Boston. On November 30, 1996, he was found dead in his cell, where he had asphyxiated himself with a plastic garbage can liner tied around his head. Prison authorities maintained that there was "no indication that Mr. Salvi was mentally ill or in need of any special intervention." This had been Salvi's second suicide attempt. Shortly before Christmas 1995 he had slipped a noose made from a pillowcase around his neck before being apprehended by a guard. It was not considered a serious suicide attempt.

In our justice system, it seems, there is an additional penalty for madness.

Traditionally, the only factors that come close to leveling the field for the mentally ill have been gender and wealth. Women were always more likely to be acquitted on grounds of insanity than men. Sadly, the victims of their crimes were usually infants, children, or lovers and spouses. After insanity defense reform, this is even more likely to occur. The wealthy, presumably by hiring more competent legal experts, often are successful in pleading the insanity defense. But the backlash against the defense has been so strong that privilege of wealth and power is no longer any guarantee of acquittal. A Philadelphia judge denied the plea of the chemical fortune heir John Du Pont to be moved to a private psychiatric hospital on bail; she felt that the security in the hospital was not sufficient to ensure that he would remain to appear at trial. Du Pont, who was charged with the shooting death of a former Olympic wrestler, David Schultz, was returned to the Delaware County Prison.

At his trial thirteen months later, all six defense and prosecution psychiatric experts concluded that Du Pont, age fifty-eight, was severely mentally ill. The defense doctors claimed that he suffered from paranoid schizophrenia which made him believe that he was the Dalai Lama and a spy for the CIA. His victim, he thought, was part of an international conspiracy to take his life; therefore, they said, he was not criminally responsible when he shot the wrestler dead at point-blank range. One of the psychiatrists hired by the defense team testified that Du Pont believed Schultz was killed by the U.S. government, a splinter group of the Buddhist church, or perhaps someone dressed up to look like him. Although uncannily reminiscent of Colin Ferguson's assertion that an unidentified white man did the Long Island Railroad shooting, John Du Pont's claims reached more attentive ears. After seven days of deliberations, the jury decided that Du Pont was guilty of third-degree murder, but mentally ill. On May 17, 1997, Du Pont was sentenced to thirteen to thirty years for Schultz's murder. At this writing he is undergoing treatment at Norristown

State Hospital and will go to prison only if the authorities decide that he has been cured. Following the announcement of the guilty but mentally ill verdict, District Attorney Patrick Meehan reassured the public: "Some thought John Du Pont, the wealthiest murder defendant in the history of the United States, would use his vast fortune to escape justice." He then added, in an uncharacteristically charitable concession for a prosecutor, "He can now get the mental treatment he needs, and that is justice."

Alice Faye Redd was a quintessential society matron — president of the PTA, the Junior League, and the Garden Club in her hometown of Lakeland, Florida. She was honored as one of ten outstanding young women in America by President Richard Nixon, and she even had her own radio show on the local Christian station: *The Happy Homemaker*. Vivacious, charming, and full of energy, she seemed to everyone a Southern superwoman. It wasn't until astounded family members found mounds of bank statements stashed in her bedroom closet that they began to realize that something was wrong. For nine years Alice Faye had been running a pyramid scheme, bilking almost $10 million from fellow church members. More than 103 people were swindled, all of them her friends and neighbors, some of them elderly.

The family felt that Alice Faye could not be in her right mind to do such a thing and spirited her off to a mental institution for evaluation. Eventually, four psychiatrists — one of them actually hired by the prosecution — agreed that Mrs. Redd suffered from manic-depression. Her condition was diagnosed as bipolar II, which meant she was almost always in an excited and elevated mood state, needed little sleep, was full of inflated notions and grandiose business schemes, and was foolish, impulsive, and extravagant in her spending. She began treatment with lithium and Prozac to control her symptoms. Exploration of her psychiatric history revealed that six generations of her family had suffered from some form of mental illness as far back as the mid-1800s. Florida State Hospital records substantiated that eleven of her first-degree relatives had been hospitalized there as well as sixty-seven collateral relatives. Her great-grandfather and a great-uncle had committed suicide. Her maternal aunts and uncles were all diagnosed with severe clinical depressions; her own mother suffered from depression and repeatedly threatened suicide. The defense experts declared that this clinical family history was critical in evaluating Mrs. Redd's illness because manic-depression is the most inheritable of mental disorders.

Alice Faye Redd pled guilty to the charges, believing that her need for psychiatric treatment was so compelling that she would receive clemency in her sentencing. She soon found the community not at all sympathetic to a person who had defrauded her neighbors out of life savings. The fifty-nine-year-old woman was sentenced to the maximum, fifteen years in prison. The prosecutor felt this was a fair decision since he believed Alice Faye would have gotten life if her case had gone to trial. In his sentencing order on March 11, 1996, the judge stated, "Through the rose-colored glasses of her bipolar disorder the defendant, perhaps, saw herself as providing her victims with benefits rather than destruction. . . . The disorder's manic states caused the defendant to view the harm she was doing as less devastating than it really was." Given the judge's clinically accurate depiction of Alice Faye Redd's mental illness, in a M'Naghten state like Florida wouldn't she have met the standard of having a mental illness that interfered with her capacity to know the nature and consequences of her actions and their wrongfulness?

With logic like this prevailing in America's courts, mental health advocates fear that there is no justice for the mentally ill. Judges seem to be either unwilling or unable to appropriately consider psychiatric diagnoses when deciding on punishment. The swelling number of mentally ill offenders in prison are not being appropriately treated and cared for in the already overstretched resources of correctional settings. One of Alice Faye's victims and a fellow church member is not concerned. She does not believe that Alice Faye was ever sick. "It really did my heart good to hear her sentenced!" she said.

California adopted a "get tough on crime" attitude in the late 1970s with mandatory sentencing laws, which flooded its prisons. The state also reformed its insanity defense standard, returning to the more stringent cognitive test of the M'Naghten rule, with the burden of proof being on the defendant without a reasonable doubt. A massive number of mentally ill offenders have since flooded the correctional system. As I have pointed out earlier, compared to mental hospitals, prisons are country clubs. That is why, depending on the state and jurisdiction, prisons carry a price tag anywhere from two to five times higher for the taxpayer. Prisons have law libraries, gyms, pools, college courses, commissaries, work-study programs. With all the brutality and harshness of prison life, an inmate still reserves some basic rights. Serial killer Ted Bundy was able to get married, have conjugal visits, and father a baby girl while on death row. Criminally insane forensic patients are not permitted to have conjugal visits. In fact, most states have laws to criminalize sexual relations for the mentally disabled. Mental patients are not viewed as being competent to consent to sexual relations, to marry, or to have children. I once had a prosecutor try to block the release of a patient from the secure unit to a regular civil ward on the grounds that he was still dangerously mentally ill. The defendant's crime was rape: This sixty-two-year-old man suffering from alcoholic deterioration had visited his wife, a mental patient at a community facility, and had sexual relations with her. The facility administrator had declared the wife incompetent to consent and had her husband arrested on charges of statutory rape. The couple had been married for forty years.

Concomitant with the national mood of getting tough on crime and the booming business in prisons is the extinction of funding for the mentally ill. In 1996, New York governor George Pataki proposed $215 million in spending cuts for mental health; the overall estimated loss, considering federal and local matching funds, would be in excess of $600 million, or about a 25 percent reduction in total mental health funding for the state. The economizing measures would require closing psychiatric hospitals and seventy-five state-run outpatient clinics. These patients require close aftercare and supervision, therapy, and monitoring of their antipsychotic medication; when those services vanish, the impact on the surrounding families and communities will be tragic. There is sure to be an increase of mentally ill homeless wandering the streets, parks, and subways. Some will commit crimes; many more will be the victims of crimes. Mental health advocates estimate that the cutbacks will result in more than twenty-five thousand emergency psychotic episodes per year. Some of those episodes will involve someone's death; the mentally ill offender will then graduate to the prison system, where his incarceration will cost anywhere from $40,000 to $75,000 per year. Not just in New York but nationwide, taxpayers are paying a high price indeed for their moment of being tough on crime and niggardly with mental health.

Putting truly psychotic individuals in prisons among the predatory psychopathic population is like feeding chum to sharks. Unless they are kept in protective custody — which involves isolation from the other prisoners and specialized housing, supervision, and staffing, adding up to an even higher tab for the taxpayer — they usually become victims of attacks by other inmates. The incarceration of the mentally ill in general-population prisons creates management problems for staff and potentially violent situations. In a disproportionate number of cases, the mentally ill offender is killed as the result of an attack by other inmates. They muck up a system that is better suited to the management of antisocial types. Frequently such ill prisoners decompensate, sinking deeper into psychosis and even attempting suicide. John Salvi is just one extreme example. Most of the time, they muddle through, receiving hit-or-miss treatment, becoming nuisances for the corrections officers, and running up bills for the taxpayer.

Compared to most state and local correctional facilities, federal penitentiaries offer deluxe accommodations. They are generally better staffed in their psychological services and do seem to be more aware of the mentally ill inmate's needs. However, their very efforts at being humane make it easy for the psychopath trying to gain special privileges through feigning mental illness. Lilly Schmidt, the colorful con artist, created quite a splash in the federal pen; hundreds of manpower hours, reams of bureaucratic reports, and thousands of dollars were expended in evaluating her declaration of faux psychosis.

Our treatment of the mentally ill in the backlash era is nothing short of "sanism." In his article "Dignity Was the First to Leave: *Godinez v. Moran*, Colin Ferguson and the Trial of Mentally Disabled Criminal Defendants" (*Behavioral Sciences and the Law*, 1996), M. L. Perlin quotes Dr. Morton Birnbaum's definition of sanism: "an irrational prejudice of the same quality and character of other irrational prejudices that cause (and are reflected in) prevailing social attitudes of racism, sexism, homophobia, and ethnic bigotry." At its heart, sanism reflects the fear, bewilderment, and discomfort we feel around mental illness, and it underlies the widespread failure to recognize mental illness as a social issue. That failure pervades every crevice of our social institutions. It is evident in how we handle the insanity defense and in how we cross the streets to avoid a mentally ill person mumbling in public. It is apparent in the halls of Congress, where funds for the research and treatment of mental illness fall far below the amounts given to any physical disease, even those diseases suffered by far fewer people. It results in discrimination in employment and health insurance benefits.

Many times when I have testified I have exhorted a jury not to suspend its common sense when being subjected to arcane designer defenses. Now I feel guilty in that I too may have unwittingly contributed to the perpetuation of the stereotypes, myths, and prejudices that characterize our attitude toward the mentally ill. Ordinary common sense is informed by experiences and the accumulation of learning from everyday life, but the diagnosis and treatment of mental illness requires years of preparation and study. It is absurd to expect a jury or a judge to grasp highly complicated and technical information presented in a contentious and emotionally charged atmosphere. This is tantamount to demanding that the jury use its common sense about the working of DNA or the movements of molecules. Legal scholar James Boudouris observed that jurors can make up their minds peremptorily to punish a defendant for the brutality of his attack and look for an expert to give them justification. In polling jurors after they convicted one defendant of a particularly gruesome crime, Boudouris recorded ignorance about mental illness and "sanist" prejudices: "Watching him, he really didn't look insane. . . . He was just damn mad because she was leaving him and he was using her."

Sanism is difficult to fight, both in others and in ourselves. The media, the public, laypeople, and even legal and psychological professionals can exhibit a knee-jerk predisposition to view the mentally ill as weak in character, lazy, slaves to their impulses, and unwilling to exercise self-control. We don't even have the vocabulary to describe the mentally ill in an honest and nonjudgmental way. Responding to a routine request, the FBI, which is responsible for collecting data about hate crimes involving race, ethnicity, religion, and sexual orientation, investigated a new category: physical and mental disability. It consulted the National Stigma Clearinghouse to select sensitive, neutral terminology that could be used in its training manuals and reports to describe mentally ill people. To thrash out these delicate issues, a conference was convened in New York City at the International Center for the Disabled in early 1996, with delegates from the fields of psychiatry, advocacy, research, government, and law enforcement. Half of the two dozen participants had been diagnosed as mentally ill. After seven hours of fierce and emotional debate, the FBI realized the nature of the "elephant in the living room" — a classic therapeutic metaphor for the denial of a huge, obvious, and messy problem. Nora Weinerth, one of the nation's leading experts on stigma, warned, "When language is used to devalue, it shapes attitudes that in turn become social policy."

Words like "psycho," "weirdo," "wacko," and "asylum" shriek from tabloid headlines, fanning bias against people with psychiatric disabilities. Mary W. Auslander, a former mental patient who is director of recipient affairs in New York City for the State Office of Mental Health, affirmed, "In the naming lies the perception of ourselves and our experience."

The blanket and automatic application of any statute, especially one dealing with a matter as complex as legal insanity, can result in a great miscarriage of justice. It's time to take a closer, empirical look at how the system really works — setting aside our sanism, our prejudices, and our irrational fears of crime and the mentally ill. The truths we see may not be pretty, but greater truth may lead to greater justice, for the mad, for the bad, and for ourselves.

Several years after the federal reform in the insanity statute, I was retained by the U.S. Department of Justice to examine George Bennet and determine whether he suffered from a mental illness that rendered him incompetent to stand trial. A two-count federal indictment had been filed against him for robbing a bank and brandishing a handgun in the commission of the crime. Bennet had walked into a New York City bank, flashed a gun, and demanded that the teller hand over the money. He was given $1,100 and got nabbed just after he hit the street.

At the time of his arrest, Bennet started acting weird. He announced he was hearing voices and getting rays from the TV; he denied that he had any criminal charges against him, said he knew nothing about the bank robbery, and talked about an extensive history of mental hospitalizations. At the time of his initial workup at the special federal facility in Springfield, Massachusetts, he impressed prison psychiatrists as being "obviously psychotic." The doctor wrote, "He starts out by relating that he is actually David Carter and that George Bennet is another person inside of him. . . . George is the good guy and David Carter is the bad guy." Bennet also told this psychiatrist that he had been hearing voices and seeing colors since he was eight or nine years old. He continued to regale the examiner with tales of being abused and locked in his room by his "mean" parents and claimed to have set the family home on fire when he was a child. The government psychiatrist did note many features that were inconsistent with a psychotic diagnosis: "Associations appear to be intact." "Oriented." "Judgment and insight into his problem appear to be intact." "The patient did not describe any delusions or unusual experiences, hallucinations." Bennet played it close to the vest. He managed to seem cooperative while at the same time claiming that he could neither read nor understand the written questions posed to him. He manifested total loss of memory in certain areas, usually those related to the crime. The psychiatrist attributed all of this to acute psychosis and never even entertained the possibility that Bennet might be faking to stonewall his case.

Bennet succeeded in being diagnosed chronic schizophrenic and declared incompetent to understand the nature and consequences of proceedings against him or to participate in his own defense. The doctor went so far as to opine that the prognosis for Bennet's ever regaining competency was poor. Six months later, Bennet was evaluated by a psychologist. By then, contact had been established with Bennet's father — who was not a postal worker, had not died of a heart attack, and had not abandoned the family, as Bennet had claimed. Mr. Bennet reported that he was a family counselor and that George had been raised in an intact family. He said that George had never served in the military as he claimed and that despite his denial, he had married and had one child. Mr. Bennet did not corroborate his son's story of childhood mental illness but stated that George had begun to experience psychiatric symptoms at about age nineteen, in connection with abusing street drugs. His father also revealed the extent of George's criminal activities and arrests.

Did the doctors take a second look at Bennet's pathology? No. As illustrated in a controversial study, "On Being Sane in Insane Places," by D. L. Rosenhan (*Science*, 1973), a preliminary diagnosis can stick to a person like flypaper — in the face of enormous evidence to the contrary. The psychologist readministered the MMPI to Bennet. The scores were identical and as improbably elevated as they had been six months earlier. This psychologist at least recognized that the profile was invalid, but he attributed it to Bennet's "marking the answer sheet in a haphazard fashion," a result of the impairment and confusion of his mental illness. If he had analyzed the test results more thoroughly, he would have discovered that Bennet carefully employed a strategy of responding to every negative and symptomatic item as true and denying any positive or healthy response. The mathematical probability of Bennet's profile being valid was 0.1 to the 30th power. Research has shown that a person's ability to dissimulate mental illness increases with exposure to psychiatric settings and information on psychiatric symptoms. Bennet had become a pro.

The U.S. attorney's office began to get impatient with the delay in bringing Bennet to trial because of the opinions of the government's own doctors, and called on me to examine Bennet to put to rest the issue of malingering. Four months later, Bennet was returned for forensic examination to the Metropolitan Correctional Center in New York. Accompanied by his attorney, a young assistant U.S. attorney, and two strapping federal marshals, I entered the cell where Bennet was waiting. Bennet was restless and annoyed; the putrid smell of garbage emanated from the adjacent incinerator. "How can a human being be expected to stay here with that smell?" he roared. There was something impressive, almost leonine, about his tawny skin and large, well-toned body. Until Bennet mentioned it, the civil servants who made up the group were oblivious to the odor; the marshals didn't flinch. Bennet was absolutely right — the odor was nauseating. He refused to proceed with the exam. The attorneys looked helplessly at me. "Let's see if they can find us another cell," I ventured. After an hour of inhaling garbage fumes, we were told there was no other single cell where we could continue. We rescheduled the exam for the next date available for all parties (two months later!) and all of us, except Bennet, went home. Justice, even in the age of the backlash, would be further delayed by the justice system itself.

On the second try at an exam, Bennet, alert and well groomed, was escorted into the spacious conference room of the U.S. attorney's offices by two federal marshals. They courteously helped him to the plush upholstered chair. I expected them to remove the handcuffs that bound Bennet's hands behind his back, but they settled back into chairs on either side of Bennet and waited. "Mr. Bennet is going to have to have his hands free to write and complete certain tests for me today," I explained. In the flat, clipped style of G-men, they intoned in unison, "He is in custody and we are not permitted to uncuff him." Again, much calling and consulting with various government officials. A court order was finally obtained to examine Bennet two days later — back at the correctional center, otherwise known as square one.

By then, Bennet seemed to be enjoying these outings. To control for the government psychologist's hypothesis that Bennet was responding randomly to test items, I read aloud each of 566 MMPI test items and closely observed in which direction (true or false) he marked his answer sheet. In scoring the tests, I found that Bennet had exaggerated and faked consistently as he had before; he obtained an invalid and absolutely faked profile.

After I finished the tests with Bennet, the alarm sounded. There had been an inmate escape. Massive emergency security measures were instituted, and no one was permitted to enter or leave the facility until the emergency was over. Along with Bennet, I was also a prisoner. I remained locked in a tiny, dark cell, alone with him for the next hour and a half.

Sensing my discomfort and frustration at the situation, Bennet underwent a remarkable transformation. He became talkative, reassuring, and sociable to the point of being warm and protective. He took pains to explain the meaning of all the alarm bell codes and the escape emergency procedure to me. Oddly, I began to feel at ease with this man, who continued to apologize in a very courtly fashion about the inconvenience he had put me through on the first two occasions of the attempted exam.

During our indeterminate sentence in this tiny cell, the differences between George Bennet, the inmate, and me, the forensic psychologist, vanished. This was a different world in here; the outside rules and realities did not apply. Here you survived on your sheer wits. He could have overpowered me in an instant, assaulted me, or worse, before a guard would ever discover it. There would have been no escape for me — but, luckily for me, no escape for Bennet either. He was basically a psychopath, albeit demented by drugs at times. But now he was clean, and there was nothing for him to gain in harming me. He was not a violent man; he had no history of rape or assault. His crimes were strictly for profit — robbery and drug dealing. For twenty years, conning had been his profession, as forensic psychology had been mine. To him we were both here practicing what we did best. Bennet knew his mental illness routine wasn't winning me over, just as implicitly I knew he wouldn't hurt me. Instead, he tried to charm me into giving him a break. "Well, I need some time to get my head together," he said. "I'm not such a bad guy. Why even the voices I used to hear were pleasant and joking companions."

I mentioned that I had worked at Creedmoor during the time Bennet had been hospitalized on the forensic unit. Pleased, Bennet nostalgically recounted his experiences there in great detail. He went on to speculate about his options within the federal system and carefully outlined for me the issue of competency and its impact upon his ability to stand trial for the bank holdup. When I asked him about the eventuality of parole, he quickly corrected me. "I'm not eligible for parole yet — I haven't even been to trial. My guess is that they'll fly me back to Springfield until I can go on with the trial."

"How long do you think that will be?" I asked.

Bennet gave a broad, engaging smile. "I guess until I get tired of it . . . but it's pretty good at Springfield."

With the sounding of an all-clear bell and the clanking of the guard's key in the door, our session ended. "You can go now, Doc," I was told. Our tête-à-tête had given me more accurate information about Bennet than his faked-bad test would ever permit. This man's criminal career reflected the vagaries of the criminal justice and mental health systems.

Coincidentally, the psychologist who had evaluated Bennet at Creedmoor was my research colleague. The materials he was able to provide me with had never even been reviewed by the government's doctors at Springfield. They revealed a vastly different clinical picture than the one the Springfield doctors had assembled. My cellmate George Bennet had a long arrest record for previous armed robbery. Long before I made his acquaintance, he had been returned to a state prison as a parole violator and had finally wended his way downstate to Creedmoor because of his acting out in jail. This was in 1983, five years before Bennet robbed the bank and began working the federal system. Bennet then wanted out — back onto parole and out into the streets. At that time he had a vested interest in appearing okay, so he had given a valid MMPI profile: no faking, no psychotic elevations, just manic impulsiveness and antisocial personality tendencies. He was recommended for discharge to the community. Weighing the odds revealed in Bennet's psychopathic test profile, psychologist Jim Audubon had predicted, "He can be expected to come into repeated difficulty with the law."

Had George Bennet become psychotic in five years? I think not. Bennet was a marginal man, a career criminal. He spent his years on parole as a heavy drug user and dealer involved in much street violence. Whenever things got hot for him on the streets, he sought voluntary admission to a psychiatric hospital, claiming that he was hearing voices telling him to kill someone. Usually, after a few days, he left of his own volition, escaped, or was discharged as "oriented and with no psychotic symptoms in evidence." Bennet had learned to use the mental health system as a time-out from his dangerous life. The federal penitentiary offered the best accommodations of all — in prison slang, "three hots and a cot," all top-of-the-line. The taxpayers were being taken for a ride, and as long as many government workers were collecting their paychecks, nobody complained or even bothered to communicate.

After my report, Bennet was declared fit to proceed, convicted, and sentenced. To my knowledge, he is still incarcerated within the federal system, playing at being mentally ill whenever it suits his purposes.

The insanity defense system after the federal reform act is even more of a crazy quilt than it was before, with inmates sent seemingly arbitrarily to either prisons or hospitals — and recently, more often to prisons, whether they belong there or not. There is no continuity, no follow-up, no consistency, and no accountability as a defendant progresses across the system, the discrete patches of which are parceled out to different institutions and agencies who have little communication and coordination among them. George Bennet is a living example of the intractable and unpleasant human truths. He took advantage of the difference between the evaluations made by people in the mental health system, whose specialty is mental illness, and those made by the correction system's specialists in criminal behavior. Why didn't the Federal Bureau of Prisons, the U.S. Department of Justice, and the New York State Office of Mental Health treatment teams just sit down and discuss Bennet? Although these systems all have computer tracking capability, they seldom coordinate their efforts to monitor mentally ill offenders.

Until there is some logic and coordination built into the insanity defense process — in fact, until it is even seen as a process — many more mentally ill offenders will not get humane or cost-effective treatment, and clever psychopaths will still disappear through the seams. The backlash ignores abuse of the mentally ill, gives carte blanche to psychopaths feigning mental illness, and causes enormous waste, duplication of services, and inefficiency. That is not what we should mean by insanity defense reform.

Social reformers, politicians, legal scholars, mental health professionals, and the citizen on the street have been clamoring for abolition of the insanity defense since it was first instituted. They have cited arguments ranging from the extreme right-wing notions of strict liability (all defendants should be held responsible for their actions regardless of their state of mind) to the far left concepts (it is unfair to cite mental illness as a mitigator to criminal intent when the legal system does not recognize race or other forms of social injustice). Those who oppose abolition of the insanity defense admit its flaws and shortcomings, but grudgingly concede that it is essential for the moral integrity of criminal law. In order to be fair about holding someone responsible for his criminal actions, we must clearly define what we mean by criminal intent. In so doing, we come upon the rare cases where it is necessary to exclude from moral blame those who lack the capacity to form intent — or what is called in the law mens rea.

Early this century, Louisiana, Mississippi, and Washington attempted to abolish the insanity defense, but their efforts were judged unconstitutional because they had not allowed for a mens rea defense. In the current climate of reform, three other states (Montana, Idaho, and Utah) have passed legislation abolishing the special insanity defense while maintaining the mens rea doctrine. Evidence of the practical effect of these new laws remains meager, since these are all small states, but an analysis of the outcomes of cases points to a hard fact: abolishing the insanity defense does not eliminate mental illness among criminals. Legal and mental health scholars predicted, shortly after reform, that attempts to replace the insanity defense with a mens rea would result in bad decisions. Apparently, regardless of legislative reform, judges and juries still sometimes react from the gut human level and view some defendants with severe mental illnesses as not morally responsible for their actions. The bureaucrats have failed to legislate away madness.

The insanity defense was changed in Montana not as a result of the hysteria produced by a notorious case but because of the public perception that insanity defendants were "beating the rap" and "getting away with murder." After the reform, it became virtually impossible for anyone, no matter how psychotically ill, to be acquitted due to lack of requisite mental state. Yet the rate of utilization of a psychological defense continued unchanged. Henry J. Steadman's research revealed some curious and contradictory results. After the get-tough-on-crime reform, fewer people were confined to either hospitals or prisons. Of those found guilty, a smaller percentage were sentenced to prison after reform and a larger percentage were placed directly on probation or conditionally released. What happened to all these defendants? In the vernacular, more of them just walked. In fact, 27 percent were released or dismissed after the reform, compared to only 5 percent before the reform. This social sleight of hand was being accomplished by eliminating most mentally ill cases from the legal system before they got to adjudication. Defendants were being found incompetent to stand trial, their charges dismissed or deferred. In the end, the severely mentally ill offenders were winding up in the same hospitals and wards as they would have had they been found not guilty by reason of insanity. Montana, like Utah, did not succeed in abolishing insanity when it dropped the insanity defense. In this case, the so-called reform produced outcomes completely opposite to those intended. But maybe the state legislators who abolished the insanity defense are happy; they got to rattle their sabers.

Until a cure for mental illness is found or we as a society are able to intervene in a preventative way, the few bizarre and heinous crimes of the mentally ill will continue. Until then, the vagaries, abuses, and insanity of the insanity defense — under whatever guise the statutes allow — will persist. There is something fundamental to human reasoning and the human sense of justice that recognizes there are simply some individuals who are too impaired to be fairly held to a moral concept of blame.

Albert Bundt was a mentally ill offender caught in the twilight zone between the mental health system and insanity defense reform. A compulsive, methodical master engraver, Bundt began to develop paranoid delusions about his young Korean bride and the handsome man who lived next door. His thoughts grew increasingly more suspicious, especially after his wife suffered an ectopic pregnancy. Bundt began to see "semen stains" on the couch, and he believed that the neighbor's penis was so large that it perforated his petite wife's stomach, causing the fetus to begin developing there. In his deluded, psychotic state, Bundt believed this was positive proof of his neighbor's crime. One day in 1967, the neighbor knocked at Bundt's door. He was greeted with two blasts from a shotgun and died instantly.

At the time of his arrest, Bundt was so psychotically delusional and out of touch with reality that he was judged incompetent to proceed and was committed to a mental hospital. Bundt spent the next sixteen years at Creedmoor, diagnosed as paranoid schizophrenic, mostly deluded and largely out of touch with the world around him. His beliefs about why he had committed his crime were still unshaken, but otherwise he kept to himself on the ward and presented no management problems. With the advent of some new antipsychotic medications, Bundt's condition suddenly improved. Although he continued to be chronically delusional, he had managed to gain enough insight to realize the error of his earlier beliefs about his neighbor. Albert Bundt's status was changed to that of a civil patient. Sixteen years after the commission of the murder, he was declared competent to proceed to trial. In a bizarre, almost double jeopardy scenario, Bundt was immediately charged with first-degree murder.

There is no statute of limitations on murder prosecutions in New York, and the Queens district attorney reinstated the original indictment. Still actively psychotic after sixteen years of treatment, delusional, and requiring psychiatric hospitalization, Albert Bundt failed to convince a jury of his insanity.

Always courteous, always precise, always psychotic, Bundt penned a twenty-five-page letter of explanation and remorse to the sentencing judge. The beauty and symmetry of his script were a tribute to his skill as a copperplate engraver. His letter looked like the Magna Carta, but its contents were gibberish. Even to the most unsophisticated Psych 1 student, it read like a primer on schizophrenic language and thought. There were neologisms — idiosyncratic, made-up words like "imperennial." There were what are called clang associations — "nudity, lewdity, and crudity" — and bizarre sensory experiences reported, like "walls whistling." Bundt still had delusions of persecution. The whole letter was in effect a colossal run-on sentence, without a pause or exhalation for twenty-five pages — circumstantial, digressive, and tangential, just like the loosening of associations in schizophrenic thinking.

Bundt attempted to give the sentencing judge an accurate account of the plot against him by "these coordinated groups organizations movements labor unions were detecting that I must be the model to woo and teach them how to love then condescend to their supremacy . . . to devoid the magic thinking ritual directed to fuse the stomach approval or disapproval driving me out of my train of thought sequence." Bundt earnestly tried to impress upon the judge that he had saved his wife, whom he loved, from rape by his neighbor: "Screaming and yelling for help from terrified hysteria causing changing of complexion of my wife's skin after she had such a beautiful refreshing hue and after I love her so much out of fear of dieing, penetrations into my wife's ears' invective due to rape and mayhem and intent murder." Finally, Bundt summoned all his courage and confronted the judge.

I think you have been stalling for time because you are wrong in anterior that this you cannot deny. What do I owe this man a lunatic whose judgment do I have to rely upon if not my own. . . . No one has the right to assume that I am totally insane to the extent that I don't know what I'm doing. . . . I had reason. This is not an irresponsible emotional eruption the way the majority of these criminal cases might be. . . . Sincerely yours, Albert Bundt.

The judge concluded that Albert Bundt did not suffer from a mental disease or defect that substantially impaired his ability to know and appreciate the nature and consequences of his actions and their wrongfulness. Bundt was sentenced to mandatory life imprisonment. None of the sixteen years he spent committed to a mental hospital counted toward his sentence. Transferred from the mental hospital that had been his home for nearly two decades, Bundt disappeared within the bowels of the correctional system at a cost to taxpayers of two to five times more per annum. "Justice" was served, Bundt did not "get away with murder," and the citizens got "tough on crime."

Outside of courtrooms I have stood with judges, prosecutors, and defense attorneys who have lowered their heads and muttered about a defendant something like, "If he were my child, it would be more merciful to just shoot him!" We brutalize the mentally ill. An Indiana court saw no reason why persons found guilty but mentally ill couldn't receive the death penalty. Many mentally ill who are sentenced to prison receive a de facto death penalty; both Colin Ferguson and Joel Rifkin believe they may share that fate. As recently as 1994, the Supreme Court ruled that juries needn't be told that people acquitted by reason of insanity will probably be confined to psychiatric hospitals for years. In fact, in most states, criminally insane people like Richard Winkler will spend more time detained involuntarily in a mental hospital than they would have spent in prison had they been convicted of a crime. We punish madness with a harsher hand.

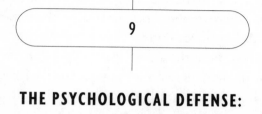

THE PSYCHOLOGICAL DEFENSE:

A MANIFESTO FOR SANITY

"*I am with you 100 percent of every step you will take*," the note affirmed. "No matter what you hear on radio or hear on TV, I am doing everything in my earthly powers to secure your well-being. I have loved you every day of my life and I love you more and more. Love, Daddy." The letter was postmarked from a maximum-security state prison where the writer was serving a life sentence for murdering his girlfriend and seriously wounding her sister as they stood together on a subway platform in 1988. It was the first time in ten years that Keith Royster had tried to contact his son, John J. Royster, who had been arrested and charged with beating a music teacher in Central Park and a computer programmer in Yonkers, pummeling a writer near a heliport in Manhattan, and killing a sixty-five-year-old dry cleaner on Park Avenue.

For days the media had featured the heart-wrenching story of an unidentified thirty-two-year-old woman, beaten beyond recognition, who languished in a coma in a New York City hospital; she turned out to be a music teacher with a close and loyal family. The story echoed that of another petite young woman, the "Central Park jogger," who was viciously raped and beaten several years before. Two other women were attacked in those early weeks of June 1996. A freelance writer, Shelby Evans, was out jogging around nine P.M. near the East Side Heliport on the eve of her fifty-first birthday. Suddenly she was attacked from behind, thrown to the ground, and her face bashed repeatedly into the pavement. Her assailant fled when the attack was interrupted by a passing motorist asking for directions. Two days later in the early evening, a twenty-six-year-old computer programmer walking across a footbridge near the border of New York City and Yonkers was attacked and sexually assaulted. She lay bloodied and unconscious for over twenty minutes before she was discovered. Her face had been so severely bashed in that police suspected she had been pounded with a rock. The following week, when I read the sad account of Evelyn Alvarez, a sixty-five-year-old Asian woman who was found beaten to death in front of her Park Avenue dry cleaning store, I thought of the comatose young woman still fighting for her life. I got a feeling in the pit of my stomach: there was a connection here between these crimes. After you have been around it for so many years, you begin to develop instincts about the logic of the psychotic killer.

Acting on those same instincts and following good police procedure, a detective made a match of fingerprints found at the dry cleaner's crime scene to a twenty-two-year-old drifter named John J. Royster, whose only brush with the law had been for jumping a turnstile and attempting to beat a subway fare three months before. Once down at the police station, Royster asked to pray and meditate, then turned to detectives and said, "Okay, I'm ready." Systematically, without a lawyer present, Royster confessed to the four crimes. Royster, by all accounts, was an angry and unfriendly loner who moved in and out of the city's homeless shelters, looked sporadically for work, and nurtured obsessions with women, Asian philosophy, and violent pornographic videos. He was reported to be very intelligent but unable to perform in school. His three-month stint in the navy the previous year resulted in a psychiatric discharge. No other record of psychiatric treatment could be found for him. A Japanese woman reading about the killings contacted the authorities, believing that her brief relationship with Royster when she visited New York might have been responsible for his attacks on the innocent women. Everyone — the press, psychologists, psychiatrists, the police — was searching for clues to Royster's state of mind, the "trigger" that sent him into his killing rage.

Royster was held at Bellevue, the city psychiatric facility, rather than at the jail. The machinery of the insanity defense process started to grind away. Public defenders were appointed for him; they contemplated whether his mental state interfered with his ability to waive his Miranda rights and give police a confession without the benefit of legal counsel. The doctors had thirty days to consider whether Royster suffered from a mental disease or defect that interfered with his capacity to understand the charges against him and participate in his own defense — that is, whether he was competent to stand trial, a harbinger of an insanity defense.

John J. Royster was charged with first-degree murder, a crime punishable by death under the state's reinstituted death penalty. Ironically, the murder of Mrs. Alvarez occurred in the jurisdiction of Robert Morgenthau, the Manhattan district attorney who had repeatedly gone on record as "loathing" the death penalty. Although an insanity defense rarely results in an outright acquittal in a gruesome murder like this, mental illness can be considered as a mitigating factor for sentencing. The law says that a background of mental illness can be used to show why a defendant should not be put to death. Some capital punishment jurisdictions have statutory "competency to be executed" hearings. The issue of mental illness muddies the already turbid waters of the death

sentence. Kevin M. Doyle, the head of New York's Capital Defender Office, whose staff lawyers represent Royster, remarked,
"Jurors perceive crazy people as scary but not absolutely evil.
They're fearful enough to put them in prison for the rest of their
lives, but they're not harsh enough to kill them." The press coverage referred constantly to the cliché that Royster's "state of
mind" would be on trial. More critical to the outcome of the impending case will be the *jurors'* states of mind and how much they
can be preprogrammed by the pretrial media and manipulated by
the lawyers on either side.

Royster's defense depicts a troubled, alienated young man,
aiming to present him as a sympathetic victim of circumstances.
Even if their research fails to turn up a solid history of diagnosable
mental illness, the uncanny fact that Royster's father is also a murderer suggests a "bad seed" leitmotif of genetic predetermination
that could point to a new kind of designer defense. Who knows?
Judge Andre Davis of the U.S. District Court for the District of
Maryland has speculated on what would happen if science could
demonstrate that bad genes controlled behavior: "Six hundred
years or more of the philosophical underpinning of our social
contract — that free will exists — may be in question. It's scary,
real scary."

The mad also frighten us for another reason. They point toward the unnervingly personal nature of the basic questions about
the bounds of individual responsibility for all of us. If he had truly
been there "100 percent" for his son, would Keith Royster have
made a positive difference in his son's life and so avoided one
death and three assaults? What responsibility does Keith Royster
have? What responsibility do *we* bear? Without religious dogma
or simplifying scientific principles to assist us, how can we know
the difference between what is mad and what is bad?

Just how sane are we when we confront the insanity defense?

Only days before John Hinckley's attack on President Reagan,
the *Congressional Record* published comments by Senator Orrin

Hatch, Republican of Utah, attacking the insanity defense, propounding "facts" and prescriptions that were clearly false but consistent with the growing blood lust for insanity defense reform. "Individuals suffering from the most serious forms of mental disabilities are unlikely to be criminally convicted under any circumstance," Senator Hatch declared, evidence to the contrary notwithstanding. Hatch complained that the concept of mental illness "has expanded steadily in this century at the expense of the concept of moral responsibility." He chose not to recognize that designer defenses, with their spurious mental illnesses and the expanding concept of mental illness, are products of those sworn to uphold justice in the courts — the lawyers themselves. The odds of a "sane" defendant being acquitted for murder through some legal loophole and walking right back into the community are significantly higher than the acquittal rate for insanity. Increasing awareness of mental illness is not what has eroded contemporary moral responsibility. Mental health experts, though some of them may aid and abet designer defenses, are not the cause of a headlong rush into diagnosing people as mentally ill so that they can evade criminal responsibility. In panic over the rise of violent crime, we have turned not only the mentally ill offender but those who treat them into scapegoats for the decline of moral responsibility. The trouble with the criminal justice system is not that we cannot handle the criminally insane but that we cannot handle the so-called normal criminals.

With regard to the insanity defense and its function in the totality of American justice, we ourselves have become insane and have lost all appreciation of context. How can we put the insanity defense in some socially responsible perspective? Through education. Starting with every police officer, judge, prosecutor, defense attorney, juror, mental health expert, and member of the media corps individually, I would tell them the good news: We don't need our legislators to enact any statutory reform or new laws. We've gotten all the "reform" our budgets and consciences can afford. Our current laws are basically workable. We do not have to pay our politicians and criminal justice system to reinvent the wheel when all it needs is a little grease to run smoothly. It's time we listen to the facts — about each insanity case, about the insanity defense itself — so we can truthfully and comprehensively apply them to the issues of law, psychology, and morality.

What really is to be gained by introducing objectivity and rationality into this hyperemotional defense? We won't sell newspapers, launch political careers, lull the public into a false sense of security, feather the nests of enterprising expert witnesses, or offer more career opportunities in criminal justice. If we make the hard and hopeful effort to apply the insanity defense sanely, who wins?

We all do. We win back our sense of rationality, responsibility, and ethics and just maybe our ability to take charge of our lives. We are no longer terrorized by the specter of the mentally ill. We are not manipulated into wasting vast amounts of our society's precious resources to "get tough on crime" and the insanity defense, at the further cost of degrading our humanity. We no longer are diverted from the real problem of violent crime in our society and the pressing need to find solutions at the root causes.

In this book, I have tried to explain, provoke, enlighten, and encourage a social dialogue — not only about the insanity defense but also about our society's fundamental interpretation of individual responsibility and free will. I want to conclude by offering a manifesto toward sanity, or what might be less grandly called a cookbook of specifics, to urge us toward a rational, sane use of the insanity defense.

Let me begin with three major proscriptions:

- There should be no TV cameras in the courtroom.
- The courts should not allow an adversarial system between defense and prosecution experts in insanity trials.
- There should be no jury trials in insanity defense cases.

Let's go through these one by one and see how they might fit into a more rational approach to the insanity defense. The media must act like responsible adults. Our instinct — and, increasingly, our independent research — shows how powerful the TV camera is in shaping public opinion. In the courtroom, the camera is not just a faceless observer; it is an active participant influencing both the process and the outcome of the trial. Everyone in the courtroom wittingly or not ends up grandstanding for the lens in ways that reduce even further the lowest common denominator of testimony and unfairly dramatize the case for both public and jury. As someone who has been subjected to death threats for testifying in an incendiary case, I know how difficult it is to find a balance among my safety and that of my family, my First Amendment rights, the rights of the media, and my professional obligation to assist the defendant in receiving a fair trial. I personally do not believe it can be done with the current intrusion of the cameras in the courtroom.

Just a cursory reading of the more notorious insanity defense cases nationwide in the mid-1990s reveals the difference in the quality of the proceedings and the ultimate verdict in cases that were televised and those in which cameras were banned from the courtroom. Cameras were allowed during testimony in these sensational trials: Lorena Bobbitt, who castrated her husband, on trial for assault; the parricidal Menendez brothers, whose first murder trial resulted in hung juries; and Joel Rifkin and Colin Ferguson, where evidence of psychosis was ignored by a court system intent on convicting two notorious killers. *Every single one of the verdicts in these televised trials was, I believe, a miscarriage of justice.* In the second Menendez trial, the infanticide trial of Susan Smith, and the trial of subway bomber Edward Leary, no cameras were allowed. In each case the trial was orderly and mannerly, and in each case the verdict was, I believe, just.

When the news media try to make "infotainment" out of our system of jurisprudence, they exercise both dramatic and social license. Though I would ban cameras from the courtroom, where they do harm, I see a constructive role for the media in restoring sanity to our legal system. The media must be held accountable for their responsibility to inform and educate the public accurately and fairly. A solution might be the retaining of mental health experts as advisers or technical consultants. By attempting to educate the public about the real issues of crime, mental illness, and the insanity defense, they could become a powerful prosocial force. Rather than inspiring copycat serial killers, they could become instrumental in the early detection and more humane treatment of the potentially criminal mentally ill.

Similarly, the representation of the mentally ill and criminally insane in dramatic television, movies, and fiction needs to eschew false and discriminating "Norman Bates" stereotypes. Certainly the public can be engaged with the real-life complexities of mental illness without bashing an entire segment of society.

The media are not the only agents, however, of social responsibility and education around the insanity defense. Core social studies curricula in the primary grades should begin with exposure to the concepts of a trial. All schoolchildren should have attended some part of an actual trial in a courtroom before they graduate. How many actually have? I applaud Court TV's innovative offering for children, where they wrestle with legal issues of actual cases as if they themselves were on the jury. Such programs are on the right track. I would like to see more specialized media attention focused on this type of project. This is a responsible investment in the future of a democratic society.

In urging a saner approach to determining insanity, I resurrect a recommendation that has been floating around since the 1830s: the abolition of the adversarial system in all trials that raise highly technical psychological issues. Our current system not only is inefficient and wasteful but propounds distortion, fallacies, and misleading information to the general public regarding mental illness and crime. What anachronistic, medieval thinking assures us that by conscripting mental health professionals into a jousting tournament we serve the best interest of justice? Surely experts have more to offer the triers of facts than the spectacle of their blood spilled in gladiatorial combat. Most other countries with advanced legal systems have abandoned the adversarial system, particularly in specialized areas such as insanity defenses. The adversarial system tends to prolong a trial with the testimony of competing and contradicting experts. This, of course, puts more money into the pockets of lawyers and experts alike. And sadly, in the end, the taxpayers finance the whole spectacle.

The practice of placing experts in an adversarial position should be replaced by an advisory panel composed of highly trained and experienced mental health professionals cited for their excellence in the areas of forensic psychology and psychiatry. The list of certified experts should contain M.D. psychiatrists and licensed Ph.D. clinical psychologists who are assigned on a random rotational basis, much the way cases get assigned to judges. The panel should be composed, as most hospital commitment committees are, of three members, including at least one psychiatrist and one psychologist. The experts on this list should not be employees of the municipality or the courts. Rather, they should be independent consultants to the courts, paid at a fixed salary rate governed by specific billing procedures as to travel time, preparation, costs, and materials, all relative to their level of experience and expertise. This rate of remuneration should be closely fixed to the going rate for other psychiatric and psychological services in the community. People should not be retained as full-time consultants such that their only means of earning income is related to the courts. The panel of experts proposal would go a long way toward leveling a playing field tilted against the indigent defendant. No longer would money be able to buy the best expert testimony. By making possible a more thorough and comprehensive uncovering of the evidence, psychological and factual, in the case, the experts would be able to render a more informed opinion.

To avoid slipshod, erratic psychological summaries and the proliferation of designer defenses, we need to overhaul the nature of forensic examinations and reports, with standardization in the format of the forensic exam and in the structure of the final report. We must ransom back our discipline from the lawyers and carve out a legitimate and respectable turf for ourselves utilizing sound, state-of-the-art scientific principles and empirical bases. We can't allow our rich scientific tradition to be molded by attorneys into a caricature of half-baked M.D.s who can't prescribe medication or peddlers of psychological snake oil, junk science, and designer defenses. In order to accomplish this, forensic psychology must have watchdog professional organizations with teeth. Although professional organizations currently exist at the county, state, and national level, I have found them to be largely impotent in applying sanctions for unethical or unprofessional conduct. Some of this may be due to a contamination of the trade with the Machiavellian attitudes of the trial attorney — a kind of wink and a nod to the notion that all's fair in love and war and the courtroom.

We need to turn our attention to designing more accurate and reliable tests for psycholegal competencies; we need to form a more precise definition of legal insanity based on the level of psychological functioning; and we need to struggle with the issues of prediction of future dangerousness. Psychologists must return to the roots of their profession as psychometricians, continuing to refine tests and measures. Useless, arcane, and subjective techniques like inkblots, sentence completions, and gloomy pictures should be outlawed in the courtroom.

Insanity defense cases should be tried not by juries but by specially trained and credentialed judges. I have seen firsthand the debacle of naive and inexperienced judges struggling with complicated psychological testimony, ineptly charging juries, and generally remaining clueless throughout the proceedings. These judges should be given on-the-job training and assistance to become proficient in the application of psycholegal principles. With the advent of the *Daubert v. Merrill Dow Pharmaceuticals* decision (1993), which entrusts judges with the "gatekeeper" function of ruling on admissibility of scientific testimony, judges will need to become more comfortable with basic scientific concepts and principles. I commend the innovative work of the Einstein Institute for Science, Health, and the Courts, which has sponsored a national program to educate one thousand federal and state judges in genetics and molecular biology. Other forensic sciences should follow suit. Mental health advocacy groups should lobby for similar programs aimed at educating judges about mental illness and the insanity defense.

The advisory panel of experts recommended above could contribute here as well, functioning as an in-service training team for judges, lawyers, and district attorneys on psychological issues. They would be available for individual consultation to the courts and would be required to conduct regular training sessions for legal personnel.

District attorneys should consider establishing separate forensic bureaus within their departments to handle all legal cases in which mental illness or psychological status is a factor. These specialized units would be assigned personnel sophisticated in psychology and psychiatry and skilled in trying insanity defense cases. And just as ignorant, ill-advised prosecutors can damage the people's case, a defendant's case is compromised by poorly prepared defense attorneys, who need access to the same sort of psychological information.

For our part, we the public must begin to focus our attention on the disposition of the mentally ill defendant both before and after the verdict. We must begin to take responsibility for balancing the rights of the institutionalized mentally ill more equitably with the demands of public safety. To break down the wall of fear and prejudice, we must have hard facts from well-designed intervention and follow-up programs. We have got to push researchers into giving us formulas that can better map the potential for violence among inmates being evaluated for privileges or release. The entire concept of forensic psychiatric settings and secure care demands a vast overhaul and a major commitment of funding and professional expertise. Given the relatively small number of criminally insane, who cost us so much more money when they go to prison rather than a hospital, maintaining our psychiatric hospital system is a bargain to the taxpayers — but only if it meets the twofold mandate of humane treatment for the inmates and protection for the community. I believe, with some renewal of effort, it can be done, and done more compassionately and cost-effectively within secure psychiatric facilities than in jails. New electronic surveillance methods, such as monitoring chips and bracelets, can be more extensively implemented in forensic psychiatric settings to minimize the risk of escape. In my years as chief of service of a facility for the criminally insane and violent mentally ill, I repeatedly saw that attention to security measures ensured not only more personal freedoms for the patients but a better working environment for the staff and ultimate safety for the surrounding community. Important mileposts on the patient's supposed journey toward rehabilitation — aftercare, outpatient clinics, community residences, adult homes — for the most part have ceased to exist in any consistent and dependable fashion. In fact, psychiatric hospitals themselves, the primary link in the chain of mental health services, are gradually becoming extinct. Balancing the rights and treatment needs of the mentally ill offender with the public safety depends on the safety net of services that we are able to construct for them.

It is not only our mental hospitals that are suffering, but our entire mental health care system. At risk are all those with severe psychological issues, whether or not they have entered a courtroom. The rise of "managed care" is wielding death blows to mental health treatment — imagine "curing" a Joel Rifkin in the maximum ten therapy sessions most insurance plans allow! Thus, our society is ensuring itself a ready supply of emotionally fragile and at-risk types just waiting to "snap." If justice, mercy, and higher values are not a sufficiently compelling inducement for us to care about the psychologically damaged among us, perhaps the more pragmatic aspects of jails filled to overflowing with mentally ill inmates might be. Janet Susin, chairwoman for managed care of the Alliance for the Mentally Ill of New York State, warns that current statewide plans to shunt severely mentally ill people into managed care health maintenance organizations with unrealistic caps on length of treatment will result in "big wreckage — which will cost the state far more than it saves in homelessness, hospitalization, and incarceration." The choice before, during, and after the verdict is ours. Are we willing to exercise it in a thoughtful, compassionate, and responsible way?

Our responsibility toward the mentally ill goes beyond reforming the criminal justice system at trial and after the verdict. The primary responsibility we possess toward the mentally ill criminal goes past policy to the personal and the moral. We have got to deal with mental illness before it intersects with crime — ideally, to keep it out of our courtrooms in the first place. We have to confront it in the family, in the schools, in our neighborhoods, on our jobs. A common theme in every one of the tragic stories recounted in this book is that each horrible act might have been prevented — if only someone had taken notice and appropriately intervened in time.

Forty people were in the fireworks store in Scottown, Ohio, getting ready for their 1996 Fourth of July celebrations, when the store exploded into an instant inferno. Bottle rockets whizzed, strings of firecrackers exploded like continuous machine-gun fire, and smoke billowed out of the cinder-block building. Eight people, including two children, were found dead, huddled around the only exit. Their bodies had to be identified from dental records. A volunteer firefighter described a woman's arms "dripping like burning plastic — her watch was melted into her arm."

Just before the explosion, three young men had been seen going into the back storeroom, where one of them used a cigarette lighter to detonate the fireworks as a "prank." Todd Hall, twenty-four, was arrested and charged with eight counts of involuntary manslaughter. The others, who egged him on, were released.

At his court arraignment, Hall, known to most residents of that small town, giggled and clowned for the cameras. As the judge explained the charges, he interrupted and said petulantly, "But I didn't do it! It's not fair."

Neighbors came forward and admitted that Hall had been be-having strangely for years. "He's the biggest nuisance you've ever seen in your life," complained the owner of the local gas station and convenience store. Employees at the store claimed that Hall would harass customers and steal cigarettes and candy. He was also known to ride his bicycle over shrubs and flower beds and barge into homes asking for food and money.

Following a fall from a skateboard in 1987, Todd Hall, then fourteen, had been lobotomized. Lobotomies as a treatment for violent mental illness have been illegal in the United States since the 1950s. However, in Hall's case, the frontal lobes of his cere-bral cortex were so damaged from his accident that they had to be removed to save what was left of his brain function and, ulti-mately, his life. The teenager was in a coma for six weeks after the surgery. He finally recovered his speech and most of his motor functioning, but he remained slow in his thinking. The Hall fam-ily sued the manufacturer for a defect in the skateboard and won an undisclosed but sizable legal settlement. They had Todd de-clared legally incompetent, became his guardians, and paid cash for a large $125,000 house.

As Hall grew older and more physically formidable, he became increasingly more violent and assaultive. In 1990 he was charged with domestic violence against his father. The charge was dis-missed after James Hall testified that his son was mentally incom-petent. Although Mr. Hall claimed that he had his son "in the best hospitals in the country," and presumably some of that insurance settlement had been earmarked for rehabilitation and custodial care for Todd, there was no indication that he was receiving any treatment at the time he blew up the fireworks store. Everybody in this small town in the American heartland — his family, neigh-bors, the sheriff, even the court system — had just seemed to ig-nore Todd Hall and look the other way, until it all blew up in their faces that tragic Fourth of July.

Speaking on behalf of her father, the owner of the fireworks business in Scottown, Dora Redmond said, "He sat up there and said, 'If I had a gun I would put it to my head and just lay down because of all those people up there!' . . . He was trying to bring happiness to people, and now it's all sadness."

Todd Hall was evaluated for his competence to stand trial, the first step toward an insanity defense plea. In a criminal justice system where insanity defenses are rare, Todd Hall's plea is rarer still, a case in which a person's mental illness can actually be ascribed to a tangible organic condition. Nearly a quarter of Hall's brain is missing. Since he has previously been declared legally incompetent due to his organic condition, this may ultimately give weight to his claims of insanity should he ever be tried. As a mental health expert, I expect that under the specific statutes that prevail in Ohio, the trial of Todd Hall could become a classic instance of an insanity acquittal. But given the vagaries of the winds of reform, I could be wrong. Todd Hall, big, oafish, and not very sympathetic, could take the fall for an entire town's grief, rage, and frustration.

The core tragedy in Scottown is that no one took responsibility for Todd Hall, a human stick of dynamite with a fuse shorter than anything he lit in that warehouse, before he claimed the lives of eight innocent people. Ironically, all this took place on Independence Day, the birthday of our system of laws, rights, and responsibilities.

Consider the solitary figure slouching along the beach. The tattered remnants of sweatpants and a shirt flapping around his frame gave him the appearance of a scarecrow, incongruously planted at seaside, perpetually bent over digging and rooting in the sand. For the last two seasons, this clammer had mined this sheltered North Shore inlet for shellfish — steamers, littlenecks, seed clams — tiny, tender, precious to restaurants but illegal to harvest. Every day he worked his rake, making his way up one side of the inlet and down the other. Some of the regular fishermen and retired family men passing the time talked about him with a mixture of suspicion, sympathy, and annoyance. No one knew his name. He was a drifter, a loner. He could be heard to brag that he hunted fox and raccoon for food, then skinned them and dried the pelts to sell. Coming upon a rabbit drowned while mired in the muck at rising tide, he tossed the carcass into his bushel, while a nearby fisherman frowned in disgust. "As long as they don't smell yet, I eat 'em," the clammer mumbled.

As soon as school let out for the summer, the inlet swarmed with small children carrying plastic pails, shovels, and nets. They caught sand fiddlers, trapped minnows, played with the horseshoe crabs, picked up mussels and shells, and tossed the terns the crusts of their sandwiches. Their mothers sat under umbrellas, their eyes trained on the inlet, listening to the ostinato of laughing gulls and children.

In the midst of this easy scene moved the clammer, a hat pulled down over his greasy hair, with even more layers of flannel clothing wrapped around him to shield him from the relentless sun. It was as if his whole being gave off a toxic aura that kept the children from getting too close to him. He mumbled and muttered constantly under his breath. Occasionally a curious or unusually friendly or forward child would approach him to ask what he was doing. Invariably, he would scare them off with some type of frightening story or threat.

He terrified one six-year-old girl by telling her there were leeches in the water that would get under her skin and suck her blood and go up into "where you pee from." Her concerned mother came over to me and asked if it was true — were there leeches on this pleasant suburban beach?

A bare-bottomed toddler, one whose mother was employing that time-honored strategy for healing diaper rash, splashed in the water with a gaggle of older children. When they got too close to the clammer, he hissed at one of the girls, "You'd better tell his mother to put some pants on him because there are snapping turtles in the water that will come and bite his wiener off!"

One particularly assertive and self-confident nine-year-old

stood up to the clammer when he told the boy to get off the beach and stop digging and picking up mussels and shells. The clammer, habitually stooped from his foraging, glared into the boy's face. "You don't have a license. I'm going to call the police and have you arrested for destroying the ecology. You are taking my livelihood away . . . you are taking food out of my mouth. I'm not going to have trouble with a rich, spoiled brat like you again this summer!"

The boy was frightened, confused, and shamed. He went back to his blanket, tears of frustration welling in his eyes.

I observed this encounter from my beach chair, where I was struggling to compose the conclusion of this manuscript. As I watched the clammer menace the boy, an alarm went off somewhere in my consciousness. It was the same alarm I felt when I read of the crimes committed by John J. Royster and knew before he confessed that they were the work of one deranged man. Was this clammer just a derelict, a weird kind of harmless guy eking out a living the best way he knew? Or would it take the disappearance of a child one day before any of us took notice of his angry and bizarre presence? He hunted, trapped, and skinned animals — he had knives, guns maybe. He could assault a child in a second while a horrified mother just watched. He could open fire randomly, like the Scottish scoutmaster who sprayed a gymnasium full of kindergartners with gunfire. Would we all then stand around wringing our hands and telling ourselves, "He just snapped"? Would the press report he had a long history of mental problems that everyone ignored — as the people who lived in Royster's neighborhood, or the villagers in Scotland, had done?

I went to the lifeguard station. The only people there were college students hired for the summer. "Who has jurisdiction over the inlet?" I asked, relating the trouble with the clammer.

"Oh, him," said the head lifeguard, a muscular young man all of nineteen. He smirked. "The guy has a license to clam," he told me, as if somehow that justified it all. "His license to clam does not entitle him to harass and intimidate children," I retorted.

"He's very possessive of the beach," the lifeguard explained. "He gets angry if anyone bothers him." It was chilling to see how this robust young man, out of fear and inexperience in dealing with someone who was so bizarre, angry, and difficult, was choosing to deny that there was any problem with the clammer and the way he menaced the children. Clearly, it was not the young man's fault — how could a teenager be equipped to deal with such a complicated problem in a man twice his age?

I resolved to take action. I immediately drove to the local police station. Fortunately, the commissioner of this private village police force was there, a retired FBI man who ran a tight ship. We had spoken on other occasions when I had dropped off materials for the district attorney with him, or when a particularly insistent judge from neighboring Nassau County had ordered the police to ferry me in a blizzard from my house to the county line so that I could testify in a homicide trial. He also had worked with Richard Taus, the FBI agent and soccer coach who had molested at least two dozen children.

"Hi, Doc, what can I do for you?" the desk officer asked. I launched into my story of the clammer. Yes, he was known to the police. "What's your take on him?" the sergeant asked.

"Drifter, vagrant — too young for Nam but a possible Section Eight from the military. Some psych history. Possible drugs, alcohol —" Before I could finish, the officer had found the file. The clammer had been picked up in the winter for trespassing and vagrancy. He had set up a shanty in the woods behind the village hall and was hunting and trapping to survive.

The commissioner dispatched a car right away to go down to the beach and look around. The man did have a legal commercial clamming license, but there was some question about the legal size limit of the clams he picked up. The conservation people and the harbormaster were called. I wondered if anything would have been done if I were just somebody's worried mother and not someone the village officials knew professionally.

The next day, the clammer was stooped over raking the sand

again. Only this time, he was far down the beach, away from the
inlet and the children. Was this the best that could be done? A little boy called out to me. "There's that bad man!" He pointed.
Was it that simple? "He's an unhappy man, an angry man," I said
to the child. "Maybe he's not bad yet. Maybe we can help him not
to do bad things."

Maybe. But it's a big maybe for all of us. The clammer has a
right to clam; the children have a right to play. Where do we draw
the line? And if this clammer needs psychiatric help, where do we
get it for him? The local state hospital has just closed. And what if
he does not even want it? Can we force him to be treated? As a
psychologist, I know that this man's anger is not just the annoyance of some grouch toward little kids getting in his way — it goes
deeper than that. It's a question of how much control over his
paranoia the clammer is willing or able to exert — and of how
much control we as citizens are willing or able to exert. A man
with his profile has a significant risk factor for acting out violently.
Do we wait until he does and then listen to a prosecutor tell us
how evil he is and how he knew exactly what he was doing? Must
we wait until the unspeakable crime is committed, the insanity defense raised, before we intervene?

Consider the young man sitting across from me on the flowered
chintz sofa in my private office. His head is shaved on the right
side, and a hank of lank, dyed black hair falls over his left eye. His
ears are studded with spikes and upside-down crucifixes. He
wears torn fishnet panty hose under his shredded black jeans.
"I'm a bisexual vampire," he tells me, showing me a dark, black-
and-white photo of himself posing in a graveyard by a tombstone.
For a split second, his aquamarine eyes sparkle, and he seems
young, wholesome, as if he is showing me a snapshot from his
soccer playoffs.

Ian, age thirteen, had been referred to me for psychological
testing by his private psychiatrist. Lately, there had been an

alarming change in the boy. He had become moody, withdrawn, bizarre in his dress and some of his actions, and violently abusive toward his mother. His doctor was puzzled and wanted some help with Ian's diagnosis and treatment. Were his behavior and dress just the normal "craziness" of adolescence exacerbated by the bitter divorce his parents were battling through the courts? Was he seriously depressed? Should Prozac be prescribed?

Even after I had spent hours with Ian, who seemed to enjoy the attention and have no trouble opening up, my clinical instincts couldn't make the sharp distinction. There was something stagy, histrionic about Ian. He purposely said things to shock me, but how much of this was a cover-up for some of the frightening thoughts and impulses that he genuinely experienced? Just what was going on in the mind of this tortured young man?

I stared at Ian's test results in shock and dread. He was in deep trouble. His psychological resources were stretched to the limit, and he was teetering on top of a volcano of rage. On his MMPI grid, scale 4, psychopathic deviate, ran neck and neck with scale 8, schizophrenia, with an enormous elevation over 100. In certain aspects, his profile already resembled that of hospitalized paranoid schizophrenics and the criminally insane. He was pathologically, nearly psychotically angry, and it went far beyond the real difficulties of his family situation or day-to-day life.

Ian was at war with himself and the universe. He stood at the crossroads of essential innocence, madness, and badness.

At face value, his concerns voiced in therapy sounded very typically adolescent. He was unhappy, afraid of trusting others, unable to accept responsibility, alienated from himself and everyone else, constantly confused and angry. However, Ian's thoughts had begun to take a peculiarly menacing turn with regard to the rights of others. He had become obsessive in his thinking that people were against him, and had started to make lists of his enemies. He had dreamed up suitable plans of revenge, some of them alarmingly vicious. His sexual feelings were strong, confused, and laced with guilt from his religious background. He denied this conflict self-defeatingly by homosexual acting out. For Ian, unbeknownst to his preoccupied parents, had started to engage in prostitution. After a breakup with another boy about his age, Ian etched a cross-hatch of razor marks on both his wrists.

Ian and his twin sister were the only children of a wealthy entrepreneur and his wife. Although his father had entered the marriage on the condition that it remain childless, he adjusted to a purported "accidental" pregnancy, which produced the twins after sixteen years of marriage, when his staunchly Catholic wife refused to get an abortion. This was the first and last time Ian's mother ever stood up to her bullying husband. The marriage, always a difficult and abusive one, deteriorated. The mother immersed herself in rearing the twins; the father turned to a series of affairs with young women. Both parents fought loudly, with no holds barred, in front of the children, who were forced to become voyeurs. Ian told me that by age four he knew everything about his parents' failed sex life and his father's other women. All of this took place in an environment of luxury and gentility.

Ian felt defective and unlovable — a "reject and a weirdo." "I hate them because they took away my childhood," he raged one day. An exceptionally bright and perceptive youngster, he escaped into fantasy and survived by lying, cheating, manipulating, and, most recently in adolescence, sexually acting out. Was Ian just another spoiled and confused suburban prince? Would he grow up and out of this "stage" and go on to take his place in his father's business? Or did he have the makings of a John Hinckley, a Joel Rifkin, a Lyle or Erik Menendez? There was no way of predicting whether Ian's rage would be turned inward in depression or possibly even suicide, or outward toward some innocent victim before he found a positive way to channel it or diffuse it.

His twin sister, Jan, an honor student, sat out in the waiting room studying her lines for the class play, a musical comedy. What was going on inside her that made her react so differently to her surroundings? Ian, although he claimed that he loved his sister and was very close to her, was an enigma to Jan. Nevertheless, she told me she accepted him unquestioningly, even though his bizarre behavior and dress embarrassed her at times. She was deeply hurt and concerned by his frequent insults and verbal abuse of her. She reported that he often interrupted her phone calls to her girlfriends by screaming obscenities at them and that he would go on rampages and tear up books and clothing in her room. Recently, she installed a lock on her bedroom door to keep her brother out. Ian smashed the door in. Jan was starting to become afraid of him.

Given the tests results, intensive, emergency treatment for Ian was essential. Prozac, however, would be out of the question. It could take the lid off his depression enough to allow all of his murderous rage to erupt — a rare but risky side effect of Prozac in potentially violent people.

Some people would insist that Ian's emotional problems are not his fault, that they are symptoms of a brain illness or chemical imbalance and should thus be destigmatized. Such a response may seem enlightened and humane. But it is ultimately disempowering and dehumanizing. Ian is not just a computer programmed by DNA or other biochemical and neural circuitry. Ian's character and mental state are the sum total of a lot of choices made not only by himself but by his parents. I agree that it is probably not productive to ask "Whose fault is it?" but I desperately want us to ask "Whose responsibility is it?"

Ian's sister is in the process of making different choices than her twin has made. Why? And how can we help Ian make better choices for himself?

I convened a meeting with Ian's parents. The charged atmosphere between them was like the electrical field preceding a thunderstorm. Conducting the session, I have never been in the presence of such hostile and rage-filled people. The father did not want to hear about Ian's strengths — his sensitivity, his intelligence, his gift with words. He wanted to see his son as "sick" and to settle it with medication and go on about his life with his new girlfriend.

I recommended that Ian's psychotherapy sessions be increased to twice a week. His psychiatrist made a recommendation that I begin to treat Ian because he seemed to have grown quite comfortable and attached to me during his evaluation. Frankly, I think she was also burned out and depleted from attempting to deal with the toxic family. Ian was encouraged by the prospect of working with me. A treatment plan was established for Ian, including family therapy and supportive counseling for his sister. Everyone seemed to be in agreement.

Ian began his sessions. For each hour, he raged and raged about his parents, his school, life in general. I encouraged him to write poetry, short stories, and songs about it. He would show them to me. Often they were well crafted and revealed a developing talent. His mother reported that he seemed less angry and there had been fewer incidents at home. He was less abusive to his sister. His grades started to improve.

Suddenly, on the eve of signing the final financial settlement in the divorce decree, Ian's parents had a huge fight. The police were called to intervene. Ian had tried to break it up and in the process punched his father. To punish Ian, his father cut off the funds for his psychotherapy. His mother called and said she could not afford to pay for his treatment; Ian would have to terminate. Ian mailed me a poem called "The Mask," about how everyone was a phony and nobody really cared.

There was something about this bristling, thorny, angry kid that was worth reaching out to. Although he had a demonstrable talent for rage, he also possessed an undeveloped aptitude for compassion and humanity. I gave Ian a "scholarship" for therapy.

The dire prognosis I fear for this boy — the extremes of madness or badness — is merely one possible outcome. It is not predetermined. It does not have to be. The alternative of healthy psychological adjustment still exists as an option for a boy so young. Ian has the right and responsibility to choose the course. We, as his caretakers, have the responsibility to do all in our power to help him make the right choices.

Index